A SUNDAY TELEGRAPH COOK BOOK

THE BEST OF

Marika Hanbury Tenison

A SUNDAY TELEGRAPH COOKBOOK

THE BEST OF

Marika Hanbury Tenison

Edited by Catherine Stott

WOMEN'S EDITOR SUNDAY TELEGRAPH

𝕋

Published by Telegraph Publications
135 Fleet Street, London EC4P 4BL

First Published 1984
© The Estate of Marika Hanbury Tenison

British Library Cataloguing in Publication Data

Hanbury Tenison, Marika
  The best of Marika Hanbury Tenison.
  1. Cookery
  I. Title   II. Stott, Catherine
  641.5   TX717

ISBN 0-86367-007-5

Photography by Eric Carter
Illustrations by Soun Vannithone

Typeset by Sunset Phototype Ltd, Barnet.
Printed and bound in Great Britain by
W. S. Cowell, Ipswich.

CONTENTS

Foreword

I T WAS SUCH FUN to read Marika's weekly pieces in the *Sunday Telegraph*. You simply couldn't begin to guess what she might be writing about, where she had been, or in what direction her flights of inspiration had led. Yet it has always been difficult to describe in detail the food I ate at Maidenwell, the great pantiled house high on Bodmin Moor – I can't remember much of it. But that is a high accolade, for just as you should barely recall the details of a well-dressed woman's clothes, hers was the *haute couture* of food. Once you had finished your meal, whether a sumptuous dinner party of many courses or a cosy kitchen supper of sausages and mash, you didn't feel obliged to rave about the food. The feeling of welcome and well-being her hospitality engendered said it for you. Indeed, Marika was adamant that her food was never to be the star of the table; guests were there to talk to one another, not talk about what was in front of them. It was an early lesson I was shown by Marika – guests who insist on talking about the food have little else to say. She would be infinitely polite and hospitable – she couldn't be otherwise – but that person was 'off the list', no matter how rich or famous or celebrated others thought them.

Talking about other people's food was different, but only if it were just the two of us. Each meal could be a time to learn, to compare and to create. It didn't have to be fancy food. We once nearly missed her station through remembering too well bacon sandwiches we had eaten around the world. She loved them, and meant always to write suggesting how British Rail might improve their sandwiches.

Marika was a savoury cook and preferred to eat savoury food. Her favourite meal, ordered oblivious of surroundings, was a procession of starters.

Her instinct was for the clear, clean flavour, achieved with the minimum of fuss and the best possible ingredients. It was extraordinary that she could stick so firmly to her peerless style and yet create enough original recipes to satisfy the constant flow of books and articles. Her inspiration came not from fashion or fad, but from travel – hers, her husband's and her friends'.

Marika liked being famous for soups and took infinite care to make stocks that were brilliantly unfussed concentrations of flavour. To them she added her talent for revealing rather than concealing, and created revelations in taste. I also like what she served with them. With a fish soup we once had hot brioches stuffed with wild mushrooms; that I *do* remember.

The Chinese respect for intrinsic flavour, translated into Western dishes, was very much Marika's style. Her palate was so alive to the subtleties of food's unadulterated flavour that she often worried whether others thought her food underseasoned. Usually it wasn't. But once I made pâtés with her for a picnic in the bluebell woods of Maidenwell. She stood aghast at the large amount of herbs and spices I used. Boldness with herbs and spices was the single thing I taught her.

Of all the good things we cooked together, the only one we regularly recalled was created that same day. It was a boned duck stuffed with three layers of pâté. The bottom layer was veal with herbs, the top was pork with spices. The middle was celeriac root puréed with seed mustard, curd cheese and eggs; it was to have had breadcrumbs, but Marika refused. She was right of course.

It was a joy to cook with Marika, or to cook for her. Her praise for others' food was quick and generous. She was the same about her own too. A new recipe was pronounced 'a triumph' or, ultimate accolade, 'an absolute poem'. She would put down her tasting fork and declare: 'We'll print that one', and the beam of satisfaction warmed the kitchen.

There were four vital ingredients in Marika's kitchen: the old solid-fuel Aga, the Magimix food processor, the wok, and the sparkling clean saucepans. Marika was truly fanatic about clean saucepans – they had to be scoured and gleaming inside and out – *especially* the bottoms.

The Aga was loved because Marika knew that if her recipes worked in the vagaries of its several ovens and hobs they could be trusted to perform in ordinary domestic ovens.

The Magimix, with which she was so associated, increased the possibility of fine food overnight, allowing anyone to make purée and pastries, or to slice and shred in seconds. Many times she told me that she could not have created quite so much if the Magimix hadn't been there to free her from the various mundane chores of cooking.

Foreword

As to the wok, everywhere Marika went, her wok went too. She refused to give 'demonstrations', instead she came along 'to entertain', usually for charity. Each performance combined comedy, outrage and the chance of watching her create – she always invented as she went along and was delighted if something didn't quite work. It made the act more fun for everyone. To Marika the wok more than anything else helped her achieve a concentration of simple flavours with ease. The inspiration it gave helped to crystallise the idea for her greatest book, *Cooking with Vegetables*. This was a genuinely new approach, based on meat as an adjunct to vegetables, rather than the other way around. She was proud of it, and rightly so, just as she was proud of being totally untrained.

As part of her steady creative process, Marika changed her mind dramatically over the fifteen years I knew her. A great early success was her book on deep-freezing. But about the time she began her affair with the wok she realised the deep-freeze had taken away the anticipation and enjoyment of the summer's first pea or strawberry. She no longer wanted to eat peas in the winter. The kitchen gardens of Maidenwell were replanted, and were amongst the first to grow yellow tomatoes and golden beetroot. The deep-freeze remained important as storage for non-seasonal and cooked foods, but fresh rather than frozen ingredients became absolutely standard in her kitchen.

There was a wonderful wickedness in Marika, too. She loved to tease people into sharing her passions, especially for offal. Her assistant Rosa still recalls, with unfailing dismay, how she was tricked into eating testicles. She admits to enjoying them, as Marika said she would, but now eats more carefully at certain times of year! Neither did she mind being teased; she felt she had 'made it' when *Private Eye* called her 'Paprika Cranberry Venison' and promptly cooked a dish named just that!

When it came to the sweet course Marika admitted to being less interested, and cake-baking remained a mystery. The puddings she liked were simple – meringues and profiteroles. Once we made a sumptuous pudding of profiteroles stuffed with cream and flavoured with rosewater and orange-flower water. They were stuck to one another with melted sugar to make a sort of hollow coronet, and in the middle were tumbled masses of raspberries, straight from her own canes. Definitely a poem to be printed.

Her pet dislikes were pompous, fancy names and over-

Foreword

decoration in food, both consistent with her mission to make food taste of itself. It had to look like itself too . . . unless it was sea bass baked in wet pages of the *Sunday Telegraph*. That looked like last night's rubbish until you opened it. It was one of her best – both practical and a joke.

Marika adored a good story and recognised one in everything. She loved telling you things, but not as a teacher or for self-glorification. She wanted to share what interested her. It needed philanthropy of the first order to share more than forty cook books and fourteen years of weekly articles.

Frankly, the burden of that responsiblity suited Marika just fine. She loathed cooking the same dish twice and boasted that she never had.

There are many more things I should like to tell you about Marika. But this book is probably as genuine a portrait as any I could draw, for what you read is what she was. It is infused with her spirit of creation and fascination, with her delight in sharing the good things of life. Nothing could be a more fitting tribute than her own words and recipes, for from her you will find the unexpected and the outrageous, the innovative and the cosy and the story-teller. They are here because she cared to share. How good it is to have this book.

Glynn Christian

INTRODUCTION

When MARIKA HANBURY TENISON died in 1982, she was only 44. She had been the cookery editor of the *Sunday Telegraph* for fourteen years, building up a huge and loyal following among our readers.

They felt they knew her personally since she had a rare gift of writing about herself and her family in a way that was intimate and charming but never self-conscious. This had the advantage of ensuring an excellent response to everything she wrote, particularly her cookery competitions, but was a bit galling for those readers who thought of her as a friend and didn't understand why she couldn't give them five minutes advice over the telephone on their dinner parties.

Marika did not work in Fleet Street but from her rambling pink farmhouse in the middle of Bodmin Moor in Cornwall. It was living in such isolation that led to her career. Her husband, Robin, the explorer, was often leading a lengthy expedition on the other side of the world, which left Marika marooned with a small daughter and time on her hands.

She could cook and she could write, so what could be more logical than combining the two? She was to joke later that it was 'either getting into trouble or writing cookery books'.

The adjective that most accurately summed up Marika's character is 'indomitable'. She saw what she wanted, saw how to achieve it and got on with it. Within a year of becoming a £1-a-week cookery writer on a local paper, she had written a book on deep-freezing, a regular magazine column and, by sheer hard work, had become cookery editor of the *Sunday Telegraph*.

No one I have ever known worked as hard as Marika. She rose at 5 am, tasted, tested and wrote until mid-day when she sprinted to the kitchen to make lunch for family, friends, farmhands, staff – or however many happened to be around. In the afternoon uncompromisingly, she slept. Another feverish burst of work and then she would often prepare a lavish dinner for what seemed like half of Cornwall.

Introduction

At weekends there might be a dozen people staying – clever, glamorous friends from the world of art, literature, exploration or big business – and somehow she contrived to provide them with round-the-clock food of a matchless quality, as if by magic. She never looked harassed, and her entertaining was like great acting – you could never see the mechanics.

Hypercompetent women like Marika are often abrasive and intolerant, but she was saved by her wonderful ability to laugh at herself. When *Private Eye* nicknamed her 'Paprika Cranberry Venison', she wore an apron printed with these words.

Her style was superb. When in the last year of her life she had a true cook's accident and broke her thigh by slipping on an onion skin, she had her crutches gaily painted. It was an unforgettable sight to see her park her large Mercedes on a double yellow line in Knightsbridge and hop deftly into a restaurant, wearing a doublet and hose, to hand the crutch to a waiter as if it were a sable coat.

For some years she had struggled against anorexia, an ironic illness for a cook as she appreciated. She never cared much for wine, but you could tempt her with a dozen oysters and a 'vodka martini straight up with a twist' that she would command in her gravelly, authoritative voice. Oh, and how the waiters jumped!

Truly Marika had nine lives. She had fought death with a passion on many occasions. She married Robin when she was 20, but it wasn't for twelve years that she first accompanied him on an expedition. This was when she used up the first of her lives, when she was at her most indomitable. Her son Rupert had been born a few weeks before and the Caesarean section resulted in serious illness. Still in pain, she spent three months visiting jungle tribes in Brazil in appalling conditions. She remembered it afterwards only for having shot and cooked a crocodile.

Undaunted, she embarked on a gruelling three-month trek through Indonesia. After two months she became exhausted but had to go five days in the jungle without food to reach a village of head-hunters. She swam through swollen rivers where the rain was so intense you couldn't see through it.

There wasn't much Marika couldn't or wouldn't cook. In her time she had to devise ways with giant red ant, iguana, monkey, croc – and she once cooked a ten foot python in a pressure cooker, serving it with *pommes frites*, which gave rise to an article called 'Snake and Chips'.

Her health had been precarious for many years, but she met each

Introduction

new onslaught on her delicate physique with laconic wit and formidable courage. Unable to walk, she cooked by whizzing round the kitchen in her typing chair on castors.

When she first learned she had cancer, she announced she was going to treat it like a case of flu. She made no secret of it, indeed she spoke movingly about it on radio and television, telling people not to be afraid. She fought it like a lion and we almost came to believe that with her outrageously cheeky courage she might perform yet another miracle and cock a snook at death.

In the last days of her life her assistant Rosa wrote to me, 'It is obviously a very, very sad time here. Marika continually amazes me with her absolute determination and pure guts to keep going'.

After the fatal brain tumour was diagnosed she kept on working, even when she could barely see and was totally immobile. The ideas kept on fizzing.

She was the most fun imaginable. Fun to *be* with, fun to *work* with. Her memory will live on through her wonderful cookery books. Above all Marika proved that it is *how* you live your life, not the length of it, that matters – which is a secret the contemporary world often forgets.

After she died shoals of letters from readers poured in. They took her death very personally because the bond between writer and reader had been so close. Many contributed, as we suggested at the time as an apt way of commemorating her life, to Marika's favourite charity, Survival International, of which Robin Hanbury Tenison is President. One reader suggested that we name a dish after her; many more asked for reprints of her work.

It seemed appropriate, therefore, that we should have something more to remember Marika by; and with that in mind I have collected together these recipes and articles which to me reflect the very best work of a much lamented friend and an inspired cookery writer.

Catherine Stott
Women's Editor
Sunday Telegraph
London
June 1984

Soups & Starters

Countryside Vegetable Soup

SERVES 4

1 onion
3 carrots
1 small turnip
3 stalks celery
2 leeks
450 g (1 lb) potatoes
3 tomatoes

3 tablespoons olive oil
1.5 litres (2½ pts) chicken or
    vegetable stock
1 tablespoon tomato purée
1 teaspoon dried mixed herbs
salt and freshly ground black pepper
pinch nutmeg

Peel and finely chop the onion. Peel and coarsely grate the carrots and turnip. Very finely chop the celery and very thinly slice the leeks. Peel and coarsely grate the potatoes, skin the tomatoes and chop the flesh, removing all tough cores. Heat the oil in a saucepan, add the onion and cook gently until soft and transparent. Add the other vegetables, mix well and cook for 3 minutes over a medium-low heat, stirring continually. Pour over the stock and mix in the tomato purée and herbs. Season with salt, pepper and a pinch of nutmeg, bring to the boil, cover and simmer gently for about 30 minutes until all the vegetables are tender. Check the seasoning.

Soup for All Seasons

SERVES 4

Remember to make this soup in the summer by substituting an onion for the leeks; it has a marvellous colour and a delicious subtle flavour which is as good chilled as it is hot.

1 potato
1 carrot
2 leeks
1 clove garlic
1 Cox's apple
½ teaspoon curry powder
juice of 1 orange

1 tablespoon olive oil
400 g (14 oz) tin tomatoes
750 ml (1¼ pts) water
1 chicken stock cube
salt, pepper and a pinch each of
    oregano and basil
milk if required

Peel and finely dice the potato and carrot. Thinly slice the leeks and crush the garlic. Peel and dice the apple and dissolve the curry powder in the orange juice. Heat the olive oil and add potato, carrot, leeks and garlic. Cook over a medium heat for about 5 minutes until the leeks are soft and all the oil has been absorbed into the vegetables. Add the remaining ingredients except the milk, mix well, season and bring to the boil. Cover and simmer gently until the vegetables are soft. Leave to cool and then purée in a blender. Reheat and thin the soup if necessary with a little milk.

Plate 1. Fair Isle Soup, Rich Vegetable Soup

Plate 2. Natalia Polonski's Soup Sensation

Rich Vegetable Soup

SERVES 8

Plate 1, illustrated facing page 16.

The charm of this kind of recipe is that no two brews will taste the same and each will be an individual masterpiece of goodness.

1 large onion
1 clove garlic
1 leek
225 g (8 oz) Swiss chard,
* spinach or cabbage*
2 stalks celery
175 g (6 oz) runner beans
50 g (2 oz) firm button mushrooms
1 carrot
3 tablespoons vegetable oil

2 × 400 g (14 oz) tins tomatoes
450ml (¾ pt) tomato juice
few drops Worcestershire sauce
about 1.2 litres (2 pts) water
2 or 3 chicken stock cubes
salt and freshly ground black pepper
pinch each oregano and thyme
50 g (2 oz) vermicelli,
* small pasta shells or*
* Chinese soup noodles*

Peel and finely chop the onion and garlic. Trim and thinly slice the leek. Finely shred the Swiss chard. Peel and coarsely grate the celery. Thinly slice the beans, mushrooms and carrot. Heat the oil in a large saucepan, add the onion, leek and garlic and cook over a low heat until the onion is soft and transparent. Add the Swiss chard, carrot, beans and celery and cook over a low heat, stirring for 3 minutes. Add the tomatoes (roughly cut them in the tin with kitchen scissors to break them up), the tomato juice and Worcestershire sauce. Add the water and the chicken stock cubes, bring to the boil, season with salt and pepper, add the oregano and thyme and cook over a high heat for 15 minutes. Add the mushrooms and pasta and continue to cook over a medium heat for a further 10 minutes. Taste the soup, and if it needs more flavour, add a further stock cube or some tomato purée; if the soup is too thick, add some more water.

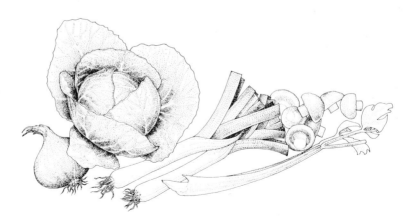

Marika's Onion and Parsley Soup
SERVES 4

1 very large onion
50 g (2 oz) butter
1½ tablespoons flour
450 ml (¾ pt) chicken stock
300 ml (½ pt) milk

3 tablespoons chopped parsley
salt and white pepper
1 egg yolk
2–3 tablespoons single cream

Peel and finely chop the onion. Melt the butter in a saucepan, add the onion and cook gently over a low heat, stirring to prevent browning, until soft and transparent. Add the flour and mix well. Gradually blend in the stock, stirring continuously until the soup is slightly thickened and comes to the boil. Lower the heat, add the milk and parsley, season with salt and pepper and simmer for 20 minutes. Beat the egg yolk with the cream, add a couple of spoonfuls of the hot soup and mix well, then add to the soup, stirring in with a wire whisk, and on no account allowing the soup to boil.

Italian Tomato Soup
SERVES 4

2 leeks
1 clove garlic
900 g (2 lb) firm, ripe tomatoes
3 tablespoons olive oil or
    sunflower oil
900 ml (1½ pts) water
1 chicken stock cube

1 bouquet garni
2 bay leaves
pinch basil or oregano
salt and freshly ground black pepper
3 tablespoons vermicelli
2 tablespoons double cream

Wash, trim and thinly slice the leeks. Peel and finely chop the garlic. Cover the tomatoes with boiling water, leave to stand for 2 minutes, drain, skin and chop. Heat the oil in a saucepan, add the leeks and garlic and cook over a low heat without browning, until the leeks are soft. Add the tomatoes, water, stock cube and herbs; bring to the boil, stirring. Cover and simmer for about 30 minutes. Remove bouquet garni and bay leaves, strain off and reserve the excess liquid and purée the vegetables. Return the purée to a clean pan. Add the liquid, season and thin with a little water if necessary. Cook vermicelli in a little boiling water until tender and drain well. Add to the soup, stir in the cream and heat through without boiling. Serve hot.

Peperonata Soup

SERVES 4

175 g (6 oz) tin pimientos
450 ml (¾ pt) tomato juice
600 ml (1 pt) water
1½ chicken stock cubes
salt and freshly ground black pepper

3 tablespoons orange juice
¼ teaspoon dried tarragon

Garnish
4 very thin slices of lemon

Drain the pimientos. Purée two-thirds of the pimientos with the tomato juice through a food mill, or in a processor or blender. Combine the purée, water, stock cubes, salt, pepper, orange juice and tarragon in a saucepan, bring to the boil, stirring to dissolve the stock cubes, and simmer for 3 minutes to develop the flavours. Meanwhile, drain and finely chop the remaining pimientos and add them to the soup. Garnish each bowlful with a thin slice of lemon.

Lentil and Vegetable Soup

SERVES 6

100 g (4 oz) lentils
1.2 litres (2 pts) stock
2 onions
2 carrots
1 stalk celery
4 bay leaves
pinch dried mixed herbs

300 ml (½ pt) milk
100 g (4 oz) lean cooked ham or bacon
salt and freshly ground black pepper

Garnish
croûtons

Put lentils into a bowl. Bring half the stock to the boil and pour over the lentils. Peel and roughly chop the onions and carrots. Roughly chop the celery, including leaves. Combine the lentils, soaking liquid, remaining stock, onions, carrots, celery and herbs in a pressure cooker, bring to pressure and cook at medium pressure for 25 minutes. Reduce pressure slowly. Drain off the liquid and reserve, discard bay leaves and purée the lentils in a blender. Return the purée to a clean pan, add liquid and milk and bring to the boil stirring all the time. Simmer for 10 minutes. Cut the ham or bacon into small dice. Season the soup with salt and pepper, thin with some milk or stock if necessary – the soup should be the consistency of thin cream – and add the ham. Serve in heated bowls with croûtons.

Golden Gorgeous Soup
SERVES 6

200 g (7 oz) chick-peas
2.1 litres (3½ pts) chicken stock
1 clove garlic
50 g (2 oz) rashers streaky bacon
2 frankfurter sausages

4 tablespoons sunflower oil
salt and freshly ground pepper
275 g(10 oz) short-cut macaroni
2 tablespoons finely chopped parsley

Cover the chick-peas generously with cold water and leave to soak overnight. Drain the chick-peas well, combine with stock and cook for about 1½ hours until they are tender. Drain and reserve stock. Purée half the chick-peas. Peel and finely chop the garlic. Remove rind from the bacon and very finely chop the rashers. Cut frankfurters into very thin slices. Heat the oil, add the garlic and bacon and cook gently until the garlic is softened; add the chick-peas, the purèe and the stock, bring to the boil, season with salt and pepper; add the macaroni and frankfurters and boil for about 10 minutes or until the pasta is tender. Check seasoning and mix in parsley at the last minute. Grated Parmesan can be served on the side.

Gorgeously Green Soup
SERVES 6–8

2 onions
2 cloves garlic
2 stalks celery
3 tablespoons sunflower oil
2 sprigs parsley
225 g (8 oz) spinach or
 Swiss chard leaves
350 g (12 oz) dried green beans
 (flageolets)

2.7 litres (4¼ pts) light stock or
 water and chicken stock cubes
salt and freshly ground black pepper
small pinch each of grated nutmeg
 and sage
50 g (2 oz) cooked tongue

Peel and roughly chop the onions and garlic. Reserve celery leaves and chop the stalks. Heat the oil in a pressure cooker. Add the onion and garlic, and cook over a low heat until the onion is soft and transparent. Add the parsley, spinach and celery and cook for a further 3 minutes. Add the beans and stock, season with salt, pepper, nutmeg and sage (go easy on the salt if you are using stock cubes), bring to pressure and cook at low pressure for 45 minutes. Drain off the stock, purée the ingredients and return the purée and stock to a clean pan. Cut the tongue into very small dice and finely chop the celery leaves. Reheat the soup, add the celery leaves and tongue, and check the seasoning. Serve with plenty of hot crusty bread.

Broad Bean Soup

SERVES 4

1 small onion
40 g (1½ oz) butter
900 ml (1½ pts) chicken stock
½ teaspoon sugar

salt and freshly ground black pepper
½ teaspoon chopped savory
350 g (12 oz) shelled broad beans
4–5 tablespoons double cream

Peel and finely chop the onion. Heat the butter in a saucepan, add the onion and cook over low heat until soft and transparent. Add the stock, sugar, pinch of salt and savory. Bring to the boil, add the beans and cook until they are quite tender. Remove and skin about a dozen beans for garnishing and purée the remainder in a sieve, food mill or blender. Return the purée to a clean pan, heat through, season with salt and pepper and blend in the cream before serving.

Smoky Pea Soup

SERVES 4

Large frozen peas are ideal for using in this warming and nourishing soup.

1 onion
4 smoked bacon rashers
40 g (1½ oz) butter
225 g (8 oz) frozen peas
1.2 litres (2 pts) water
1 chicken stock cube

1 teaspoon sugar
salt and freshly ground black pepper
pinch grated nutmeg
1 egg yolk
4–5 tablespoon single cream

Peel and finely chop the onion. Remove rind and finely chop the bacon. Cook onion and bacon gently in the butter until the onions are transparent. Add the peas, water, stock cube and sugar; season with salt, pepper and nutmeg. Bring to the boil and simmer gently for 20 minutes. Purée the soup in a blender or through a food mill and return it to a clean pan. Beat the egg yolk with the cream, add to the soup and heat through without boiling, stirring well until the soup is piping hot and slightly thickened. Serve at once.

Fair Isle Soup

SERVES 6

Plate 1, illustrated
facing page 16.

1 small lettuce
40 g (1½ oz) butter
700 g (1½ lb) shelled peas
4 mint leaves
pinch sugar
1.2 litres (2 pts) chicken stock

1 tablespoon lemon juice
salt and freshly ground black pepper
1 tablespoon flour
2 tablespoons single cream
shredded lettuce

Wash, dry and shred the lettuce. Melt 15 g (½ oz) butter in a large saucepan, add the lettuce and cook slowly over a low flame for 2 minutes, stirring to prevent browning. Add the peas, 3 of the mint leaves, sugar, stock and lemon juice. Bring to the boil, cover and cook for about 15 minutes until the peas are tender. Purée soup in a blender or through a fine sieve and season with salt and pepper. Melt 25 g (1 oz) butter in a clean saucepan, add flour and mix well. Gradually blend in puréed soup, stirring continually until the soup comes to the boil and is thick and smooth. Lower the heat, blend in the cream and pour into hot serving bowls. Garnish with the remaining mint leaf and shredded lettuce.

January Saturday Soup

SERVES 8

2 cloves garlic
2 onions
2 potatoes
2 stalks celery
450 g (1 lb) pork belly with skin removed
450 g (1 lb) dried haricot beans, soaked
400 g (14 oz) tin tomatoes

bouquet garni
1.8 litres (3 pts) water
3 chicken stock cubes
salt and freshly ground black pepper
¼ small cabbage
175 g (6 oz) ham

Peel and finely chop the garlic. Peel and chop the onions. Peel and dice the potatoes. Thinly slice the celery. Trim excess fat from the pork and cut it into small dice. Gently melt the pork fat in a saucepan. Add the garlic, onions, potatoes and celery and stir over a low heat until the fat has been absorbed by the vegetables. Add the haricot beans, pork meat, tinned tomatoes and bouquet garni. Stir in the water and chicken stock cubes. Bring to the boil, stirring to dissolve the stock cubes and season with salt and pepper. Simmer gently for about 45 minutes until the beans are soft and the meat tender. Shred the cabbage and finely chop the ham. Add these to the soup, check the seasoning (if the soup is not rich enough for your taste add some tomato purée), and simmer for 10 minutes until the cabbage is just cooked.

Jerusalem Artichoke Soup

SERVES 4–6

Peeling Jerusalem artichokes is always a problem. Use a peeler to remove every particle of skin, since the soup should be almost pure white in colour.

700 g (1½ lb) Jerusalem artichokes
25 g (1 oz) butter
450 ml (¾ pt) milk
salt and freshly ground black pepper
pinch grated nutmeg

450 ml (¾ pt) chicken stock
150 ml (¼ pt) single cream

Garnish
thin lemon slices

Wash and peel artichokes, chop into small pieces and place in acidulated water. Melt the butter in a heavy saucepan, add drained artichokes and cook over a low flame, shaking the pan occasionally, for 5 minutes. Pour over the milk, season with salt, pepper and nutmeg, cover and simmer until artichokes are tender. Purée in a blender. Pour the purée into a clean pan, blend in the stock and cream, and heat through without boiling. Check the soup for seasoning and serve really hot with a thin slice of lemon floating on the top of each serving.

Potato Soup with Orange

SERVES 5–6

A small quantity of orange peel adds an interesting flavour to many soups.

900 g (2 lb) potatoes
1 large onion
15 g (½ oz) butter
1.2 litres (2 pts) well-flavoured
 meat stock

1 bay leaf
rind of ½ orange
salt and white pepper
2 tablespoons double cream

Boil the potatoes until tender and drain well. Mash until smooth. Peel and finely chop the onion and cook over a low heat in the butter until soft and transparent. Add the stock and bay leaf, bring to the boil and simmer gently for 10 minutes. Add the mashed potatoes and cook for a further 10 minutes. Cut the orange rind into very fine strips and soak these in boiling water for 5 minutes and drain well. Remove the bay leaf and pass the soup through a fine sieve. Return to a clean pan and season with salt and pepper. Blend in the cream and heat through. Pour into heated bowls and scatter orange strips over the top.

Sunset Soup

SERVES 4

700 g (1½ lb) carrots
1 small onion
4 ripe tomatoes
50 g (2 oz) butter
900 ml (1½ pts) chicken stock
pinch thyme and chervil

salt and freshly ground black pepper
2 tablespoons single cream

Garnish
1 tablespoon finely grated orange rind

Peel and roughly chop the carrots. Skin and chop the onion. Peel the tomatoes, squeeze out the seeds and roughly chop the flesh. Melt the butter, add the carrots and onion and cook over medium heat until the onion is soft and transparent. Add the tomatoes, mix well and cook slowly for 10 minutes, stirring every now and then. Add the stock, herbs, salt and pepper. Bring to the boil and simmer for about 20 minutes or until the carrots are soft. Purée the soup in a blender or through a fine sieve. Add the cream, adjust the seasoning and gently heat through without boiling. Pour into heated soup bowls and sprinkle with a little grated orange rind.

Potage Dubarry

SERVES 4

450 g (1 lb) cauliflower florets
750 ml (1¼ pts) chicken stock
salt and freshly ground black pepper
thin slices of lemon

paprika
thin slices of lemon
1 tablespoon mixed finely chopped
    parsley, chervil and chives

Cook the florets in the stock until tender. Drain and purée. Put the purée in a clean pan, blend in the stock and season with salt and pepper. The soup should have a rich, creamy texture. If necessary, thin it with a little more light stock. Pour the soup into bowls, sprinkle a little paprika over the surface and float a slice of lemon on the top of each serving, then sprinkle with the finely chopped herbs.

Crab Soup
SERVES 4

Not as extravagant as it sounds since the strong flavour of crab can be stretched by the addition of potatoes when this soup is made in a food processor. The result is a rich aromatic soup which can be further enhanced by the addition of a little brandy poured into each bowl just before serving. Serve with slices of buttered brown bread.

350 g (12 oz) potatoes
1 onion
40 g (1½ oz) butter
600 ml (1 pt) fish fumet or
   chicken stock
50 g (2 oz) brown crabmeat
   fresh, frozen or tinned
300 ml (½ pt) milk
salt and freshly ground black pepper

few drops Tabasco sauce
few drops anchovy essence
50 g (2 oz) white crabmeat,
   fresh, frozen or tinned
150 ml (¼ pt) single cream

Garnish
chopped fresh parsley

Peel and roughly chop the potatoes. Peel and roughly chop the onion. Melt the butter in a heavy saucepan. Add the potatoes and onion and cook over a low heat, stirring now and then, until the butter is all absorbed into the vegetables. Add the stock, bring to the boil and simmer until the potatoes are soft. Strain off most of the stock and process the potatoes and onion until smooth. Mix the brown crabmeat with a little of the stock until smooth. Return the purée to a clean pan with the stock and crab mixture, add the milk and bring to the boil. Season with salt, pepper and a little Tabasco and anchovy essence. Mix in the white crabmeat and cream. Heat through without boiling and ladle into bowls. Sprinkle with chopped parsley.

Cream of Celery and Walnut Soup
SERVES 4

1 head celery
1 onion
25 g (1 oz) butter
1.2 litres (2 pts) good chicken stock

celery salt and freshly ground
   black pepper
50 g (2 oz) shelled walnuts
150 ml (¼ pt) double cream

Finely chop some of the celery leaves for garnish. Roughly chop the stalks. Peel and chop the onion. Melt 15 g (½ oz) butter in a saucepan, add the celery and onion and cook over a low heat, stirring occasionally until the onion is soft and transparent. Add the stock, bring to the boil, season with celery salt and pepper and simmer for about 30 minutes until the celery is soft. Purée the soup. Very finely chop the walnuts. Heat the remaining butter in a clean pan. Add the walnuts and cook over medium heat for 3 minutes, stirring. Add the puréed soup, check seasoning and heat through. Stir in the cream and serve with a garnish of celery leaves.

Royal Soup

SERVES 6

This is a real culinary masterpiece which looks as though it took two days to prepare and was made by a chef of the utmost fame, but it is in fact incredibly easy to do yourself. Fragrant consommé in which a chicken liver is lightly poached is crowned by a golden dome of flavour-sealing puff pastry. In the upper echelons of haute cuisine the pastry is removed and discarded by the diner, but I always eat mine!

2 chicken livers
900 ml (1½ pts) good quality beef or
*   chicken consommé*
4 tablespoons medium-dry sherry

2 teaspoons lemon juice
salt and freshly ground black pepper
375 g (13 oz) packet frozen puff pastry
1 egg, beaten

Cut each chicken liver into three slices and place a slice in each bowl. Combine the consommé, sherry and lemon juice in a saucepan, season if necessary and heat through. Pour the hot consommé into the bowls. Roll out the pastry to about 0.5 cm (¼ in) thickness and cut into rounds 1 cm (½ in) larger than the bowls. Dampen the edges of the pastry lightly, stretch it over the bowls and press down the edges firmly all round, indenting them with a fingertip. Brush with beaten egg and bake in a hot oven (200°C / 400°F / Reg 6) for about 20 minutes, until the pastry has risen into domes and is a beautiful golden brown. Serve at once.

Natalia Polonski's Soup Sensation

SERVES 6

Plate 2, illustrated facing page 17.

When I first experimented with this soup, I found it so fabulous that we had it three nights running without losing our enthusiasm for its sparkling summer taste.

1 cucumber
3 tomatoes
2 cloves garlic
450 ml (¾ pt) water
1 chicken stock cube
1 tablespoon tomato purée
1 tablespoon gelatine powder

juice of ½ lemon
freshly ground black pepper
150 ml (¼ pt) sour cream
175 g (6 oz) peeled prawns

Garnish
fennel sprigs

Peel and grate the cucumber. Peel the tomatoes (nick the skins, cover with boiling water for 2 minutes and slide the skins off), remove tough cores and finely chop the flesh. Squeeze the garlic through a press. Combine the water, stock cube and tomato purée in a saucepan; simmer for 5 minutes, stirring occasionally. Remove from the heat, add the gelatine and stir until melted. Leave to cool, then mix in the cucumber, tomato, garlic and lemon juice; season with pepper. Refrigerate until lightly set. Mix up gently with a fork and spoon into individual bowls, leaving a hole in the centre of each one. Fill the holes with sour cream and top with prawns. Garnish with fennel sprigs. Serve well chilled.

Soups & Starters

Watercress and Ham Soup

SERVES 4

A substantial green soup that makes a good start to a meal when the day is cold.

1 large onion
2 large potatoes
1 rasher bacon
3 bunches of watercress
50 g (2 oz) butter

1.2 litres (2 pts) rich chicken stock
50 g (2 oz) cooked ham
100 ml (4 fl oz) single cream
salt and freshly ground black pepper
milk if required

Peel and finely chop the onion. Peel and dice the potatoes. Remove the rind and finely chop the bacon rasher. Cut stalks from the watercress and reserve some leaves for garnishing. Melt butter in a large saucepan, add the onion, potatoes, bacon and watercress stalks, simmer over a low heat, stirring occasionally to prevent browning, for 15–20 minutes until the potatoes are soft and the butter has been absorbed. Add the watercress leaves and stock, bring to the boil and simmer for 10 minutes. Purée in a blender, return to a clean pan and add the ham and cream, season with salt and pepper and heat through, diluting with a little milk if the soup is too thick. Garnish with watercress leaves before serving.

Chicken and Lemon Soup

SERVES 4

A real winner this, combining warmth, goodness and flavour; a soup with all the pick-you-up of a strong whisky and soda or two, and none of the after-effects.

1 small onion
20 g ($\frac{3}{4}$ oz) butter
1 tablespoon flour
900 ml (1$\frac{1}{2}$ pts) strong chicken stock
juice of 1 lemon
2 egg yolks

4 tablespoons single cream
salt and freshly ground black pepper

Garnish
fresh parsley

Peel and finely chop the onion. Melt the butter in a medium-sized saucepan, add the onion and cook over a low heat until transparent. Add the flour, mix well and gradually blend in the chicken stock, stirring continuously until the mixture is smooth. Add the lemon juice, bring to the boil and simmer gently for 10 minutes. Strain the soup through a fine sieve. Beat the egg yolks and cream together until smooth. Whisk stock into the egg and cream mixture a little at a time. Return to a clean saucepan and heat gently, stirring continuously, until heated through. Do not boil. Add salt and pepper if necessary and sprinkle a little finely chopped parsley over the top before serving.

Bull's Eye
SERVES 4

A light, colourful and elegant soup.

2 × 400 g (14 oz) tins consommé
1 tablespoon tomato purée
juice of ½ lemon
1–2 tablespoons dry sherry
1 tablespoon finely chopped chives
 or grated onion

150 ml (¼ pt) sour cream
salt and freshly ground black pepper

Garnish
1 small jar red lumpfish roe

Heat half a tin of consommé in a saucepan. Add the tomato purée, lemon juice and sherry and stir until well blended. Remove from the heat and mix in the remaining consommé. Pour into four bowls and chill until set firm. Mix the chives or grated onion into the sour cream and season lightly with salt and pepper. Place a dollop of sour cream in the centre of each serving and top with a generous spoonful of red lumpfish roe. Serve well chilled.

Avocado Soup
SERVES 4

Although this soup is more usually served chilled it can be heated through and served hot with small croûtons. If you like a spicy flavour then try adding 2 teaspoons of curry powder to the chicken stock.

1 chicken stock cube
450 ml (¾ pt) water
2 ripe avocados
juice of ½ lemon

150 ml (¼ pt) sour cream or yoghourt
1 teaspoon finely grated raw onion
salt and freshly ground black pepper

Dissolve the stock cube in the water. Peel avocados thinly, remove stones and mash the flesh with a fork. Combine avocados, stock and lemon juice and purée in a blender. Beat in the sour cream or yoghourt and grated raw onion. Season with salt and pepper and chill before serving.

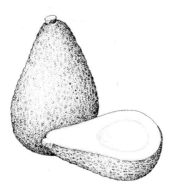

28

Patio Soup
SERVES 6

Beautiful to look at, cool and sophisticated to taste. Make sure it is served icy cold.

2 ripe avocados
juice of ½ lemon
450 ml (¾ pt) chicken stock
150 ml (¼ pt) single cream
150 ml (¼ pt) sour cream
100 g (4 oz) peeled prawns

½ teaspoon finely grated onion
½ teaspoon finely chopped mint
salt and freshly ground black pepper

Garnish
6 mint leaves

Mash avocados with a fork and beat in lemon juice, stock, cream and sour cream. Purée the mixture until absolutely smooth in a blender or food mill. Roughly chop prawns and add them to soup with onion and chopped mint. Season with salt and pepper, mix well and pour into individual soup bowls. Chill in the fridge for at least an hour and garnish each bowl with a leaf of fresh mint.

Iced Cucumber and Mint Soup
SERVES 4–6

2 cucumbers
1 small onion
300 ml (½ pt) water
salt and white pepper
450 ml (¾ pt) chicken stock
2 tablespoons flour
juice of ½ lemon

2 bay leaves
150 ml (¼ pt) plain yoghourt
3 mint leaves

Garnish
thin slices of lemon

Peel and chop the cucumbers and onion. Combine the cucumber, onion and water in a saucepan. Season with salt and pepper, bring to the boil, cover and simmer until the cucumber is soft. Purée the cucumber in a blender or through a fine sieve and return to a clean saucepan. Add enough chicken stock to the flour to make a thin, smooth paste. Blend in the rest of the stock and add to the purée with the lemon juice and bay leaves. Bring the soup slowly to the boil, stirring continually, and simmer gently for 2 minutes. Remove the bay leaves and leave to cool. Stir the yoghourt and mint leaves into the soup, check the seasoning and chill for at least two hours. Garnish with thin slices of lemon.

Iced Cucumber and Watercress Soup
SERVES 4

1 large cucumber
1 small bunch watercress with stalks removed
1 clove garlic, crushed
1 tablespoon finely chopped mint

150 ml (¼ pt) strong chicken stock
150 ml (¼ pt) plain yoghourt
salt and freshly ground black pepper
pinch ground coriander seeds

Peel and chop the cucumber, purée it with the watercress and garlic in a blender or food processor until smooth. Add the mint, chicken stock and yoghourt, season with salt and pepper and coriander and mix well. Served really well chilled.

Cucumber Soup
SERVES 4–6

Served chilled in summer, hot in winter.

1 small onion
1 clove garlic
1½ cucumbers
350 g (12 oz) spinach
2 tablespoons sunflower oil
900 ml (1½ pts) chicken stock

pinch oregano
salt and freshly ground black pepper
pinch nutmeg
300 ml (½ pt) milk
150 ml (¼ pt) single cream
1 tablespoon chopped chives

Peel and finely chop the onion and garlic. Peel 1 cucumber and cut it into small dice. Wash and drain the spinach. Heat the oil and add the onion and garlic. Cook over a low heat until the onion is soft. Add the cucumber and spinach, mix well and simmer for 3 minutes. Add the stock and oregano, season with salt, pepper and nutmeg, bring to the boil and simmer for 20 minutes. Purée soup until smooth. Turn into a clean pan, add the milk and cream and heat through. Just before serving add the remaining cucumber, peeled, with the seeds removed and cut into small dice, and the chives.

Chilled Borsch
SERVES 4

450 g (1 lb) beetroot
2 carrots
1 onion
1.2 litres (2 pts) strong beef stock
1 teaspoon red wine vinegar

salt and freshly ground black pepper
50 g (2 oz) cooked ham
Garnish
4 tablespoons sour cream
1 tablespoon finely chopped chives

Peel the beetroot and chop into small pieces. Peel and finely chop the carrots and onion. Simmer vegetables in the stock until tender and the soup is a deep red. Strain through a fine sieve. Add the vinegar and season with salt and pepper. Chill well.

Cut the ham into thin strips and add to the soup. Garnish each serving with a spoonful of sour cream mixed with the chives.

Beetroot and Pickled Cucumber Soup

SERVES 4

1 onion
1 clove garlic
1 stalk celery
4 large tomatoes
2 tablespoons vegetable oil

bouquet garni
900 ml (1½ pts) chicken stock
salt and freshly ground black pepper
350 g (12 oz) cooked beetroot
2 dill-pickled cucumbers

Peel and chop the onion and crush the garlic. Chop the celery. Skin the tomatoes and remove the seeds. Heat the oil in a saucepan, add the garlic and onion and cook over a low heat, stirring occasionally to prevent sticking, until the onion is soft and transparent. Add the celery, tomatoes, bouquet garni and stock, season with salt and pepper, bring to the boil and simmer for 20 minutes. Strain off the liquid and purée vegetables in a blender or food processor. Blend the liquid into the purée and mix well. Coarsely grate the beetroot and dill-pickled cucumber. Add them to the soup, mixing well. Check the seasoning and chill well before serving.

Chilled Smoked Haddock Soup

SERVES 4

A spoonful of red caviar on the top of each serving turns this soup into something really special.

100 g (4 oz) smoked haddock fillet
600 ml (1 pt) milk
300 ml (½ pt) plain yoghourt
4–5 tablespoons finely chopped
 pickled cucumber

2 tablespoons finely chopped chives
½ tablespoon grated onion
1 teaspoon lemon juice
freshly ground black pepper

Poach haddock gently in the milk until soft. Drain off the milk and flake the fish (make sure you remove all the bones). When the milk has cooled, skim off any fat from the surface and mix in the yoghourt. Add the pickled cucumber to the milk and yoghourt with the fish, chives, grated onion and lemon juice. Season with a little pepper and chill well.

Iced Melon Tea

SERVES 4

1 ripe cantaloup melon
300 ml ($\frac{1}{2}$ pt) dry white wine
1 tablespoon sugar
juice of $\frac{1}{2}$ lemon
pinch ground ginger

pinch ground cinnamon
300 ml ($\frac{1}{2}$ pt) water

Garnish
chopped mint leaves

Cut the melon in half. Remove all seeds and scoop out the flesh. Combine the melon and other ingredients in a saucepan, bring to the boil and simmer gently for 20 minutes. Cool and purée in a blender until completely smooth. Chill until ice cold and serve in bowls with a scattering of finely chopped mint leaves over the surface.

Lightly Curried Apple and Apricot Soup

SERVES 6

1 onion
2 cooking apples
1 tablespoon sunflower oil
1 tablespoon mild curry powder
225 g (8 oz) dried apricots

400 g (14 oz) tin tomatoes
900 ml (1$\frac{1}{2}$ pts) chicken stock
salt and freshly ground black pepper
1 teaspoon lemon juice
sugar or honey, to taste (optional)

Peel and chop the onion. Peel, core and chop the apples. Heat the oil in a very large frying pan, add the onion and cook gently until it is soft and transparent. Stir in the curry powder and mix well. Add the apricots and apples, mix in the tomatoes, bring to the boil and add the chicken stock, seasoning and lemon juice. Simmer for 30 minutes and at this point check the liquid. If it is too sharp add a little sugar or honey. Strain off the liquid and purée the fruit and tomatoes in a blender. Add the liquid to the fruit and chill really well.

Chilled Apple Soup

SERVES 4

900g (2 lb) Granny Smith apples
1 litre (1$\frac{3}{4}$ pts) clear
    chicken stock
2 teaspoons curry powder

juice of $\frac{1}{2}$ lemon plus 1 teaspoon
150 ml ($\frac{1}{4}$ pt) dry white wine
4 tablespoons double cream

Peel, core and roughly chop the apples. Combine them with the chicken stock, curry powder and juice of half a lemon. Bring to the boil and simmer gently for 30 minutes until the apples are soft and transparent. Line a sieve with a piece of muslin and place it over a large bowl. Pour the apples and liquid through it and when the liquid has drained through, gather the edges of the cloth together and gently squeeze the cooked apples to extract the remaining juices. Discard the pulp. Add the wine to the soup and chill in the fridge until ice-cold. Before serving, whip the cream, blend in a teaspoon of lemon juice and add a spoonful to each serving.

Plate 3. Circe Cocktail

Plate 4. Marinated Herring

Chilled Melon Soup
SERVES 4

1 Ogen melon
600 ml (1 pt) water
1 chicken stock cube
1 teaspoon curry powder
juice of ½ lemon

¼ teaspoon ground ginger
2 tablespoons double cream

Garnish
chopped mint leaves

Halve the melon and scoop out the seeds. Scrape out all the flesh and combine it in a saucepan with the water, stock cube, curry powder, lemon juice and ground ginger. Bring slowly to the boil and simmer gently for 20 minutes. Purée in a blender or through a fine sieve and leave to cool. Blend in the cream, pour into soup bowls and leave to chill in the refrigerator for at least an hour; garnish with chopped mint just before serving.

Green Pepper Soup
SERVES 4

2 green peppers
1 parsnip
1 onion
2 rashers streaky bacon
150 ml (¼ pt) white wine

600 ml (1 pt) chicken stock
1 bay leaf
150 ml (¼ pt) gold top milk
  or single cream
salt and freshly ground black pepper

Remove the cores and seeds from the green peppers and roughly chop the flesh. Reserve a few pieces chopped finely. Peel and chop the parsnip and onion. Remove rinds and chop the bacon. Cook the bacon without added fat in a saucepan for 3 minutes, then add the vegetables and cook in the bacon fat, stirring occasionally, for 5 minutes. Add the wine, stock and bay leaf. Bring to the boil and simmer gently for 20 minutes until the vegetables are tender. Remove the bay leaf and purée the soup in a blender or food processor. Return to the cleaned plan and stir in the milk. Heat through without boiling, season to taste and stir in the reserved green pepper. Refrigerate and serve chilled.

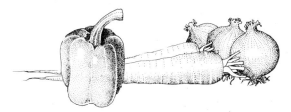

Serendipity Cocktail
SERVES 4

This refreshing drink has only 30 calories per serving.

600 ml (1 pt) tomato juice
1 sprig parsley
1 slice lemon
2 drops Tabasco and 2 of
  Worcestershire sauce
¼ green pepper with seeds removed
1 stalk celery, chopped

1 teaspoon grated raw onion
salt

Garnish
4 tender stalks celery
4 lemon slices

Combine all the ingredients in an electric blender and process until smooth. Strain into four goblets, chill well and garnish with a stick of celery and a slice of lemon.

Charlestown Salata
SERVES 6

Made in the manner of the delicious Greek taramasalata, this can also be used as a sandwich filling. Serve it in a mound on crisp lettuce leaves; garnish with olives and accompany with plenty of hot toast.

2 slices white bread, crusts removed
350 g (12 oz) smoked mackerel
200 ml (7 fl oz) olive oil
juice of ½ lemon

1 teaspoon grated raw onion
1 clove garlic, crushed
1 tablespoon sour cream
salt and freshly ground black pepper

Dip the bread in warm water to soften it. Squeeze out all excess water. Remove the skin from the mackerel and fillet the fish, removing all bones. Pound the flesh until smooth in a mortar with a pestle. Add the bread and continue to pound to a smooth paste (this can be done in a blender). Gradually beat in the oil as for a mayonnaise, so that the mixture emulsifies. After half the oil has been used, beat in the remainder with the lemon juice. The mixture should be smooth, creamy and thick. Add the grated onion, crushed garlic and sour cream. Season with salt and pepper, mix well and chill before serving.

Guacamole
SERVES 4

Serve with hot toast or hot cream crackers. It also works well as a dip for crudités.

2 ripe tomatoes
1 clove garlic
1 small onion
1 large or 2 small avocados
1 tablespoon finely chopped celery

2 tablespoons very finely chopped
*   parsley*
2 tablespoons lemon juice
drop Tabasco sauce
salt and freshly ground black pepper

Peel the tomatoes, discard the core and seeds and finely chop the flesh. Crush the garlic. Peel and very finely chop or grate onion. Peel the avocado, remove the stone and mash flesh with a fork until smooth. Combine all the ingredients, mix well and season with salt and pepper. Pile into a serving dish and serve at once.

Cucumber with Sour Cream
SERVES 4

This is an old summer favourite. Serve it as a sauce for fish or barbecued food; use it as a dip with sticks of crisp green pepper; serve it as part of a hot weather hors d'oeuvre or as a salad side dish. To make it into a delicious starter cocktail add prawns, a little tomato ketchup and a dash of Worcestershire sauce and Tabasco and serve on a bed of chopped lettuce.

   The garlic is optional and if you don't have any fresh dill available (a herb well worth growing if you can) soften a little dried dill in lemon juice before adding.

1 large cucumber
salt
1 small clove garlic
150 ml ($\frac{1}{4}$ pt) sour cream
1 tablespoon finely chopped dill

1 tablespoon finely chopped chives
1 tablespoon finely chopped mint
$\frac{1}{4}$ teaspoon caster sugar
freshly ground black pepper
paprika

Peel and coarsely grate the cucumber. Place in a sieve, sprinkle with salt and leave to stand for 30 minutes in a cool place. Rinse well and press firmly to remove excess water, pat dry with kitchen paper. Squeeze the garlic through a garlic press or crush with a fork. Combine all ingredients, mix lightly and season with pepper. Sprinkle the top with paprika and chill well before serving.

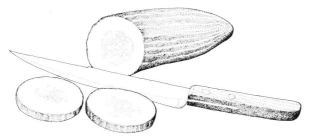

Cold Artichokes with Prawn Mayonnaise

SERVES 4

4 globe artichokes
1 onion
1 tablespoon white wine vinegar
1 teaspoon lemon juice
1 tablespoon tomato ketchup

200 ml (7 fl oz) mayonnaise
100 g (4 oz) peeled prawns
2 spring onions
salt and freshly ground black pepper

Trim the artichokes. Bring 2.5 cm (1 in) of water to the boil in a saucepan that is just large enough to take them all. Add the onion, peeled and finely chopped, and the vinegar. Place the artichokes upside down in the water, cover and cook over a medium heat for 30–45 minutes until tender. Drain well and leave to cool. Carefully remove the centre leaves of the artichokes and the fibrous hairs from the centre. Add the lemon juice and tomato ketchup to the mayonnaise and mix well. Roughly chop the prawns and finely slice the spring onions. Add them to the mayonnaise and season with salt and pepper. Fill the centre of the artichokes with the prawn mayonnaise and chill well before serving.

Stuffed Tomatoes

SERVES 4

4 small firm ripe tomatoes
2 spring onions
100 g (4 oz) cottage cheese
pinch dried mixed herbs

salt and freshly ground black pepper

Garnish
fresh parsley or red caviar

Cut a slice off the top of the tomatoes and scoop out the core and seeds. Very finely chop the spring onions. Combine the cottage cheese with the onions and herbs, season with salt and pepper and mix well. Fill the tomatoes with this mixture and garnish with a sprig of parsley or with a teaspoon of red caviar.

Soups & Starters

Melodia
SERVES 4

4 small ripe melons
1 ripe avocado
150 ml (¼ pt) plain yoghourt
½ teaspoon made English mustard

½ teaspoon lemon juice
2 anchovy fillets
1 tablespoon finely chopped mint
freshly ground black pepper

Cut a thin slice off the top of each melon and scoop out the seeds. Using a small ball scoop, remove all the flesh and transfer to a bowl. Halve the avocado, remove the stone and scoop out the flesh with the ball scoop. Add the avocado to the melon. Combine the yoghourt, mustard and lemon juice. Finely chop the anchovies and add to the yoghourt with the mint. Season with pepper and pour the sauce over the melon and avocado. Mix lightly, fill melon shells with the mixture and chill in the fridge for at least an hour before serving.

Cocktail Caravancia
SERVES 4

1 small honeydew melon
½ cucumber
3 tomatoes
1 tablespoon white wine vinegar
4 tablespoons olive or sunflower oil
1 teaspoon lemon juice
½ teaspoon Dijon mustard
1 tablespoon tomato ketchup

1 teaspoon curry powder
1 tablespoon finely chopped chives
salt and freshly ground black pepper
100 g (4 oz) peeled prawns

Garnish
lemon slices

Halve the melon and remove the seeds. Cut the flesh into small dice. Peel and halve the cucumber lengthwise; remove the seeds and dice the flesh. Immerse the tomatoes in boiling water for 2 minutes, drain well and slide the skins off. Halve the tomatoes, scoop out the seeds and tough cores and dice the flesh. Combine the vinegar, oil, lemon juice, mustard, tomato ketchup, curry powder and chives in a screw-top jar, season with salt and pepper and shake vigorously. Toss all the ingredients with the dressing, divide between four glass goblets and chill well for at least an hour before serving. Garnish with thin slices of lemon.

Circe Cocktail

SERVES 6

Plate 3, illustrated facing page 32.

Serve with buttered brown bread or hot brown rolls.

1 small Ogen melon
3 kiwi fruit
175 g (6 oz) seedless green grapes
2 avocados
1½ tablespoons lemon juice
4 tablespoons olive oil

1 teaspoon honey
salt and freshly ground black pepper
1 tablespoon chopped parsley
small pinch ground aniseed
1 tablespoon vodka

Halve the melon, remove the seeds and scoop out the flesh. Cut into small cubes. Peel and slice the kiwi fruit. Cut the grapes in half. Halve and remove the stones from the avocados, then peel and cut the fruit into 1 cm (½ in) slices. Combine all the fruit in a bowl. Mix the remaining ingredients together and toss with the fruit. Transfer to six glass goblets and chill well.

Avocado with Cottage Cheese

SERVES 4

A good slimmers' salad which can be served as a first course.

4 spring onions
100 g (4 oz) cottage cheese
salt and freshly ground black pepper

2 ripe avocados
pinch cayenne pepper

Trim and finely chop the spring onions. Add them to the cottage cheese, mix well, seasoning with salt and black pepper. Halve the avocados, remove the stones and fill the cavities with cottage cheese, spreading it over the surface of the avocados to prevent discolouring. Sprinkle a pinch of cayenne pepper over each one. Serve at once.

Devilled Avocado and Prawns

SERVES 4

2 avocados
1 tablespoon lemon juice
2 tablespoons olive oil
pinch mustard powder
1 tablespoon white wine vinegar
few drops Worcestershire sauce

few drops Tabasco sauce
salt and freshly ground black pepper
100 g (4 oz) peeled prawns
½ tablespoon finely chopped chives
or parsley

Cut the avocados in half lengthwise and discard the stones; spoon out the flesh and cut into small dice. Toss the avocado with the lemon juice. Combine the olive oil, mustard, vinegar, Worcestershire and Tabasco sauces. Season with salt and pepper and add the avocado, prawns and finely chopped chives or parsley. Heap the mixture into the avocado shells and chill before serving.

Baked Avocados with Creamed Prawns
SERVES 4

2 large avocados
2 tablespoons lemon juice
pinch grated nutmeg
few drops Worcestershire sauce
few drops Tabasco sauce

150 ml (¼ pt) white sauce
salt and freshly ground black pepper
100 g (4 oz) peeled prawns
50 g (2 oz) grated cheese
pinch paprika

Halve the avocados, remove the stones and brush the flesh with lemon juice. Slightly enlarge the centre cavities. Add a pinch of nutmeg and the Worcestershire and Tabasco sauces to the white sauce. Season with salt and pepper, if necessary, and add the prawns. Fill the centres of avocados with the prawn mixture, top with grated cheese and sprinkle with a little paprika. Place on a lightly greased baking dish and bake in a moderately hot oven (190°C / 375°F / Reg 5) for 10–15 minutes until the avocados are heated through and the cheese has melted.

Shuimono
SERVES 4

You can make this seafood dish with crab too.

1 large cucumber
salt
225 g (8 oz) peeled prawns
juice of 1 large lemon
1 teaspoon caster sugar

freshly ground black pepper

Garnish
4 spring onions

Peel the cucumber, cut into thin slices and then matchstick strips, sprinkle with salt and leave to drain in a colander for 30 minutes. Rinse and dry on kitchen paper and combine with the prawns, lemon juice and sugar. Season with salt and pepper and garnish with spring onions, cutting down through the green part to give a tasselled appearance. Arrange in four bowls and chill before serving.

Prawns in Lemon Consommé
SERVES 4

400 g (14 oz) tin consommé
juice of 1 lemon
1 tablespoon dry sherry

225 g (8 oz) peeled prawns
finely shredded lettuce or watercress

Combine the consommé, lemon juice and sherry and leave in the fridge until the mixture begins to gel. Mix in peeled prawns, pour into a mould and chill until set firm. Turn out on to a bed of finely shredded lettuce or watercress.

Tuna and White Bean Salad

SERVES 4

200 g (7 oz) tin tuna in oil
½ teaspoon dried basil
1 teaspoon lemon juice
2 onions (preferably mild ones)
12 black olives

1 crushed clove garlic
3 tablespoons olive oil
1 tablespoon white wine vinegar
salt and freshly ground black pepper
425 g (15 oz) tin butter beans

Drain off and reserve the oil from the tuna. Soak the basil in lemon juice. Peel and very thinly slice the onions and divide into rings. Halve the black olives, removing stones. Combine the garlic, oil, tuna oil, vinegar and lemon juice with basil; season with salt and black pepper and mix well. Break the tuna into chunks and toss with the onions and beans in the dressing. Arrange on four dishes, garnish with olives and chill before serving.

Three-Bean Salad with Tuna Fish and Herbs

SERVES 6

425 g (15 oz) tin
   French beans
425 g (15 oz) tin butter beans
425 g (15 oz) tin red kidney beans
100 g (4 oz) tin tuna fish
1 small mild onion
1 teaspoon Dijon mustard
1 tablespoon white wine vinegar
3 tablespoons olive oil
1 tablespoon tomato chutney

garlic salt and freshly ground
   black pepper
2 tablespoons finely chopped
   parsley
pinch dried basil and oregano

Garnish
12 black olives
1 hard-boiled egg

Drain all the beans. Drain and coarsely flake the tuna. Peel and very thinly slice the onion. Combine the mustard, vinegar, oil and tomato chutney and mix well; season with garlic salt and pepper and mix in the parsley and dried herbs. Pour the dressing over the beans, onion and tuna and toss lightly. Turn into a serving dish and garnish with olives, finely chopped egg white and yolk rubbed through a sieve. Serve with French bread.

Marinated Herring

SERVES 4

Plate 4, illustrated facing page 33.

2 carrots
2 onions
300 ml (½ pt) dry white wine
300 ml (½ pt) dry cider
bouquet garni
3 bay leaves
10 black peppercorns
2 cloves
salt

150 ml (¼ pt) white wine vinegar
4 fresh herrings, filleted
2 tablespoons olive or sunflower oil
2 red onions
1 green pepper
300 ml (½ pt) sour cream
white pepper
1 tablespoon finely chopped
    spring onions

Peel and thinly slice the carrots and onions. Simmer wine and cider with carrots, onions, herbs, peppercorns, cloves and a little salt for 30 minutes. Add vinegar and bring to the boil. Arrange the fish in a shallow pan, pour over it the boiling liquid and boil for 2 minutes. Remove from heat. Add the oil and leave until cool. Refrigerate for 24 hours. Peel and very thinly slice the red onions. Deseed the pepper and thinly slice. Remove the fish from the marinade and cut or leave whole, if preferred. Beat cream and season with salt and pepper. Arrange herrings on serving plate, pour over cream and arrange the peppers and onions on top. Sprinkle with chopped onions.

Mussels Provençal

SERVES 4

Mussels cooked in the style of snails and just as delicious.

3 litres (5 pts) mussels
    (about 10–12 per person)
150 ml (¼ pt) dry white wine
1 small bunch parsley
2 cloves garlic

50 g (2 oz) butter
50 g (2 oz) sliced bread
    with crusts removed
2 teaspoons green peppercorns
salt

Scrub the mussels with a wire brush, pull out the beards which protrude from the opening side of the shell. Place the mussels in a large, heavy saucepan, pour over the wine and bring to the boil over a high heat. Cook over high heat for about 6 minutes, shaking the pan, until all the mussels have opened. Discard any unopened ones. Remove the mussels one at a time onto a flat open serving dish, pulling off the top, empty shells. Remove the coarse stems from the parsley. Peel the garlic. Finely chop the parsley and garlic together, add the butter, the bread and peppercorns and blend to a smooth paste. Season with salt. Spread a teaspoon of the mixture onto each mussel and put under a hot grill until golden brown. Serve at once.

Saumon Fumé Empress Charlotte
SERVES 4

175 g (6 oz) smoked salmon
2 small leeks
6 tomatoes
150 ml (¼ pt) white wine vinegar
150 ml (¼ pt) water
2 teaspoons sugar

¼ teaspoon mustard powder
6 crushed coriander seeds
cayenne pepper

Garnish
hard-boiled egg yolk

Cut the smoked salmon into thin strips. Remove the outer leaves of the leeks and very thinly slice the tender hearts. Cover the tomatoes with boiling water and leave for 2 minutes, drain, slide the skins off and slice. Arrange alternate slices of tomato, salmon and leeks in small dishes or glass goblets. Combine vinegar, water, sugar, mustard and coriander in a saucepan and bring to the boil. Season with a little cayenne pepper. Pour the hot dressing over the other ingredients, cover and refrigerate for at least 5 hours before serving. Decorate each dish with a 'mimosa' of coarsely sieved egg yolk. Serve with hot pitta bread.

Ceviche
SERVES 6

1 sea bass or any firm white fish, about 1.5 kg (3 lb)
4 spring onions
1 tablespoon finely chopped fresh coriander or parsley
juice of 1 lime

1 wineglass dry white wine
4 tablespoons sunflower oil
sea salt and freshly ground black pepper
lettuce

Ask the fishmonger to fillet the bass (take the bones home to use for a delicious fish soup) and remove the skin from the fillets. Chill the fillets in the deep freeze until they begin to stiffen and then cut the flesh into 1 cm (½ in) diagonal strips. Arrange these in a shallow dish. Trim and thinly slice the spring onions and scatter over the fish. Combine lime juice, coriander, white wine and oil. Season with salt and pepper and pour the dressing over the fish, which should become opaque. Cover with cling film and refrigerate for 4 hours, turning the fish after 2 hours. Drain off most of the dressing and serve the fish, which will have 'cooked' in the marinade, on large lettuce leaves.

Soups & Starters

Sardines and Tomatoes
SERVES 4

3 × 125 g (4 oz) tins sardines
8 ripe tomatoes
1 clove garlic

4 tablespoons olive oil
  plus extra for drizzling
salt and freshly ground black pepper
2 tablespoons dried breadcrumbs

Drain the oil from the sardines and arrange them in a lightly greased baking dish. Skin the tomatoes, remove seeds and chop flesh roughly. Crush the garlic, combine with the olive oil and tomatoes in a saucepan with salt and pepper and cook over a low heat for 8 minutes without stirring. Pour the tomato mixture over the sardines, sprinkle thickly with breadcrumbs and moisten with a little olive oil. Brown in a hot oven (200°C / 400°F / Reg 6) for 10 minutes.

Kamano Miko (Pickled Smoked Salmon)
SERVES 6

Serve with thin slices of buttered brown bread.

175 g (6 oz) smoked salmon trimmings
2 bunches spring onions
4–6 tomatoes
150 ml (¼ pt) water

150 ml (¼ pt) white wine vinegar
2 teaspoons sugar
½ teaspoon ground dried red chillies

Remove any hard dry edges from the smoked salmon and cut the rest into thin strips. Cut about 1 cm (½ in) off the green tops of the spring onions and trim the stems. Slice each onion into three, lengthwise. Peel and thinly slice the tomatoes. Combine the water, vinegar, sugar and ground chillies in a saucepan and bring to the boil. Arrange layers of tomatoes, onions and smoked salmon in a glass serving dish, pour over this the hot vinegar mixture, cover and refrigerate for at least 8 hours.

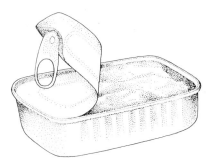

Smoky Stuffed Eggs
SERVES 4

6 hard-boiled eggs
300 ml ($\frac{1}{2}$ pt) mayonnaise
1 cooked kipper
1 teaspoon lemon juice
freshly ground black pepper

1 bunch watercress

Garnish
lettuce leaves

Cut the eggs in half lengthwise and remove the yolks. Mash the yolks to a smooth paste with 1 tablespoon of the mayonnaise. Discard the skin and bones and put the kipper through the blender. Beat together the kipper, egg-yolk mixture and lemon juice and season with pepper. Trim the watercress and cook in fast-boiling salted water for 3 minutes. Drain well and rub through a fine sieve. Leave to cool, then mix the watercress purée into the mayonnaise. Fill the egg whites with the fish mixture. Place the eggs flat side down on a serving dish and surround with crisp lettuce leaves; cover with the mayonnaise and serve.

Quail Eggs in Gelée
SERVES 4

400 g (14 oz) tin beef consommé
2 tablespoons dry sherry
1 tablespoon tomato purée
pinch oregano
2 teaspoons lemon juice
1 teaspoon powdered gelatine
4 large tinned artichoke hearts

12 cooked quail eggs
(these can be bought in tins or jars and should be drained)
2 tablespoons chopped red pepper

Garnish
4 teaspoons sour cream
paprika

Combine the consommé, sherry and tomato purée in a small saucepan. Add the oregano and lemon juice and simmer, stirring, for 5 minutes. Soften the gelatine in a little of the warm consommé mixture. Stir the gelatine into the liquid. Leave to cool until beginning to set. Drain artichokes and arrange them in the bottom of four large ramekin dishes, place 3 quail eggs on the centre of each artichoke and sprinkle with finely chopped red pepper. Pour over enough of the setting consommé mixture to cover the ingredients and chill until set firm. Garnish each serving with a teaspoon of sour cream and a light dusting of paprika.

Mimosa Mousse

SERVES 4–6

7 hard-boiled eggs
1 teaspoon curry powder
1 teaspoon lemon juice
1 tablespoon warm water
1 teaspoon gelatine powder
2 × 400 g (14 oz) tins consommé

1 tablespoon tomato purée
150 ml ($\frac{1}{4}$ pt) double cream
150 ml ($\frac{1}{4}$ pt) mayonnaise
salt and freshly ground black pepper
few drops Worcestershire and Tabasco
sauces

Peel the eggs, reserve one yolk and roughly chop the remaining whites and yolks. Combine the curry powder, lemon juice, water and gelatine and heat gently, stirring until gelatine has dissolved. Add one tin of consommé and the tomato purée and heat just long enough for the consommé to melt. Leave to cool. Beat the cream until thick; add to the mayonnaise and combine with the consommé mixture in a glass bowl; chill in the fridge until set. Spoon over the remaining consommé and garnish with the reserved egg yolk rubbed through a coarse sieve.

Egg and Cucumber Mousse

SERVES 6

This dish is very pretty garnished with thin slices of pimiento-stuffed olives, or topped with a thin layer of sour cream and some caviar.

5 hard boiled-eggs
$\frac{1}{2}$ cucumber
1 teaspoon gelatine powder
150 ml ($\frac{1}{4}$ pt) plain yoghourt

2 tablespoons mayonnaise
1 tablespoon lemon juice
salt and white pepper
dash Tabasco sauce

Chop the hard-boiled eggs. Peel the cucumber and cut the flesh into small dice. Dissolve the gelatine in 1 tablespoon hot water. Mix the yoghourt with the mayonnaise and lemon juice, season with salt and pepper, add the Tabasco and mix in the gelatine. Fold in the eggs and cucumber, spoon into cocotte dishes and chill until set.

Mousse de Jambon

SERVES 4–6

700 g (1$\frac{1}{2}$ lb) cooked lean ham
2 tablespoons tomato purée
paprika
200 ml (7 fl oz) double cream
1 tablespoon gelatine powder

5 tablespoons water
salt and freshly ground black pepper

Garnish
chopped aspic jelly

Mince the ham. Add the tomato purée and a pinch of paprika. Put the mixture through a fine sieve. Whip the cream. Melt the gelatine in a little water. Add the cream, then the gelatine to the ham mixture, stirring well. Season well with salt, pepper and a little paprika. Turn into a dampened mould and chill until set. Then turn on to a serving plate, garnish the border with aspic jelly and serve.

45

Mushroom Tartlets with Saffron and Cream

SERVES 8

Plate 5, illustrated facing page 48.

*350 g (12 oz) frozen puff pastry,
  thawed*
350 g (12 oz) button mushrooms
1 small onion
40 g (1½ oz) butter
4 tablespoons dry white wine
salt and freshly ground black pepper

pinch ground saffron
150 ml (¼ pt) double cream
2 teaspoons flour

Garnish
chopped coriander or parsley

Thinly roll out the pastry and line eight patty tins about 13 cm (5 in) in diameter and bake blind until a light golden brown. Slice the mushrooms. Peel and very finely chop the onion. Melt the butter in a saucepan, add the onion and cook over a low heat until the onion is soft and transparent. Add the wine, increase the heat, season with salt and pepper, mix in the saffron and boil until the liquid has almost completely disappeared. Add the mushrooms and toss them over a high heat for 3 minutes (they should be cooked but still firm). Mix the cream with the flour to a smooth paste and stir it into the mushrooms. Continue to stir over a high heat until the sauce is thick. Turn the mushroom mixture into the patty cases, garnish and serve at once, or leave the mixture to cool, fill the cases and reheat in a moderate oven (180°C / 350°F / Reg 4) for about 15 minutes until heated through.

Camembert Fritters

SERVES 4

1 × 350 g (12 oz) firm Camembert
1 teaspoon cayenne pepper
1 egg, beaten

3 tablespoons dried breadcrumbs
oil for deep-frying

Thinly pare the rind of the Camembert and cut the cheese into 4 cm (1½ in) finger-size lengths. Sprinkle the cheese with cayenne. Dip the cheese into the beaten egg and then into the breadcrumbs. Chill until firm, then egg and breadcrumb a second time, shaking off the excess crumbs. Deep-fry the Camembert in very hot fat for just a few minutes until golden brown and drain at once on kitchen paper, serving as quickly as possible.

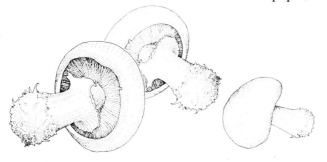

Tagliatelli Alla Carbonara

SERVES 6 AS A STARTER,
4 AS A MAIN COURSE

50 g (2 oz) ham
3 eggs
50 g (2 oz) finely grated cheese
salt and freshly ground black pepper

450 g (1 lb) tagliatelle
50 g (2 oz) butter
2 tablespoons double cream

Finely chop the ham, beat the eggs with a fork and combine the ham, eggs and half the cheese; season with salt and pepper. Cook the tagliatelle in boiling salted water until just tender, drain well and rinse in cool water. Return the pasta to a saucepan with the butter and stir gently over a slow flame until the butter melts. Pour over the egg mixture and continue to stir, without breaking the pasta, until the egg is on the point of setting (the sauce should be liquid, not scrambled). Add the cream, check the seasoning, turn into a serving dish and sprinkle with the remaining grated cheese before serving.

Potted Cheese with Port

SERVES 4

These pots may be kept in the fridge for up to two weeks and make marvellous presents if you top the pots with a piece of patterned cotton.

350 g (12 oz) mature Cheddar cheese
3 tablespoons port
100 g (4 oz) butter
1 teaspoon dried mixed herbs

1 tablespoon finely chopped parsley
pinch ground mace and cayenne pepper
freshly ground black pepper
4 small bay leaves

Grate the cheese coarsely. Combine the cheese, port, butter and herbs in a bowl over a saucepan of hot water and stir over a medium heat until the cheese has melted. Add parsley and season with a little mace, cayenne, and freshly ground black pepper. Mix well until the cheese is smooth. Pour into pots, top with a bay leaf and leave to cool. Cover tightly with cling film and refrigerate.

Potted Shin of Beef

SERVES 4

A good dish for winter and spring picnics. Serve with French bread.

450 g (1 lb) shin of beef
150 g (5 oz) streaky bacon
salt, pepper and a pinch nutmeg

bouquet garni
clear stock or water
1 bay leaf

Cut the meat into very thin slices. Remove the rinds and chop bacon. Arrange alternate layers of meat and bacon, seasoning each layer with salt, nutmeg and pepper. Add bouquet of herbs and lay the bacon rinds on top. Pour in just enough stock to cover, cover very tightly and cook in a slow oven (150°C / 300°F / Reg 2) for 3 hours or until the meat is fork-tender. Remove the bacon rinds, bouquet garni and bay leaf, leave to cool and then refrigerate until the juice has set to a clear jelly.

Barbecued Spare Ribs
SERVES 4

A substantial first course which should be followed by a light main course.

900 g (2 lb) spare ribs of pork
  (American cut)
2 cloves garlic
1 large onion
2 tablespoons olive oil
3 tablespoons brown sugar
2 tablespoons malt vinegar

$\frac{1}{4}$ teaspoon chilli powder
pinch sage
2 tablespoons tomato ketchup
150 ml ($\frac{1}{4}$ pt) strong stock or water
  and stock cube
salt and freshly ground black pepper

Part boil the spare ribs in boiling salted water for 4 minutes, drain well and pat dry on kitchen paper. Divide the ribs up by cutting between the bones with kitchen scissors. Crush the garlic. Peel and finely chop the onion. Heat the olive oil in a saucepan, add the onion and garlic and cook over a medium heat until the onion is soft and transparent. Add the remaining ingredients, season with salt and pepper, bring to the boil and simmer for 5 minutes. Place the spare ribs in a baking dish, brush with some of the sauce and cook in a moderately hot oven (190°C / 375°F / Reg 5) for 30 minutes. Pour over the remaining sauce and cook for a further 45–60 minutes, basting frequently. Transfer the spare ribs to a heated serving dish and serve the sauce separately after spooning off any excess fat from the surface.

Smoked Fish Pâté
SERVES 6

The smoked fish you use depends on your purse but the basic recipe remains the same. Try this with smoked mackerel, smoked salmon trimmings, kipper, cooked smoked haddock or even smoked eel. Serve with hot toast.

$\frac{1}{2}$ small onion
$\frac{1}{2}$ clove garlic
150 g (5 oz) butter
225 g (8 oz) smoked fish
  with skin and bones removed

juice of $\frac{1}{2}$ small lemon
150 ml ($\frac{1}{4}$ pt) double cream
freshly ground black pepper
pinch each mace and cayenne
  pepper

Peel and roughly chop the onion and garlic. Heat half the butter in a saucepan, add the onion and garlic and cook over a low heat until the onion is soft and transparent. Combine the onion, garlic, fish and remaining butter in the food processor bowl and process until smooth. Add the lemon juice and cream, season with pepper, mace and cayenne and process until well mixed. Pack into small pots and chill until firm.

Plate 5. Mushroom Tartlets with Saffron and Cream

Plate 6. Slimmers' Lettuce and Cheese Mousse

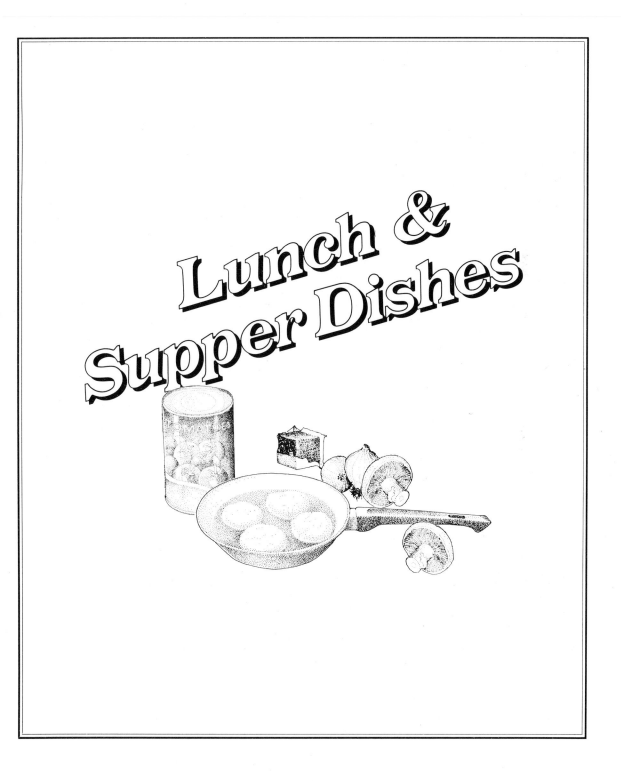

Lunch & Supper Dishes

Prawn and Cucumber Jelly

SERVES 4

½ cucumber
salt
2 red peppers
juice of ½ lemon
1 teaspoon powdered gelatine
1½ × 400 g (14 oz) tins consommé
1 tablespoon medium-dry sherry
225 g (8 oz) peeled prawns

150 ml (¼ pt) home-made mayonnaise
2 tablespoons double cream
1 teaspoon horseradish sauce
few drops Tabasco sauce
salt and freshly ground black pepper

Garnish
lettuce leaves

Peel the cucumber and grate it coarsely. Put into a sieve or colander, sprinkle with a little salt and leave to drain for 20 minutes. Rinse and lightly pat dry with kitchen paper. Remove the core and seeds of the red peppers and very finely chop the flesh. Combine the lemon juice and gelatine with a little of the consommé. Heat over a low flame until the gelatine has melted. Remove from the heat and mix in the remaining consommé and the sherry. Pour a little of the consommé into a ring mould that has been rinsed in cold water. Chill the mould in the fridge until the jelly has set. Spread half the prawns over the set jelly and pour on enough jelly to cover. Return to the fridge until set. Combine the cucumber and peppers and spread over the set prawns and jelly. Pour over enough consommé to cover and leave to set once more. Finish with a layer of prawns and the remaining consommé. Refrigerate for at least an hour. Combine the mayonnaise with the cream and horseradish. Flavour with a few drops of Tabasco and salt and pepper, if necessary. Mix well. Dip the mould quickly into very hot water and turn out onto a serving dish. Fill the centre with the mayonnaise mixture and surround with crisp lettuce leaves.

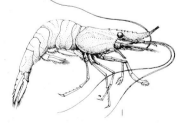

Slimmers' Lettuce and Cheese Mousse

SERVES 4

Plate 6, illustrated facing page 49.

Serve with a tomato, pepper and onion salad.

2 small iceberg lettuces, shredded
4 spring onions
225 g (8 oz) cottage cheese
3 tablespoons freshly grated
    Parmesan cheese
4 tablespoons sour cream

salt and freshly ground black pepper
pinch cayenne
Worcestershire and Tabasco sauces
1 tablespoon powdered gelatine
2 tablespoons hot water
2 egg whites

Very finely chop or shred the hearts of the lettuce reserving the outer leaves for serving. Very finely chop the spring onions. Combine the shredded lettuce, onions, cottage cheese, Parmesan and sour cream in a blender and process until the cottage cheese is smooth. Season the mixture with salt, pepper, a pinch of cayenne and a little Worcestershire and Tabasco sauce. Dissolve the gelatine in the hot water and add it to the cheese base. Chill until it begins to set. Whisk the egg whites until stiff and gently fold into the chilled mixture. Turn into a dampened loaf tin or ring mould and chill until set firm. Turn out and serve in slices on lettuce leaves.

Savoury Chicken Mousse

SERVES 6

A light though filling concoction which makes good use of leftover cooked chicken. It can also be served in individual ramekin dishes as a first course.

3 rashers lean bacon
275 g (10 oz) cooked chicken
150 ml ($\frac{1}{4}$ pt) strong chicken stock
salt, pepper and a pinch cayenne
1 tablespoon powdered gelatine

300 ml ($\frac{1}{2}$ pt) double cream
150 ml ($\frac{1}{4}$ pt) tinned consommé
1 teaspoon lemon juice
1 teaspoon tomato purée

Fry the bacon without extra fat over a low heat until crisp. Reserve the fat and discard rinds. Crumble the bacon rashers into small pieces. Pass the chicken twice through the fine blades of a mincer. Combine the chicken with the crumbled bacon, bacon fat and half the stock. Season with salt, pepper and cayenne. Melt the gelatine in the remaining stock. Whip the cream until thick. Blend the gelatine mixture into the chicken, mix well and fold in the cream. Spoon into a glass bowl and chill in the fridge until firm. Heat the consommé with the lemon juice and tomato purée and season with a little salt and pepper, then leave to cool. Pour over the chicken mousse and leave to set in the fridge. Serve well chilled.

Lunch & Supper Dishes

Maidenwell Club Sandwich

SERVES 4

Plate 7, illustrated facing page 64.

8 thin rashers streaky bacon
 (the thinner the better)
1 small iceberg lettuce
8 firm, ripe tomatoes
12 thin slices white bread
butter

salt and freshly ground black pepper
8 thin slices cooked chicken
mayonnaise

Garnish
pimiento-stuffed green olives

Fry the bacon rashers over a medium-high heat without extra fat until really crisp. Drain on kitchen paper and remove rinds. Clean the lettuce, remove the outer leaves for garnishing and shred the heart. Thinly slice the tomatoes. Toast the bread, remove the crusts and butter one side of each slice. Cover 4 slices of buttered side of toast with two rashers of bacon each and with slices of tomato, season with salt and pepper and top with a second layer of toast, buttered side up. Cover this layer of toast with shredded lettuce and slices of chicken. Spread with mayonnaise, season lightly and cover with the remaining slices of buttered toast. Cut the sandwiches into four triangles, holding each one together with a toothpick put through an olive. Arrange the sandwiches on a plate and garnish them with the lettuce leaves.

Sunshine Sandwiches

SERVES 2

3 eggs
salt and white pepper
40 g (1½ oz) butter
3 rashers streaky bacon

25 g (1 oz) picked-over spinach
4 slices of white or brown bread
 with crusts removed
softened butter, for spreading

Beat the eggs until they are just broken up – do not overbeat – and season with salt and pepper. Heat half the butter in a small saucepan, add the eggs and cook over a low heat, stirring frequently until the eggs are just solidified. Add the remaining butter, mix well and pack the mixture in a small oblong container which has been well-buttered. Leave to set in the refrigerator until firm, turn out, and cut the egg mixture into thin slices. Cook the bacon rashers, without extra fat, over a medium heat until they are really crisp. Drain on kitchen paper, cut off rinds and crumble the rashers. Finely chop the spinach. Spread the bread slices with a little softened butter, cover with the slices of egg, sprinkle over the bacon and spinach and sandwich firmly with a second slice of buttered bread.

Lunch & Supper Dishes

Chicken Salad Sandwiches
SERVES 4

2 cooked chicken portions
1 hard-boiled egg
1 teaspoon curry paste
4 tablespoons mayonnaise
salt and freshly ground black pepper
1 tablespoon finely chopped chives

8 thin slices of white bread
butter
crisp lettuce leaves

Garnish
sliced tomatoes

Discard the skin, remove the meat from the bones and cut it into small dice. Peel and chop the hard-boiled egg. Add the curry paste to the mayonnaise and mix well. Season with salt and pepper if necessary. Add the chicken, egg and chives to the mayonnaise and mix well. Toast the bread and butter one side of each slice. Place some lettuce leaves on half the toast, spread the lettuce leaves lavishly with the chicken mixture and top with the remaining buttered toast. Cut each sandwich into four triangles, spear each triangle with a toothpick and arrange on a plate. Garnish with slices of tomato.

Marika's Scramble
SERVES 2

4 eggs
1 small fillet smoked mackerel
3 small tomatoes
40 g (1½ oz) butter
salt and freshly ground black pepper

4 thin rashers streaky bacon
2 slices of bread, cut into circles

Garnish
1 tablespoon finely chopped parsley

Lightly beat the eggs (do not overbeat; they should just be broken up and runny). Cut the mackerel into small pieces. Cover the tomatoes with boiling water and leave for 2 minutes, drain and slide the skins off, remove the core and seeds and chop the tomato flesh. Melt the butter in a small saucepan. Season the eggs with salt and pepper and add to the butter. Cook over a low heat, stirring until they begin to thicken but are not yet set. Add the mackerel and tomatoes, stirring occasionally, scraping up the set eggs from the bottom of the pan until the mixture is just set – it is important not to overcook the eggs or they will go dry and be curdled-looking. While they are cooking, fry the bacon, rinds removed, until it is nicely crisp and drain on kitchen paper. Fry the circles of bread in bacon fat until they are crisp and golden. Pile the eggs onto the bread, surround with bacon and top with parsley.

Lunch & Supper Dishes

Oeufs à la Tripe
SERVES 4

One of the best hot hard-boiled egg dishes, so named because of its similarity in taste and texture to that of tripe and onions. Lightly cooked shredded cabbage or broccoli spears go well with this dish.

8 hard-boiled eggs
3 Spanish onions
90 g (3½ oz) butter
2 tablespoons flour
450 ml (¾ pt) milk

1 teaspoon Dijon mustard
salt and freshly ground black pepper
pinch nutmeg
4 tablespoons double cream

Shell the eggs and cut them into thin slices with an egg-slicer. Peel and very thinly slice the onions and divide into rings. Melt 40 g (1½ oz) of the butter in a saucepan. Add the onions and cook over a low heat, stirring occasionally, until the onions are soft and transparent (they must not be allowed to brown). Melt the remaining butter in a clean saucepan, add flour and mix well. Gradually blend in the milk, stirring continually, over a medium-high heat until the sauce comes to the boil and is thick and smooth. Add the mustard, season with salt, pepper and nutmeg, mix in the onions and eggs and simmer gently for 3 minutes. Remove from heat and add the cream. Turn into a shallow serving dish, cover with foil and heat through in a moderate oven (180°C / 350°F / Reg 4) for a few minutes before serving.

Crumpelettes
SERVES 2

1 small onion or shallot
4 tablespoons white wine vinegar
pinch each mace and dried thyme
2 egg yolks
90 g (3½ oz) softened butter
  plus extra butter for spreading

salt and freshly ground black pepper
3 tablespoons boiling water
4 eggs
4 crumpets

Make the sauce first: very finely chop the onion and combine with the vinegar, mace and thyme. Bring to the boil and cook over a high heat for about 5 minutes, until the vinegar has been absorbed into the onion. Beat the egg yolks until smooth, blend in the onion and softened butter. Put into the top of a double saucepan and cook over a low heat, stirring continually, until the sauce is as thick and smooth as mayonnaise. Remove from the heat, season with salt and pepper and beat in 3 tablespoons of boiling water a little at a time. Poach the eggs in boiling acidulated water, drain well and trim the edges neatly with kitchen scissors. Toast the crumpets and spread with butter. Place an egg on each crumpet, pour over the sauce and serve at once.

Braised Leeks with Poached Eggs and a Sauce Maigre

SERVES 2

4 large or 6 medium leeks
150 ml (¼ pt) chicken stock
2 egg yolks
juice of ½ lemon

150 ml (¼ pt) plain yoghourt
salt and freshly ground black pepper
2 large eggs
pinch paprika or cayenne

Clean the leeks and blanch them in boiling water for 5 minutes. Drain the leeks well (prop them upside down in a colander) and put them into a baking dish smeared with a dash of oil. Pour in the stock, cover with foil and braise in a moderate oven (180°C / 350°F / Reg 4) for about 30 minutes until the leeks are tender. Combine the egg yolks, lemon juice and yoghourt in a blender and process until smooth. Season with salt and pepper and heat, stirring, in the top of a double boiler until the sauce becomes the consistency of thin custard. Poach the eggs until just set and drain well. Place them on top of the leeks, pour on the sauce and sprinkle with a little paprika or cayenne pepper before serving.

Matrimonial Eggs

SERVES 1

When served with a salad, this makes a surprisingly substantial meal ideal for slimmers.

2 eggs
50 g (2 oz) lean ham
1 tablespoon finely chopped red pepper
½ × 400 g (14 oz) tin
   beef consommé
2 tablespoons lemon juice

1 tablespoon dry sherry (optional)
1 tablespoon tomato purée
salt and freshly ground black pepper
1 tablespoon cottage cheese
½ tablespoon finely chopped chives

Plunge the eggs into boiling water and boil them over a high heat for 5 minutes exactly. Cool them under running water to prevent them from cooking further. Chop the ham finely and mix it with the red pepper. Put this mixture in the bottom of a small, deep dish. Peel the eggs and place them on top of the ham mixture. Heat the consommé, add the lemon juice, sherry, tomato purée and seasoning and stir until the ingredients are well blended. Leave to cool and pour over the eggs. Refrigerate until the consommé is set firm. Top with a spoonful of cottage cheese and sprinkle with the chives before serving.

Gelda's Fancy

SERVES 4

4 hard-boiled eggs
150 g (5 oz) cooked chicken or ham
6 anchovy fillets
40 g (1½ oz) butter
2 tablespoons flour

300 ml (½ pt) milk
1 teaspoon Dijon mustard
salt and freshly ground black pepper
2 tablespoons double cream
50 g (2 oz) grated cheese

Roughly chop the hard-boiled eggs. Finely chop the chicken or ham and anchovies. Melt the butter, add the flour and mix well. Gradually blend in the milk, stirring constantly over a medium heat until the sauce comes to the boil and is thick and smooth. Mix in the mustard, add the eggs, chicken or ham and anchovies. Season with salt and pepper, blend in the cream and pour into a flameproof serving dish. Sprinkle with the grated cheese and brown under a grill or in a hot oven (220°C / 425°F / Reg 7) until golden brown.

Speciality Rarebit

SERVES 4

25 g (1 oz) butter
25 g (1 oz) flour
1 teaspoon English made mustard
150 ml (¼ pt) milk
225 g (8 oz) grated Cheddar cheese

1 tablespoon beer
salt and freshly ground black pepper
4 slices buttered bread
4 thin slices ham
4 eggs

Melt the butter in a saucepan, add the flour and mustard, mix well and gradually blend in the milk, stirring continually over a medium heat until thick and smooth. Mix in the cheese, beer and seasoning and cook gently until the cheese is melted. Have ready 4 slices buttered toast and 4 poached eggs. Cover the buttered toast with slices of ham, top with a poached egg and cover with the cheese mixture. Brown under a hot grill and serve at once.

Tomato and Cheese Omelette Filling

SERVES 4

450 g (1 lb) tomatoes
50 g (2 oz) Cheddar cheese
1½ tablespoons olive or sunflower oil

½ teaspoon dried oregano
salt and freshly ground black pepper

Cover the tomatoes with boiling water, leave them to stand for 2 minutes and then drain and slide the skins off. Remove the core and seeds from the tomatoes and chop the flesh. Cut the cheese into small cubes. Heat the oil in a shallow saucepan, add the tomatoes and oregano and cook over a medium heat, stirring for 15 minutes. Season with salt and pepper and keep warm. Just before your omelette is ready, add the cheese to the filling and heat just long enough for the cheese to begin to melt (it should be soft around the outside, but still firm in the centre).

Omelette Leander
SERVES 4

If you have a little left-over cooked chicken, fill an omelette with a creamy chicken sauce and a good dollop of sour cream. Serve it with special baked potatoes and a salad of lamb's lettuce, grated courgettes and spring onions tossed in a herby vinaigrette dressing.

175 g (6 oz) cooked chicken
1 onion
65 g (2 ½ oz) butter
½ tablespoon flour
4 tablespoons dry white wine
8 tablespoons top of the milk
pinch tarragon
salt and white pepper

150 ml (¼ pt) sour cream
5 eggs
1 teaspoon water
1 tablespoon sunflower oil

Garnish
finely chopped parsley or chives

Finely chop the chicken. Peel and finely chop the onion. Heat 40 g (1½ oz) butter in a saucepan, add the onion and cook over a low heat, stirring to prevent sticking, until the onion is very soft and transparent. Add the chicken and heat well. Add the flour and mix well. Gradually add the white wine and milk, stirring over a medium heat until the sauce is thick and smooth. Add the tarragon, season with salt and pepper and simmer, stirring occasionally, for 5 minutes. Beat the sour cream until smooth. Keep the sauce warm. Lightly beat the eggs with the water (they should not be fluffy). Season with salt and pepper. Heat the remaining butter and the oil in a large omelette pan until foaming. Add the omelette mixture, swirling it round the pan over a moderately high heat. Score through the omelette with a palette knife to allow the mixture to seep through to the bottom. When the omelette is beginning to solidify, spread a layer of sour cream and then chicken filling over the centre, fold it in half, slide it onto a serving plate and serve at once, sprinkled with finely chopped parsley or chives.

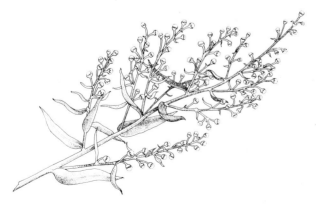

Green Omelette with Tomato Mayonnaise

SERVES 4

4 large eggs
1 tablespoon cold water
175 g (6 oz) cooked and well-drained
    spinach
pinch dried mixed herbs
25 g (1 oz) grated Parmesan cheese
salt and freshly ground black pepper
pinch nutmeg and cayenne

2 tomatoes
1 tablespoon tomato ketchup
200 ml (7 fl oz) mayonnaise
1 teaspoon finely chopped fresh
    tarragon
few drops Worcestershire and Tabasco
    sauce
sunflower oil for frying

Beat the eggs with the water. Finely chop the spinach. Add the spinach, dried mixed herbs and cheese to the eggs and season with salt and freshly ground black pepper, nutmeg and cayenne. Cover the tomatoes with boiling water and leave for 2 minutes, drain, slide the skins off, discard the cores and seeds and finely chop the flesh. Stir the ketchup into the mayonnaise and fold in the tomatoes and tarragon. Flavour with a few drops of Worcestershire and Tabasco sauces. Heat about 0.5 cm ($\frac{1}{4}$ in) oil in a large frying-pan. Add the egg mixture from a large spoon and cook until firm and lightly golden on both sides. Drain on kitchen paper and serve hot or cold, with the tomato mayonnaise.

Omelette Suzanne

SERVES 2

4 thin rashers bacon
100 g (4 oz) cream cheese
5 eggs, separated
200 ml (7 fl oz) single cream

salt and freshly ground black pepper
25 g (1 oz) grated Cheddar cheese
50 g (2 oz) butter

Remove the rinds and cut the bacon rashers into thin matchstick strips. Fry, without fat, until crisp and drain on kitchen paper. Combine with the cream cheese. Beat the egg yolks with half the cream. Lightly whisk the whites and fold them into the yolk mixture with a little salt and pepper. Add the remaining cream to the grated cheese. Heat the butter in an omelette pan, add the egg mixture and cook over a medium-high heat, cutting through the omlette with a knife as it cooks. When the eggs have just set, cover with the cream cheese and bacon, fold in half and slide onto a heated serving dish. Pour on the cream and cheese mixture and brown quickly under a hot grill. Serve at once.

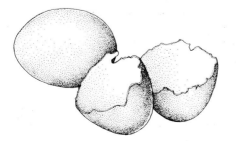

Devonshire Leek Pie
SERVES 4

This is very good served with cold meat.

225 g (8 oz) shortcrust pastry
6 large leeks
300 ml (½ pt) milk

salt and freshly ground black pepper
5 tablespoons single cream

Roll out the pastry to make a 'lid' for a large pie dish. Wash and trim the leeks and cut the white part (and a little of the green) into 2.5 cm (1 in) pieces. Put into the milk with salt and pepper and simmer gently until the leeks are just tender. Pour into the pie dish and add the cream. Cover with the pastry and bake in a hot oven (200°C / 400°F / Reg 6) for 30 minutes.

Egg, Bacon and Parsley Pie
SERVES 4

450 g (1 lb) shortcrust pastry
4 rashers bacon
6 small eggs
3 tablespoons finely chopped parsley

salt and freshly ground black pepper
40 g (1¼ oz) butter
milk

Divide the pastry into two pieces, one a little larger than the other. Roll out and use the larger piece to line a flan case. Roughly chop the bacon and fry without extra fat for 5 minutes. Cool and scatter the bacon over the bottom of the flan. Break the eggs over the top, sprinkle with the parsley and season with salt and pepper. Dot with butter, dampen the pastry edge and top with the remaining pastry. Pinch the edges together firmly. Brush the pie with milk, cut a slit in the centre and cook in a hot oven (220°C / 425°F / Reg 7) for 15 minutes, then lower the heat to 190°C / 375°F / Reg 5 and cook for a further 20–25 minutes.

Cheese, Bacon and Potato Pie
SERVES 4

Serve this pie with a green salad or cooked vegetable.

6 potatoes
2 large onions
6 rashers bacon
25 g (1 oz) butter

25 g (1 oz) flour
300 ml (½ pt) milk
225 g (8 oz) grated cheese
salt and freshly ground black pepper

Peel and thinly slice the potatoes and onions. Remove rinds, chop the bacon and cook gently for 5 minutes without additional fat. Lightly grease a fireproof dish and fill with alternating layers of potato, onion and bacon. Melt the butter, add the flour and mix well. Gradually blend in the milk, stirring continuously until the sauce comes to the boil and is thick and smooth. Stir in 175 g (6 oz) of the grated cheese and season with salt and pepper. Pour the sauce into the dish and top with the remaining cheese. Bake in a moderately hot oven (190°C / 375°F / Reg 5) for 45 minutes.

Paprika's Special Easter Quiche

SERVES 6

Plate 8, illustrated between pages 64 and 65.

Serve hot or cold with a sumptuous spring salad of lettuce, watercress, spring onions and avocado in a well-spiced dressing.

350 g (12 oz) self-raising flour
pinch salt
175 g (6 oz) butter
dry sherry

Filling
1 onion
2 leeks
3 courgettes
2 tomatoes
2 rashers streaky bacon
75 g (3 oz) ham

15 g ($\frac{1}{2}$ oz) butter
1 tablespoon oil
3 eggs
300 ml ($\frac{1}{2}$ pt) double cream
100 g (4 oz) grated Cheddar cheese
2 tablespoons grated Parmesan cheese
salt and freshly ground black pepper
pinch cayenne and nutmeg
celery leaves and chives
2 tablespoons finely chopped parsley
6 tablespoons fresh white breadcrumbs
pinch paprika

Combine the flour with a little salt and rub in the butter in small pieces with the fingertips until the mixture resembles fine breadcrumbs. Mix in enough dry sherry to make a stiff dough. Knead until smooth. Roll out the pastry on a well-floured board, line a 25 cm or 30 cm (10 in or 12 in) quiche case, prick the bottom and chill it in the freezer while you are making the filling.

Peel and thinly slice the onion. Clean and thinly slice the leeks and courgettes. Skin the tomatoes, remove the cores and seeds and chop the flesh. Finely chop the bacon and ham. Heat the butter in a frying-pan with the oil. Add the onion and leeks and cook over a moderate heat, stirring until the onion is soft and transparent. Add the bacon and fry for 2 minutes. Add the courgettes, ham and tomatoes and continue to cook for a further 5 minutes. Beat the eggs with the cream and half the Cheddar and Parmesan. Season with salt and pepper, a little cayenne and a pinch of nutmeg. Spread the vegetable mixture in the cold case, packing it in firmly. Top with celery leaves, chives and parsley and pour over the egg and cream mixture. Sprinkle with the breadcrumbs mixed with the remaining cheese and a little paprika and bake the quiche in a moderate oven (180°C / 350°F / Reg 4) for about 45 minutes until the filling is set, the pastry is golden and the topping has formed a crisp crust.

Lunch & Supper Dishes

Egg and Anchovy Pie
SERVES 4

So simple and so good!

6 hard-boiled eggs
50 g (2 oz) tin anchovies
2 boiled potatoes
25 g (1 oz) butter
2 tablespoons flour

450 ml ($\frac{3}{4}$ pt) milk
salt and freshly ground black pepper
2 tablespoons finely chopped parsley
browned breadcrumbs
a littled melted butter

Peel and roughly chop the hard-boiled eggs. Soak the anchovy fillets in a little milk for 10 minutes to remove excess salt. Squeeze out the milk and finely chop the fillets. Cut the cooked potatoes into very small dice. Melt the butter, add the flour and mix well. Gradually add the milk, stirring continuously over a medium-high heat until the sauce comes to the boil and is thick and smooth. Season with salt and pepper and simmer for 3 minutes. Add the hard-boiled eggs, anchovies, potatoes and parsley and mix lightly. Transfer to a lightly greased ovenproof dish, cover with a thin layer of breadcrumbs and dribble a little melted butter over the top. Bake in a moderate oven (180°C / 350°F / Reg 4) for 20–30 minutes.

Cheese Pinchpenny Pie
SERVES 4

900 g (2 lb) potatoes
2 large onions
2 tomatoes
25 g (1 oz) butter
25 g (1 oz) flour

$\frac{1}{2}$ teaspoon made English mustard
300 ml ($\frac{1}{2}$ pt) milk
salt and freshly ground black pepper
225 g (8 oz) grated Cheddar cheese

Peel and thinly slice the potatoes and onions. Chop the tomatoes into small pieces. Grease an ovenproof dish and fill it with alternate layers of sliced potatoes, onion rings and chopped tomatoes. Melt the butter in a saucepan, add flour and mustard and mix well; gradually blend in the milk, stirring continually over a medium heat until the sauce is thick and smooth. Season with salt and pepper and stir in the grated cheese, reserving 2 tablespoons for the topping. Pour the sauce over the other ingredients, top with the remaining cheese and bake in a moderately hot oven (190°C / 375°F / Reg 5) for 35–40 mintues or until the potatoes are tender.

Mediterranean Macaroni and Cauliflower Cheese

SERVES 6

This is a hotch-potch family dish that is quickly prepared, inexpensive, and will satisfy everyone. It can be made in advance, and the only accompaniment it needs is a green or mixed salad. Leftover chicken, cooked rashers of bacon or slices of cooked sausages can be used instead of ham.

1 small cauliflower
225 g (8 oz) macaroni
400 g (14 oz) tin tomatoes
175 g (6 oz) ham
3 hard-boiled eggs
pinch saffron
150 ml (¼ pt) boiling water

50 g (2 oz) butter
50 g (2 oz) flour
450 ml (¾ pt) milk
100 (4 oz) grated Cheddar cheese
salt and freshly ground black pepper
50 g (2 oz) fresh white breadcrumbs
a little melted butter

Steam the cauliflower until just tender but still firm. Cook the macaroni in boiling salted water until tender and drain well. Drain off the tomato juice, reserving for soups and stews, and roughly chop the tomatoes. Chop the ham and quarter the hard-boiled eggs. Combine these ingredients in a fireproof serving dish. Infuse the saffron in the boiling water. Melt the butter in a heavy pan. Add the flour and mix well. Gradually blend in the milk, stirring continuously, and cook gently until thick and smooth. Add half the cheese and continue to stir until it has melted. Blend in the saffron water and season with salt and pepper. Pour the sauce over the cauliflower and macaroni mixture, tossing lightly. Scatter the breadcrumbs and remaining cheese over the top and dribble over a little melted butter. Bake in a moderate oven (180°C / 350°F / Reg 4) until heated through and golden brown on the surface, about 20–30 minutes.

Italian Risotto

SERVES 6

3 aubergines
200 g (7 oz) mozzarella cheese
100-175 g (4-6 oz) uncooked gammon
  or lean bacon
1 small onion
2 cloves garlic
oil for frying
2 × 400 g (14 oz) tins tomatoes

1 teaspoon dried basil
salt and freshly ground black pepper
2 tablespoons tomato purée
275 g (10 oz) Italian Arborio rice
900 ml (1½ pts) chicken stock
50 g (2 oz) butter
50 g (2 oz) grated Parmesan cheese

Thinly slice the aubergines, place them in a colander, sprinkle with salt and leave to stand for an hour. Cut the mozzarella cheese into thin slices. Very finely chop the gammon. Peel and finely chop the onion. Crush the garlic. Drain the aubergines and pat dry with a clean towel. Fry the slices in a little oil until soft and drain on kitchen paper. Heat 2 tablespoons of oil in a large saucepan, add the gammon or bacon and cook until the fat is transparent. Add the tomatoes and basil, season with salt and pepper, mix in the tomato purée and cook, uncovered, over a high heat, stirring every now and then, for 30 minutes. Remove two-thirds of the sauce and reserve. Add the rice to the sauce in the pan and stir until the rice is transparent. Cook the rice over a low heat, adding some of the stock every now and then until it is absorbed (this will take about 30 minutes) and the rice is tender but not mushy. Add the butter and two-thirds of the Parmesan cheese and mix well. Place a layer of rice in the bottom of a baking dish, cover with the aubergines and half the reserved tomato sauce. Add the mozzarella in a layer and then top with the remaining rice and sauce. Sprinkle with Parmesan and bake in a moderate oven (180°C / 350°F / Reg 4) for 20 minutes, until the cheese is melted and the dish is heated through.

Spinach and Ricotta Gnocchi

SERVES 4–6

Plate 9, illustrated between pages 64 and 65.

Gnocchi, light, mouth-melting, cork-shaped dumplings cooked in broth or water are among my favourite pasta recipes. In this version ricotta cheese is used but you can substitute any good soft cream cheese.

450 g (1 lb) fresh spinach
350 g (12 oz) ricotta cheese
225 g (8 oz) flour
1 egg yolk

1 egg
salt and freshly ground black pepper
100 g (4 oz) butter
100 g (4 oz) grated Parmesan cheese

Cook the spinach and drain very thoroughly, then purée in a blender. Work the spinach purée with the ricotta, flour, eggs, salt and pepper to make a smooth dough. Using wetted hands, form into little cork-shaped pieces and cook in plenty of boiling water. Remove with a slotted spoon as they float to the surface. Toss the gnocchi in the butter and Parmesan cheese and serve immediately.

Crumpet Pizza

SERVES 2

Plate 10, illustrated
facing page 65.

Ham can be added, and so can a little crushed garlic, if you like. This recipe works equally well with split baps.

1 small onion
4 button mushrooms
1 dessertspoon olive oil
3 skinned, seeded, cored,
  chopped tomatoes
salt and freshly grond black pepper

small pinch oregano
50 g (2 oz) mozzarella or
  Gruyère cheese
4 crumpets
4 anchovies
2 black olives, halved

Very finely chop the onion. Thinly slice the mushrooms. Heat the oil in a small saucepan. Add the onion and cook for about 5 minutes until soft and transparent. Add the mushrooms and cook for a further 3 minutes. Add the tomatoes, stir well with a fork to break up the flesh, season with salt and pepper and add the oregano. Bring to the boil, cover and simmer for about 20 minutes, stirring occasionally, until the tomato sauce is thick. Cut the cheese into wafer-thin slices. Lightly toast the crumpets, cover them generously with a thick layer of tomato sauce and top with cheese slices. Top with anchovies and olives. Cook under a hot grill until the cheese is melted and golden brown.

Crostini di Fegatini di Pollo

SERVES 4

For a special occasion, a little brandy can be added while the chicken livers are cooking, and flamed to provide an even richer flavour.

225 g (8 oz) chicken livers
50 g (2 oz) bacon fat
1 clove garlic
1 small onion
1 tablespoon olive or sunflower oil
25 g (1 oz) butter

pinch dried sage
15 g ($\frac{1}{2}$ oz) grated Parmesan cheese
few drops lemon juice
6 slices white bread with crusts
  removed

Remove any fibres and discoloured areas from the chicken livers. Chop the livers very finely (do not mince them as this will destroy their texture). Chop the bacon fat, garlic and onion very finely. Heat the oil and butter, add the fat, garlic and onion and cook gently until the onion is golden. Add the chicken livers and sage, season with salt and pepper and cook over a low heat for 10 minutes. Add the Parmesan cheese and a few drops of lemon juice and mix well. Halve the slices of bread and toast them lightly. Spread the chicken livers on the bread, pour any remaining juice over the top and bake in a hot oven (200°C / 400°F /Reg 6) for about 3 minutes until heated through.

Plate 7. Maidenwell Club Sandwich

Plate 8. Paprika's Special Easter Quiche

Plate 9. Spinach and Ricotta Gnocchi

Plate 10. Crumpet Pizza

Ham Rolls with Leek, Mushroom and Apple Filling
SERVES 4

Serve with a watercress and celery salad or with calabrese.

100 g (4 oz) firm button mushrooms
1 small onion
½ tablespoon oil
1 large cooking apple
300 ml (½ pt) dry cider

salt and freshly ground black pepper
8 small leeks
8 cabbage leaves
½ teaspoon made English mustard
8 thin slices very lean ham

Finely chop the mushrooms. Peel and finely chop the onion. Heat the oil in a small pan. Add the onion and cook until soft. Add the mushrooms, raise the heat and cook for 2 minutes. Peel and grate the apple and add it to the mushrooms with 50 ml (2 fl oz) cider. Season with salt and pepper and simmer until the apple is soft. Clean and cook the leeks until just tender and drain well. Blanch the cabbage leaves until just tender and drain well. Place a leek and some of the mushroom filling on each slice of ham, roll up neatly in the cabbage leaves and arrange in a baking dish. Bring the remaining cider to the boil and reduce to half the quantity. Mix the mustard into the cider, pour the sauce over the ham rolls, cover with foil and bake in a moderate oven (350°C / 180°F / Reg 4) for about 20 minutes.

Red Cabbage with Bacon
SERVES 6

For a more substantial dish, you can add some well-browned and thickly sliced sausages to the other ingredients when adding the cider and vinegar. Serve with jacket potatoes.

225 g (8 oz) rashers streaky bacon
1 red cabbage
1 large onion
2 cooking apples
15 g (½ oz) lard or dripping

1 teaspoon caraway seeds
salt and freshly ground black pepper
2 tablespoons cider
1 tablespoon white wine vinegar
2 teaspoons honey

Remove the rinds from the bacon and chop the rashers. Halve the cabbage, cut out the core and shred the leaves. Peel and chop the onion. Peel, core and dice the apples. Heat the lard or dripping in a large saucepan. Add the bacon and cook over a low heat until the fat has melted. Add the onion and stir until soft and transparent. Add the cabbage and apple, mix in the caraway seeds, season with salt and pepper and toss over the heat for about 5 or 6 minutes, until the cabbage is just tender (it should still remain crisp). Add the cider, vinegar and honey, mix well and heat through.

Lunch & Supper Dishes

Savoury Ham Croquettes

SERVES 4

A good savoury supper dish to be served with either a tomato or mushroom sauce.

225 g (8 oz) cooked ham
2 hard-boiled eggs
25 g (1 oz) grated cheese
½ teaspoon dried mixed herbs
1 tablespoon minced onion
1 teaspoon dry mustard
1 large egg
milk if necessary

flour seasoned with salt and pepper
2 egg whites, beaten
dry breadcrumbs
oil for frying

Garnish
parsley or fried parsley sprigs

Mince the ham and finely chop the hard-boiled eggs. Combine these with the grated cheese, herbs, onion and mustard, mix well and bind with a raw egg. If the mixture is too dry, add a little milk. Season and shape into thick rolls. Dip the rolls into seasoned flour, coat in beaten egg white and roll in the breadcrumbs. Fry the croquettes in very hot fat until crisp and golden brown and drain on crumpled kitchen paper. Serve as soon as possible with a garnish of fresh parsley or fried parsley sprigs.

Kosfit Ferakh

SERVES 4

I serve these small crispy chicken balls as a main course with a mixture of peppers, tomatoes and aubergines topped with a delicious yoghourt mixture. (The chicken balls freeze most successfully.)

350 g (12 oz) cooked chicken
    off the bone
50 g (2 oz) pistachio nuts
100 g (4 oz) fresh white breadcrumbs
pinch dried mixed herbs
2 teaspoons lemon juice
1 tablespoon olive oil

salt and freshly ground black pepper
flour
oil for frying

Garnish
lemon wedges
parsley sprigs

Very finely mince the chicken. Very finely grind or chop the nuts. Soak the bread in a little warm water until soft and squeeze out the excess water. Combine the chicken, bread, nuts, herbs, lemon juice and oil; season with salt and pepper and mix until smooth and sticky. Rub your hands with a little olive oil. Shape the mixture into balls the size of small walnuts and roll in seasoned flour. Fry the balls in hot oil about 0.5 cm (¼ in) deep until they are crisp and golden. Drain well on kitchen paper, pile into a warm serving dish and garnish with wedges of lemon and sprigs of parsley.

Savoury Chicken Patties

SERVES 4

This economical dish uses only the meat from one chicken leg, thigh and wing.

225 g (8 oz) raw chicken
100 g (4 oz) streaky bacon,
  rinds removed
175 g (6 oz) cooked rice
2 eggs

salt and freshly ground black pepper
pinch dried mixed herbs
flour
dried breadcrumbs
oil for frying

Finely chop the the chicken and bacon and mix them together. Add the rice and one of the eggs, beaten until smooth. Season with salt and pepper. Add a pinch of mixed herbs and mix well. Chill in the fridge for 30 minutes. Using very well-floured hands, divide the mixture into four or six portions and form them into flat cakes. Place the cakes between two sheets of greaseproof paper (dust the bottom sheet with a little flour) and flatten the cakes gently with a rolling pin until they are about 0.5 cm ($\frac{1}{4}$ in) thick. Chill the patties in the fridge for a further hour to stiffen them. Brush the patties with beaten egg, lightly coat them with breadcrumbs and fry until golden-crisp on both sides in about 0.5 cm ($\frac{1}{4}$ in) hot oil.

Savoury Potato Cakes with Ham and Eggs

SERVES 4

A high-tea recipe that makes a mouth-watering supper dish.

450 g (1 lb) potatoes
50 g (2 oz) butter
salt and freshly ground black pepper
75 g (3 oz) self-raising flour

50 g (2 oz) ham
50 g (2 oz) rashers bacon
bacon fat, lard or dripping for frying
4 eggs

Peel, roughly chop and boil the potatoes until tender. Drain well and mash until smooth, with the butter. Season. Beat in the flour to make a stiffish dough and leave to cool. Chop the ham, remove rinds from the bacon and finely chop the rashers. Fry the bacon without extra fat over a low heat for about 5 minutes until cooked. Drain on kitchen paper and mix into the dough. Roll out the dough on a well-floured board to about 0.5 cm ($\frac{1}{4}$ in) thickness and cut into twelve 8 cm (3 in) diameter cakes. Fry in the bacon fat, lard or dripping for 3–4 minutes a side until crisp and golden brown. Arrange on a warm serving dish, top with the ham and keep warm while frying the eggs, then slide them neatly onto the top of the potato cakes. Serve at once.

Pork Stuffed Cabbage
SERVES 4–6

1.5 kg (3 lb) Savoy cabbage
450 g (1 lb) cold roast pork
1 small onion
2 slices white bread,
  crusts removed
3 tablespoons milk

1 clove garlic
100 g (4 oz) lard
salt and freshly ground black pepper
flour
2 eggs, beaten
dried breadcrumbs

Carefully remove the large leaves of the cabbage and cook them in lightly salted boiling water until soft. Drain well and cut out the coarse white ribs. Dry the leaves with kitchen paper. Finely mince the cooked meat and onion. Soak the bread in the milk, squeeze out excess milk, then mince the bread. Crush the garlic. Heat 1 tablespoon of the lard, add the onion and cook over a low heat, stirring every now and then, for 2 minutes. Add the meat, garlic and bread, season with salt and pepper, remove from the heat and mix well. Place 1 generous tablespoon of stuffing on each cabbage leaf, turn in the sides and then roll up neatly, pressing the open end firmly. Coat each roll in lightly seasoned flour, beaten egg and breadcrumbs. Heat the remaining lard in a deep saucepan, add the rolls and cook over a high heat, turning them carefully, for about 10 minutes.

Butter Bean Bake
SERVES 4

For many people, butter beans hold unfortunate memories of tasteless school meals, but this is a very un-school-like way of cooking them.

2 rashers bacon
2 hard-boiled eggs
425 g (15 oz) tin butter beans
25 g (1 oz) butter
1 tablespoon flour

300 ml ($\frac{1}{2}$ pt) milk
1 tablespoon finely chopped parsley
salt and freshly ground black pepper
40 g ($1\frac{1}{2}$ oz) grated cheese

Fry the bacon until crisp, remove rinds and chop into small snippets. Chop the hard-boiled eggs. Drain the juice from the butter beans. Heat the butter, add flour and mix well. Gradually blend in the milk, stirring continually over a medium heat until the sauce is thick and smooth. Bring to the boil, reduce the heat and mix in the bacon, hard-boiled eggs, parsley and butter beans. Season and turn into a lightly buttered flameproof dish. Sprinkle with grated cheese and brown under a hot grill.

The Duke's Mushroom Savoury

SERVES 4–6

4 large 5 cm (2 in) slices of
white bread
2 spring onions
225 g (8 oz) firm button mushrooms
3 anchovy fillets

75 g (3 oz) butter
2 tablespoons finely chopped parsley
1 teaspoon lemon juice
freshly ground black pepper and
pinch cayenne

Remove the crusts from the bread, cut each slice in half, then make croustades by carefully cutting three-quarters of the way through each side of the rectangles 0.5 cm ($\frac{1}{4}$ in) from the outer edge. Remove the bread from the centre to leave a neat box-shaped rectangle. Finely chop the spring onions and mushrooms. Very finely chop the anchovy fillets. Melt the butter in a frying-pan and use some of it to brush the sides and centres of the bread cases. Add the spring onions and anchovies to the remaining butter and cook over a medium-high heat for 1-2 minutes. Add the mushrooms and cook, tossing every now and then, for a further 4 minutes. Add parsley and lemon juice and season with a small pinch of cayenne and a generous twist of pepper. Mix lightly and divide between the cases. Place the cases on a baking sheet and bake in a moderately hot oven (190°C / 375°F / Reg 5) for about 15 minutes or until crisp and golden brown.

Potato and Ham Pancakes

SERVES 6–8

900 g (2 lb) potatoes
2 cloves garlic
2 eggs
75 g (3 oz) flour
1 tablespoon finely chopped parsley

50 g (2 oz) cooked ham,
finely chopped
salt and freshly ground black pepper
vegetable oil for frying

Peel and grate potatoes coarsely. Wrap in a towel and squeeze out all excess moisture. Crush the garlic. Beat the eggs. Put the potatoes into a bowl, add the flour, garlic, eggs, parsley and very finely chopped ham, season with salt and pepper and mix well. Heat 0.5 cm ($\frac{1}{4}$ in) vegetable oil in a large frying-pan until it is smoking. Drop the potato mixture into the pan from a tablespoon and cook the pancakes for a few minutes on each side until crisp and golden. Do not try to do too many at a time. Drain on kitchen paper and keep warm while frying the next batch. Serve promptly, top with fried eggs for a more filling supper.

Cauliflower with a Sauce of Chicken and Onion
SERVES 4

1 large onion
225 g (8 oz) uncooked chicken breast
50 g (2 oz) butter
1 teaspoon hot curry paste

1 tablespoon flour
300 ml ($\frac{1}{2}$ pt) milk
salt
1 cauliflower

Peel and chop the onion. Cut the chicken breast into 0.5 cm ($\frac{1}{4}$ in) wide strips. Melt the butter in a saucepan. Add the onion and cook over a low heat until the onion is soft and transparent. Add the chicken and stir over a medium heat until the flesh just loses its transparent quality. Add the curry paste and flour and mix well. Gradually mix in the milk, stirring constantly over a medium-high heat until the sauce comes to the boil and is thick and smooth. Season with salt and simmer the sauce for 10 minutes. Meanwhile, cut the cauliflower into quarters and steam it until it is just tender. Place the cauliflower in a serving dish, pour over the sauce and serve at once.

Stuffed Courgettes
SERVES 4

4 large or 8 small courgettes
450 (1 lb) cooked lean meat
1 large onion
2 tomatoes

1 tablespoon olive oil
celery or garlic salt
freshly ground black pepper

Cook the courgettes in boiling water for 10 – 20 minutes, depending on size, drain and leave to cool. Cut a thin slice off the top of each courgette and scoop out the flesh from the centre of each courgette. Finely chop the flesh. Mince the cooked meat, peel and finely chop the onion; peel and finely chop the tomatoes. Heat the olive oil, add the onions and cook until soft. Mix in the meat, tomatoes and chopped courgettes, season and cook over a medium heat for 5 minutes. Stuff the courgettes with the mixture and arrange them in a baking dish. Cover with foil and bake in a moderate oven (180° C/ 350° F/ Reg 4) for about 30 minutes until the courgettes are tender.

Flippit Cakes

SERVES 4

The mashed potato and parsnip combination is one I am very fond of. In this recipe, these leftover vegetables go towards producing a delicious supper dish.

50 g (2 oz) cooked mashed potato
100 g (4 oz) cooked mashed parsnips
50 g (2 oz) flour
100 g (4 oz) cooked ham

1 tablespoon finely chopped parsley
salt and freshly ground black pepper
lard or dripping for frying

Combine the potato and parsnip, add the flour and beat until the mixture is smooth. Finely chop the ham and add to the mashed vegetables with the parsley. Season with salt and pepper and mix well. Using well-floured hands, shape the mixture into eight round flat cakes. Fry the cakes in hot lard or dripping for about 3 minutes on each side until crisp and golden brown.

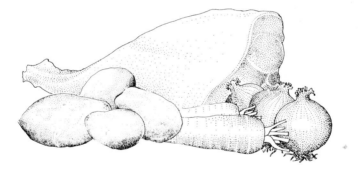

Fish

Fish

Sole Vèronique

SERVES 4

Plate 11, illustrated
facing page 80.

A scaled-down version of the classic dish which all the family will enjoy.

175 g (6 oz) green grapes
1 small onion
50 g (2 oz) small button mushrooms
4 fillets sole, plaice or small whiting
bouquet garni
salt and white pepper
150 ml ($\frac{1}{4}$ pt) medium-dry white wine

150 ml ($\frac{1}{4}$ pt) water
40 g (1$\frac{1}{2}$ oz) butter
1$\frac{1}{2}$ tablespoons flour
150 ml ($\frac{1}{4}$ pt) milk
squeeze of lemon juice
2 tablespoons single cream

Peel, halve and seed the grapes with the curved end of a hairpin. Peel and finely chop the onion, thinly slice the mushrooms. Place the fish in a lightly buttered shallow saucepan. Add the onion and bouquet garni season with salt and pepper and pour over the wine and water. Bring slowly to the boil and simmer gently for 10–15 minutes until the fish is just cooked. Discard the bouquet garni and remove the fish with a slotted spoon. Take off any black skin and arrange the fish in a shallow serving dish. Cover with foil and keep warm. Strain the stock into a clean pan, reserving the onion. Add the mushrooms and boil the stock until reduced to half. Strain the stock, reserving the mushrooms. Melt the butter in a clean pan, add the flour and mix well. Gradually add the stock and milk, stirring continually over a medium-high heat until the sauce is thick and smooth. Check seasoning, add the onion, mushrooms and three-quarters of the grapes, mix in the lemon juice and cream and heat through without boiling. Pour the sauce over the fish and garnish with the remaining grapes.

Soufflé of Sole Fillets

SERVES 2

A light fish dish which will tempt the most fragile of appetities.

4 small fillets of sole
150 ml ($\frac{1}{4}$ pt) milk
40 g (1$\frac{1}{2}$ oz) fresh white breadcrumbs
$\frac{1}{2}$ tablespoon finely chopped parsley

25 g (1oz) finely grated cheese
salt and freshly ground black pepper
2 eggs

Poach the fillets in a the milk until tender (about 8 minutes). Drain well and flake the fish with a fork. Combine the breadcrumbs and the milk in a saucepan and stir over a moderate heat until the mixture is smooth. Remove from the heat and mix in the fish, parsley, grated cheese and seasoning. Separate the eggs; whip whites until stiff but not dry, and add yolks one by one to the fish mixture. Fold in the beaten whites lightly and pour mixture into a greased soufflé dish. Bake in a moderate oven (180°C / 350°F / Reg 4) for 40 minutes. Serve at once.

Goujons of Sole

SERVES 6

4 large fillets sole
salt and freshly ground black pepper
1 egg, beaten
fine dried breadcrumbs
oil for deep-frying

Garnish
sprigs of parsley
lemon wedges

Remove any black skin from the sole (the white skin should not be stripped off). Cut the fish into thin diagonal strips about 2.5 cm (1 in) wide. Season the strips lightly with salt and pepper, dip them in beaten egg and then coat them evenly with breadcrumbs. Make sure the parsley sprigs are completely dry. Heat the oil until a haze rises from the surface. Fry the goujons (not too many strips at a time) in the hot oil until they are crisp and golden brown, drain them well on kitchen paper and keep each batch warm while frying the rest. When all the strips are cooked, deep-fry the parsley for 1 minute until it is crisp and drain well on kitchen paper. Serve the goujons at once with a garnish of fried parsley sprigs and lemon wedges. Serve with tartare sauce.

Grilled Fillets of Fish Japanese Style

SERVES 4

The Japanese have an unusual way of grilling fish with a glaze of egg yolk and rice wine which makes an exciting dish. This is an anglicised version using dry sherry rather than sake; any fillets of firm white fish can be used. The coating gives a golden finish and imparts a delicate taste to the fish as well as sealing in the natural juices.

8 small fillets white fish
salt and freshly ground black pepper
2 egg yolks

1 tablespoon sherry
pinch cayenne pepper

Rub the fish fillets with salt and leave to stand for 15 minutes. Combine the egg yolks with the sherry and season with a little salt, pepper and a pinch of cayenne. Arrange the fillets on a flameproof dish and brush them with half the egg mixture. Grill under a medium heat for 5 minutes, turn over, brush with the remaining glaze and continue to grill for a further 5 minutes until cooked through and golden brown.

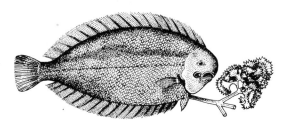

Monkfish à l'Americaine

SERVES 6

For a very attractive dish, serve the fish and sauce in the centre of a moulded rice ring.

1.5 kg (3 lb) boned monkfish
flour
salt and freshly ground black pepper
pinch cayenne pepper
3 onions
2 cloves garlic
4 tablespoons olive or sunflower oil
3 tablespoons brandy
450 ml (¾ pt) dry white wine

pinch dried thyme and majoram
2 bay leaves
400 g (14 oz) tin chopped tomatoes
1 tablespoon tomato purée
few drops Tabasco sauce
3 tablespoons double cream

Garnish
finely chopped parsley

Cut the fish into 0.5 cm (¼ in) slices. Season the flour with salt, pepper and cayenne and coat the fish with it. Peel and finely chop the onions; peel and crush the garlic. Heat the oil in a large frying-pan and cook the onions and garlic over a low heat, stirring occasionally, until the onions are soft and transparent, then remove with a slotted spoon and keep hot. Raise the heat to high and cook the fish in the pan juices until lightly browned on both sides. Add half the brandy, bring to the boil and set it on fire. Shake the pan until the flames die down and immediately remove the fish. Return the onions and garlic to the pan and add the wine, herbs, tomatoes, tomato purée and a few drops of Tabasco sauce. Bring to the boil and cook, uncovered, over a fairly high heat for about 30 minutes or until the sauce has thickened. Remove the bay leaves, add the fish and remaining brandy to the sauce, check seasoning and simmer for 5 minutes or until the fish is just cooked. Stir in the cream and heat through without boiling. Garnish with parsley and serve.

Grilled Plaice with Orange Juice

SERVES 4

The flavouring of citrus fruits goes particularly well with most white fish.

4 large or 8 small fillets of plaice
40 g (1½ oz) butter
salt and freshly ground black pepper

juice of 1 large orange
juice of ½ lemon

Lay the fillets in a lightly greased flameproof dish and dot with the butter. Season the fish with salt and black pepper. Combine the orange and lemon juice and pour half over the fish. Grill under a hot grill, as near to the flame as possible for 4 minutes. Turn the fish over, pour over the remaining fruit juice and continue to grill for 4 minutes until the fish is cooked through and golden.

Fish

Whiting alla Bagna Cauda
SERVES 4

You can serve this summer dish hot or well chilled. Accompany it with a green salad and crusty bread.

1.1 kg (2½ lb) whiting
3 cloves garlic
1 large onion
8 anchovy fillets

1 red pepper
3 tablespoons sunflower oil
150 ml (¼ pt) double cream
freshly ground black pepper

Steam the whiting until just tender. Remove the skin and bones and flake the fish into large pieces while it is still warm. Peel and crush the garlic. Peel the onion, cut it into thin slices and separate the rings. Pound the anchovies to a paste. Put the pepper under a hot grill and cook, turning it every now and then until the skin blackens and loosens. Remove the skin, halve and remove the core and seeds and cut the flesh into thin strips. Heat the oil. Add the garlic and onion and cook over a low heat until the onion is soft and transparent. Add the pepper and the anchovy paste and continue to cook over a low heat for 10 minutes. Stir in the cream and season with pepper – do not boil. Arrange the whiting in a serving dish and pour the sauce over it.

Baked Halibut with Sauce Antonia
SERVES 4

75 g (3 oz) butter
900 g (2 lb) halibut on the bone
salt and freshly ground black pepper
40 g (1½ oz) flour
300 ml (½ pt) milk
2 tablespoons tomato pickle or chutney

1 tablespoon Dijon mustard
2 tablespoons double cream

Garnish
parsley sprigs
lemon wedges

Grease a large sheet of aluminium foil with 15g (½ oz) of the butter. Place the fish on the foil, dot with 25 g (1 oz) butter, season with salt and pepper and wrap up in a neat parcel. Bake the parcel of fish in a moderate oven (180°C / 350°F / Reg 4) for 30 minutes until the fish is just tender. Meanwhile, make the sauce by melting the rest of the butter, adding the flour and mixing well. Gradually add the milk, stirring continually over a medium heat until the sauce is thick and smooth. Add the tomato pickle and mustard, bring to the boil and cook for 2 minutes. Season with salt and pepper, add the cream and remove from the heat. Remove any skin from the fish, arrange on a serving dish and spoon over the sauce. Garnish with fresh parsley and lemon wedges.

Fish

Fritto di Pesci
SERVES 4

Serve with tartare sauce. Accompany with a fresh tomato and raw onion salad, garnished with some black olives.

450 g (1 lb) cod fillet
3 tablespoons olive oil
100 g (4 oz) flour
pinch salt

225 ml (8 fl oz) water
1 egg white
oil for deep-frying

Remove any bones from the cod fillet and place it skin-side down on a board. Using a sharp knife, cut the fillet lengthwise into finger-sized strips about 0.5 cm ($\frac{1}{4}$ in) wide. Cut the strips into 5 cm (2 in) lengths. Mix the olive oil with the flour and salt and blend in the water. Whisk the batter until smooth with a wire whisk and leave to stand for 30 minutes. Whisk the egg white until stiff and fold lightly into the batter. Dip the cod striplets into the batter and fry them in very hot oil until crisp and light golden brown. Drain on kitchen paper and serve at once.

Fritto Misto di Mare
SERVES 4

350 g (12 oz) small squid
225 g (8 oz) coley
2 red mullet
salt

flour
oil for deep-frying
wedges of lemon

To clean the squid, gently pull the heads away from the body and cut off the tentacles just in front of the eye, thus removing the brain and all the other nasties. You now have the tentacles ready for cooking and can deal with the bodies. Remove the plastic-like quill and wash the inside thoroughly to get rid of any white substance. Using a small sharp knife, score the outer purplish skin and peel it off, leaving only the white, opaque flesh behind. Cut the squid into thin rings. Cut the coley into thin strips about 1.5 cm ($\frac{1}{2}$ in) wide. Clean the mullet leaving in the liver. Remove their heads and tails and cut each fish into 5 cm (2 in) pieces. Lightly salt, then coat the fish in flour. Heat the oil until a haze rises from the surface and deep-fry the fish, a little at a time, until crisp and golden brown. Drain on kitchen paper and keep each batch hot while cooking the remaining fish. Pile the fish on to a white damask napkin and serve at once with lemon wedges.

Fish

Scandinavian Baked Cod
SERVES 4

Serve with mashed potatoes.

700 g (1½ lb) cod fillets
3 stalks celery
1 large onion

2 large cooking apples
salt, pepper and a pinch of celery salt
300 g (10 oz) tin tomato soup

Cut the fillets into 8 pieces. Thinly slice the celery. Peel and thinly slice the onion. Peel, core and dice the apples. Combine the apples and vegetables and arrange them in the bottom of a well-buttered baking dish. Cover with the fish and season with salt, pepper and a pinch of celery salt. Pour over the tomato soup, cover with foil and bake in a hot oven (220°C / 425°F / Reg 7 for 30 minutes.

Poached Codling
SERVES 4

Cod often needs a lot of titivating to make it into an elegant meal. Codling, baby cod weighing about 1 kg (2 lb) is delicate and delicious, with a texture almost as smooth as turbot.

1 shallot
700 g (1½ lb) codling fillet
600 ml (1 pt) milk
salt
1 bay leaf
4 peppercorns
50 g (2 oz) butter
2 tablespoons flour

1 egg yolk
2 tablespoons double cream
½ teaspoon lemon juice

Garnish
lemon wedges
sprigs parsley

Peel and chop the shallot. Put the fish, milk, a little salt, the shallot, bay leaf and peppercorns in a lightly greased frying-pan. Bring slowly to the boil, cover and simmer gently until the fish is just soft, about 15 or 20 minutes. Remove the fish carefully and place on a warm serving dish. Remove all the skin and cover with tin foil to keep warm while making the sauce. Strain the milk. Heat the butter, add the flour and mix well without browning. Gradually blend in the milk, stirring continually over a medium heat until thick and smooth. Remove from the heat and beat in the egg yolk, cream and lemon juice. Taste for seasoning and reheat without boiling. Pour over the fish and serve at once with a garnish of lemon wedges and parsley.

Fish

Sea Bass with Olive Sauce

SERVES 4–6

2 sea bass, about 700 g (1½ lb) each
salt and freshly ground black pepper
flour
2 spring onions
1 clove garlic
1 red pepper
50 g (2 oz) black olives
100 g (4 oz) stuffed green olives

7 tablespoons vegetable oil
2 tablespoons finely chopped parsley
1 tablespoon chopped capers
150 ml (¼ pt) dry white wine
2 teaspoons tomato purée
25 g (1 oz) butter
4 tablespoons fresh white
  breadcrumbs

Clean the fish, removing heads and tails and cut each fish across into four chunks. Wash the pieces and pat dry with kitchen paper. Season some flour and coat the fish pieces with it. Trim and finely chop the spring onions. Peel and crush the garlic. Remove the core and seeds of the red pepper and cut the flesh into thin strips. Remove the stones from the black olives and finely chop along with the green olives. Heat 4 tablespoons oil in a saucepan, add the spring onions, garlic and red pepper and cook gently until the onion is soft and transparent. Add the parsley, capers and olives and continue to cook gently for 5 minutes, stirring to prevent sticking. Add the wine and tomato purée and simmer for 5 minutes. Heat the remaining oil with the butter in a shallow frying-pan. Add the fish and cook over a low heat until it is browned on both sides, about 6 minutes on each side. Pour over the sauce and simmer for a further 3 minutes. Place the fish in a heated serving dish, cover with the sauce, sprinkle with the breadcrumbs and place under a hot grill for 1–2 minutes until golden brown.

Baked Mackerel with Onions and Potatoes

SERVES 4

8 small filleted mackerel
salt and freshly ground black pepper
450 g (1 lb) potatoes
2 large onions
2 tablespoons vegetable oil

2 tablespoons finely chopped parsley
75 g (3 oz) butter
2 tablespoons fresh white breadcrumbs
150 ml (¼ pt) single cream
juice of ½ lemon

Season the fish with salt and pepper. Peel and slice the potatoes. Peel and thinly slice the onions and divide into rings. Heat the oil in a frying-pan, add the onion rings and cook over a low heat until the onions are soft and transparent. Layer the fish, potatoes and onions in a well-buttered baking dish with the parsley, dot with the butter and sprinkle with the breadcrumbs. Bake in a moderately hot oven (190°C / 375°F / Reg 5) for 20 minutes. Pour on the cream and continue to cook for a further 8 minutes. Sprinkle with the lemon juice just before serving.

Plate 11. Sole Vèronique

Plate 12. Lorenzo's Red Mullet

Plate 13. White Fish Salad

Plate 14. Brochette de Moules

Fish

Baked Mackerel from Makassar
SERVES 4

Serve with rice and a green salad.

2 cloves garlic
salt and freshly ground black pepper
4 filleted mackerel
50 g (2 oz) butter

2 tablespoons soy sauce
1½ tablespoons lemon or lime juice
pinch chilli powder

Pound the garlic to a paste with the salt and pepper. Rub the mixture into the flesh of the fish and arrange the fillets in a well-buttered ovenproof dish. Bake them in a moderately hot oven (190°C / 375°F / Reg 5) for 20 minutes. Melt the butter, add the soy sauce, lemon juice and chilli powder, mix well and pour the sauce over the mackerel. Return to the oven and continue to cook for a further 15–20 minutes, basting with the juices every now and then.

Cold Baked Mackerel
SERVES 4

4 small mackerel
50 g (2 oz) butter
salt and freshly ground black pepper
100 g (4 oz) button mushrooms
1 clove garlic
300 ml (½ pt) sour cream

2 tablespoons grated onion
1 teaspoon English made mustard
pinch paprika

Garnish
finely chopped parsley

Clean and gut the mackerel, leaving the heads and tails on. Soften 40 g (½ oz) of the butter and season with salt and pepper. Rub both insides and outsides of the fish with the butter, wrap in foil and bake in a moderately hot oven (190°C / 375°F / Reg 5) for 20 minutes. Unwrap and leave to cool. Arrange the fish in a shallow serving dish. Cut the mushrooms into very thin slices and cook gently for 3 minutes in the remaining butter. Drain well and leave to cool. Press the garlic and combine with the sour cream, onion and mustard. Season with salt, pepper and a pinch of paprika and fold in the mushrooms. Spread the sauce over the mackerel. Sprinkle with parsley and serve chilled.

Japanese Grilled Mackerel
SERVES 2

In the East grilling is usually done directly over a charcoal burner, but this recipe responds equally well to the overhead heat of our Western, less aromatic and exotic, electric heat or gas flame.

450 g (1 lb) mackerel fillets
salt
1 tablespoon finely grated raw turnip

½ teaspoon very finely chopped parsley
1 tablespoon soy sauce
olive oil

Divide each fillet in half lengthwise. Rub both sides with a little salt. Combine the grated turnip with the parsley and soy sauce and brush the sauce all over the fish, then leave to marinate for 2 hours. Cover the wire rack of the grill with foil and brush the foil over with a thin film of olive oil. Pre-heat the grill. When really hot, place the pan as near as possible to the heat without the fish actually touching it. Grill the fillets for 5 minutes until crisp and golden.

Baked Stuffed Herrings in Foil
SERVES 4

Mackerel can be used in place of herrings.

4 large herrings
juice of ½ lemon
salt and freshly ground black pepper
1 shallot or small onion
175 g (6 oz) firm button mushrooms

50 g (2 oz) butter
½ teaspoon lemon juice
pinch cayenne pepper
2 tablespoons finely chopped parsley
1 tablespoon tomato purée

Ask your fishmonger to remove the head, tail and backbone of the fish. Rub the insides with the lemon, salt and pepper. Peel and very finely chop the shallot; very thinly slice the mushrooms. Melt the butter in a frying-pan, add the shallot and cook over a moderate heat until soft. Add the mushrooms and cook for a further 2 or 3 minutes. Mix in the lemon juice, cayenne, parsley and tomato purée. Season and simmer for 5 minutes. Place each herring on a piece of lightly greased foil and spread the stuffing on one side. Fold the foil over neatly and seal to make a parcel. Bake in a moderate oven (180°C / 350°F / Reg 4) for 20 minutes and serve in the foil parcels.

Fish

Grey Mullet Cooked in Wine and Orange Juice

SERVES 4

2 grey mullet
2 sprigs fennel
salt and freshly ground black pepper
4 tablespoons olive oil
3 tablespoons dry white wine

juice of $\frac{1}{2}$ orange
8 black olives
4 thin slices lemon
2 thin slices orange

Clean and scale the fish (your fishmonger will probably do this) and lay it in a lightly oiled ovenproof serving dish. Place a sprig of fennel inside each fish and season with salt and pepper. Pour over the oil, white wine and orange juice and bake in a moderate oven (180°C / 350°F / Reg 4), without covering, for 20 minutes. Stone and chop the olives, sprinkle them over the fish and continue to cook for a further 5 minutes. Arrange the slices of lemon and orange over the fish and serve at once.

Lorenzo's Red Mullet

SERVES 6

Plate 12, illustrated between pages 80 and 81.

6 red mullet
50 g (2 oz) butter
salt and freshly ground black pepper
150 ml ($\frac{1}{4}$ pt) dry white wine
1 small onion
50 g (2 oz) tin anchovies
225 g (8 oz) tin tomatoes

1 tablespoon olive oil
juice of 1 lemon
1$\frac{1}{2}$ tablespoons finely chopped parsley

Garnish
lemon slices

Using a sharp knife, scrape the scales off the mullet by running a knife along the fish towards the head. Cut off the fins and barbs with a pair of kitchen scissors. Wash but do not gut the fish. Use 25 g (1 oz) of the butter to grease a baking dish and a piece of greaseproof paper. Place the fish in the dish, season with salt and pepper and pour over the wine. Cover with greaseproof paper and cook in a hot oven (200°C / 400°F / Reg 6) for 15–20 minutes. While the fish is cooking, finely chop the onion and anchovies and roughly chop the tomatoes. Heat the oil in a saucepan and cook the onion for about 5 minutes until soft and transparent. Add the tomatoes with juice and anchovies, season with freshly ground black pepper and simmer for 15 minutes. Remove the fish to a warm serving dish and keep hot. Add the lemon juice, parsley and the remaining 25 g (1 oz) butter to the juices in the pan, bring to the boil and cook, stirring all the time, over a medium heat for 2 minutes. Pour the juices and the tomato sauce over the fish and garnish with lemon slices.

Fish

Skate in Black Butter

SERVES 4

This is the classic way to cook skate but it must be very fresh and the pieces should be cut from the centre of large skate wings.

4 pieces of skate wings
65 g (2½ oz) butter
1½ tablespoons white wine vinegar
1 tablespoon finely chopped capers
2 tablespoons finely chopped parsley

Court bouillon
225 g (8 oz) white fish trimmings
  and bones

1 carrot
1 stalk celery
2 onions
2 sprigs parsley
1 bay leaf
1 teaspoon salt
½ teaspoon black pepper
150 ml (¼ pt) dry white wine

To make the court bouillon, break up the fish bones and put them along with the trimmings into a large saucepan. Peel and chop the carrot and chop the celery including any leaves. Peel the onions. Combine all the ingredients for the court bouillon in the saucepan and cover with cold water. Bring to the boil, cover tightly and simmer for about 1 hour to develop all the flavours. Strain through a muslin-lined sieve. Place the skate wings in a large shallow pan, cover with the court bouillon and bring gently to the boil, turning down the heat immediately any bubbles appear on the surface. Simmer very gently for about 10-15 minutes until the flesh is opaque and will just flake from the bones. Transfer to a heated serving dish and keep hot. Melt the butter in a frying-pan and cook over a medium heat until golden (do not allow it to blacken). Pour the butter over the fish. Quickly add the vinegar to the pan and stir until it boils, then pour it over the fish. Sprinkle with the chopped capers and parsley and serve at once.

Truite aux Amandes

SERVES 4

Please don't attempt this unless you have a large frying-pan because the fish must be fried together and served at once.

4 trout
150 ml (¼ pt) milk
flour seasoned with
  salt and pepper

100 g (4 oz) butter
75 g (3 oz) split blanched almonds
2 teaspoons lemon juice

Clean and gut the fish (or ask your fishmonger to do it). Keep the heads and tails on. Dry well, dip in milk and roll in the seasoned flour. Heat 50 g (2 oz) of the butter in a frying-pan until foaming, add the trout and cook until golden brown on both sides. Lift the fish out onto a heated serving dish and keep warm. Quickly add the remaining butter to the pan juices, put in the almonds and cook over a medium heat until the almonds are a golden brown. Add the lemon juice and pour the sauce over the fish.

Fish

Sprats in Batter
SERVES 6

Cooked in this way, the sprats can also be served as a first course, accompanied with brown bread and butter.

900 g (2 lb) sprats
100 g (4 oz) flour
pinch salt
1 tablespoon vegetable oil
oil for deep-frying
5 tablespoons water

5 tablespoons pale ale
2 egg whites

Garnish
12 sprigs parsley
lemon wedges

Wash and dry the sprats but do not remove the heads or tails and do not gut. Combine the flour, salt, vegetable oil, water and pale ale in a bowl and beat until smooth with a rotary whisk. Beat the egg whites until stiff and fold them lightly into the batter mixture. Dip the fish a few at a time into the batter and fry in very hot oil until crisp and golden brown. Drain the fish on kitchen paper and keep warm while frying the remaining sprats. Do not fry too many fish at one time. Drop the parsley sprigs one by one into the hot oil and cook for just about 1 minute until crisp. Pile the sprats onto a serving dish and garnish with parsley and wedges of lemon.

Smoked Mackerel Fillets in White Wine and Lemon Juice
SERVES 4

4 smoked mackerel
150 ml ($\frac{1}{4}$ pt) white wine
2 teaspoons lemon juice

2 teaspoons grated orange rind
40 g ($1\frac{1}{2}$ oz) butter

Place the mackerel skin-side down on a lightly buttered shallow baking dish. Combine the white wine, lemon juice and orange rind and pour over the fish. Dot the fish with butter and bake them in a hot oven (200°C / 400°F / Reg 6) for 8 minutes. Serve as soon as possible.

Chilled Kedgeree
SERVES 6

Cold kedgeree may seem a little unusual, but it is in fact delicious; it makes a perfect light dish for a hot day.

900 g (2 lb) smoked haddock
600 ml (1 pt) milk
$\frac{1}{2}$ teaspoon tarragon
juice of $\frac{1}{2}$ lemon

300 ml ($\frac{1}{2}$ pt) double cream
salt and freshly ground black pepper
350 g (12 oz) cooked rice
2 hard-boiled eggs

Poach the haddock in milk until tender. Drain off the milk, remove the skin from the fish and leave to cool. Flake the fish with a fork. In a large bowl soak the tarragon in the lemon juice for 5 minutes, add the cream, mix well and season with salt and pepper. Stir in the fish and rice and arrange in a serving dish. Garnish with quarters of hard-boiled egg. Chill before serving.

Fish

White Fish Salad

SERVES 6

Plate 13, illustrated
between pages 80 and 81.

For this dish you can use any firm-fleshed white fish. Sea bass is good, so is haddock, halibut or chicken turbot. You could also use cod, or whiting, which is economical and just as good.

1 onion
1 carrot
1 stalk celery
fish bones
bouquet garni
1 wineglass dry white wine
salt and freshly ground black pepper
900 g (2 lb) white fish fillets
½ teaspoon dry English mustard

3 tablespoons sunflower oil
1 tablespoon white wine vinegar
1 tablespoon finely chopped parsley
1 tablespoon finely chopped chives
6 black olives
50 g (2 oz) peeled prawns
lettuce leaves
2 cloves garlic
150 ml (¼ pt) mayonnaise

Peel and slice the onion. Peel and roughly chop the carrot, roughly chop the celery. Combine the fish bones with the vegetables and bouquet garni, pour over the white wine, add enough water to cover and season with salt and pepper. Bring to the boil, cover and simmer for 1 hour. Strain and leave to cool. Cover the fish fillets with the cooled stock, bring to the boil and gently simmer for about 10 minutes until the fish has become tender (do not overcook). Drain, remove any skin and bones, and leave to cool. Cut the fish into bite-sized pieces. Combine mustard, oil, vinegar, parsley and chives in a screw-top jar, season with salt and pepper and shake until well mixed. Stone and slice the black olives. Combine the fish, prawns, olives and dressing in a bowl and toss lightly to mix. Line a plate with lettuce leaves, pile the salad on the leaves and chill well. Crush the garlic, mix it with the mayonnaise and serve with the salad.

Fish

A Good Fish Pie

SERVES 6–8

900 g (2 lb) cod, haddock or coley
2 onions
50 g (2 oz) butter
1½ tablespoons flour
450 ml (¾ pt) milk
6 anchovy fillets
½ teaspoon coriander seeds
pinch grated nutmeg

pinch dill weed
salt and freshly ground black pepper
450 g (1 lb) spinach
2 hard-boiled eggs
50 g (2 oz) Cheddar cheese

Garnish
2 tablespoons finely chopped parsley

Steam the fish over boiling water until just cooked. Remove the skin and flake the flesh. Peel and finely chop the onions. Melt the butter in a saucepan, add the onions and cook over a low heat until they are soft and yellow. Stir in the flour and gradually blend in the milk, stirring continuously over a medium heat until the sauce is thick and smooth. Pound the anchovies, coriander, nutmeg and dill in a mortar with a pestle until a thick paste forms. Blend this paste into the sauce and season lightly with pepper. Cook the spinach in a very little boiling, salted water until tender, then drain well and coarsely chop. Chop the eggs. Add the fish and hard-boiled eggs to the sauce and stir lightly to mix the ingredients. Spread half the mixture in a lightly greased baking dish, cover with spinach and spread the remainder on top. Sprinkle with the cheese and bake in a moderate oven (180°C / 350°F / Reg 4) for 20 minutes until the dish is heated through and the cheese is bubbling. Sprinkle with parsley and serve.

Caribbean Smothered Fish

SERVES 6

1 large onion
65 g (2½ oz) butter
225 g (8 oz) tin tomatoes
salt and freshly ground black pepper
900 g (2 lb) white fish fillets
5 tablespoons water
2 tablespoons lemon juice

1 tablespoon white wine vinegar
pinch chilli powder
1 egg, beaten
dried breadcrumbs

Garnish
finely chopped parsley

Peel and finely chop the onion and fry in half the butter until yellow and transparent; add the tomatoes and mix well. Season with salt and pepper and simmer for 5 minutes. Cut the fish into 2.5 cm (1 in) strips and score each piece lightly with a sharp knife. Combine the water, lemon juice and vinegar, pour over the fish and leave to stand for 5 minutes. Drain off the liquid and wipe the fish dry; season with salt and freshly ground black pepper and a small pinch of chilli pepper. Dip the pieces in beaten egg, then in breadcrumbs and fry until golden brown in the remaining butter. Pour the sauce over the fish and garnish with a little finely chopped parsley.

Fish

Swedish Fish Pies
SERVES 6

Make these in individual ovenproof soup bowls.

6 thinly sliced rashers bacon
700 g (1½ lb) potatoes
4 onions
freshly ground black pepper
6 cod steaks

100 g (4 oz) butter
150 ml (¼ pt) double cream
2 tablespoons milk
12 anchovy fillets

Remove rinds and chop the bacon finely. Peel the potatoes and cut into wafer-thin slices. Peel the onions, slice as thinly as possible and divide into rings. Place a layer of potatoes in six bowls, cover with a layer of onions and season with freshly ground black pepper. Place the cod steaks in the centre of each dish, sprinkle with the bacon, season with more pepper, cover the steaks with a layer of onions and the remaining potato slices and season with pepper. Dot the top layers with butter. Combine the cream with the milk. Pour the liquid over the layered ingredients and top each dish with a cross made from two anchovy fillets. Cover with foil and bake in a hot oven (200°C / 400°F / Reg 6) for 30 minutes. Remove the foil and leave for a further 5–10 minutes until the tops are golden brown.

Prawns in Cider
SERVES 4

Serve with slices of buttered brown bread, hot toast or French bread.

350 g (12 oz) best quality
    frozen prawns
2 slices onion
pinch dried mixed herbs
300 ml (½ pt) medium-dry cider

2 hard-boiled eggs
65 g (2½ oz) butter
1½ tablespoons flour
salt and freshly ground black pepper
pinch mace

Leave the prawns to thaw at room temperature for 3 hours. Combine the onion, herbs and cider in a heavy saucepan and boil until the cider is reduced by half (this takes about 15 minutes over a high flame). Drain through a fine sieve. Chop the hard-boiled eggs. Melt the butter in a saucepan, add the prawns and heat through well until the mixture bubbles. Sprinkle with the flour and stir until it is well mixed with the prawns. Gradually pour over the reduced cider, stirring continually over a high heat until the sauce is smooth; add the seasoning, mace and hard-boiled eggs. Simmer for just 3 minutes to incorporate the flavours.

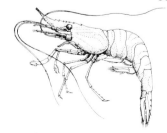

Fish

Prawn Curry
SERVES 4

1 large onion
3 cloves garlic
2 tablespoons sunflower oil
½ teaspoon turmeric
1 teaspoon mustard seed
1 teaspoon chilli powder
½ teaspoon fenugreek
50 g (2 oz) desiccated coconut
150 ml (¼ pt) plain yoghourt

225 ml (8 fl oz) water
salt
450 g (1 lb) frozen prawns
juice of ½ lemon

Garnish
finely chopped coriander, celery
  leaves or parsley

Peel and chop the onion. Peel and crush the garlic cloves. Heat the oil. Add the onion and cook until dark golden brown. Add the spices, garlic, coconut and yoghourt together with the water. Season with salt, bring to the boil and boil for 10 minutes. Add the prawns and lemon juice and simmer for a further 10 minutes. Garnish with finely chopped coriander leaves, celery leaves or parsley.

Cod and Prawn Chowder
SERVES 6

Frozen fish is particularly suitable for this dish where that evocative salty freshness of fish straight from the sea is not of paramount importance.

100 g (4 oz) frozen prawns
3 leeks
4 thin rashers streaky bacon
450 g (1 lb) potatoes
15 g (½ oz) butter
1 tablespoon flour
300 ml (½ pt) chicken stock
600 ml (1 pt) milk
salt and freshly ground black pepper

pinch mace
bouquet garni
½ teaspoon saffron strands
2 tablespoons boiling water
700 g (1½ lb) cod
150 ml (¼ pt) double cream

Garnish
1 tablespoon finely chopped parsley

Thaw the frozen prawns. Clean the leeks and cut into thin slices. Remove rinds and finely chop the bacon. Peel the potatoes and dice. Heat the butter, add the bacon and cook over a low heat for 5 minutes until the bacon fat has oozed out. Add the leeks and potatoes and cook over a low heat until the leeks are softened. Add the flour, mix well and gradually blend in the stock and milk, stirring continually over a high heat until thickened and smooth. Season with salt and freshly ground black pepper and a pinch of mace. Add the bouquet garni and simmer for 20 minutes. Infuse the saffron in the boiling water for 15 minutes. Remove the skin and any bones from the cod and cut the flesh into 1 cm (½ in) cubes. Strain liquid from the infused saffron and add it with the cod to the soup. Simmer for about 8 minutes or until the cod is just tender. Add the prawns, bring to the boil and take off the heat; stir in the cream. Pour the soup into a large tureen and sprinkle with parsley.

Fish

Cullen Skink
SERVES 4–6

A traditional Scottish recipe which I sometimes serve cold in summer.

1 onion
700 g (1½ lb) smoked haddock fillets
900 ml (1½ pts) milk
225 g (8 oz) mashed potatoes
2 bay leaves

salt, white pepper and nutmeg
150 ml (¼ pt) single cream

Garnish
1 tablespoon finely chopped parsley

Peel and thinly slice the onion and divide into rings. Place the haddock fillets in a lightly greased baking dish, top them with the onion rings and pour over just enough water to cover. Cover with foil and bake in a moderate oven (180°C / 350°F / Reg 4) for about 20 minutes or until the fish is just tender. Drain and reserve the liquid, discarding the onion. Remove the skin from the fish and gently flake the flesh. Place the milk in a saucepan with the potato and heat, stirring continuously, until the mixture comes to the boil and is creamy and smooth. Add the bay leaves and fish liquid and simmer for 5 minutes. Remove bay leaves and add the fish, season with salt, pepper and a little grated nutmeg. Add the cream and heat through. Sprinkle with chopped parsley and serve.

Salmon Kedgeree
SERVES 6

350 g (12 oz) long-grain rice
salt and freshly ground black pepper
1 large onion
350 g (12 oz) cooked salmon

3 hard-boiled eggs
175 g (6 oz) butter
1 teaspoon curry powder
1 teaspoon lemon juice

Put the rice into a saucepan with enough cold water to come 2 cm (¾ in) above it. Season with salt and stir well. Bring slowly to the boil. Stir well, cover tightly and cook over a low heat for 20 minutes. Give the rice another stir, cover tightly again and leave on the edge of the stove for 10 minutes, by which time all the water should have been absorbed and the rice should be dry and fluffy. Peel and roughly chop the onion, roughly flake the salmon, quarter the hard-boiled eggs, melt 25 g (1 oz) of the butter in a heavy pan or casserole. Add the onion and cook over a low heat for 2 minutes. Add the remaining butter, the curry powder and lemon juice and mix in the rice. Lightly fold in the salmon and hard-boiled eggs and season with salt and pepper. Cover with a damp cloth and a tight lid and heat through very gently for 20 minutes to incorporate the flavours.

Fish

Croquettes de Saumon
SERVES 4

This dish is especially good when served with a thick tomato sauce.

40 g (1½ oz) butter
2 tablespoons flour
150 ml (¼ pt) milk
250 g (9 oz) cooked flaked salmon
100 g (4 oz) finely chopped mushrooms
1 tablespoon finely chopped parsley
salt and freshly ground black pepper
2 egg yolks, beaten

1 tablespoon double cream
1 egg, beaten
dry breadcrumbs
oil for deep-frying

Garnish
parsley sprigs

Melt the butter, add the flour and mix well. Gradually add the milk, stirring continually over a moderate heat until the sauce is smooth and very thick. Add the salmon, mushrooms and parsley. Season with salt and pepper and mix well. Cook over a low heat for 10 minutes. Cool and mix in the beaten egg yolks and cream. Chill the mixture in the fridge for at least 2 hours, then form into cork-shaped croquettes. Dip in beaten egg and coat in breadcrumbs. Deep-fry in very hot oil until really crisp, drain well on kitchen paper and arrange on a dish lined with a white napkin. Deep-fry the parsley until crisp and use to garnish the croquettes.

Hungarian Fish Salad
SERVES 4

Serve with hot French bread.

350 g (12 oz) white fish
425 g (15 oz) tin butter beans
1 green pepper
1 tinned pimiento
4 spring onions
50 g (2 oz) firm buttom mushrooms
1 small clove garlic

2 tablespoons Dijon mustard
salt, pepper and pinch paprika
1½ tablespoons lemon juice
4 tablespoons olive or sunflower oil
1 tablespoon finely chopped parsley
100 g (4 oz) prawns, fresh cockles
   or mussels in brine

Steam the fish until just tender. Cool, remove fish skin and bones and roughly flake the flesh. Drain the butter beans. Remove the core and seeds from the pepper and cut the flesh into thin strips. Cut the pimiento into thin strips. Thinly slice the onions and mushrooms. Blanch the mushrooms in boiling, acidulated water for 3 minutes, drain and leave to cool. Crush the garlic and mix it to a paste with the mustard, a little salt, pepper and paprika. Mix in the lemon juice and oil. Combine all salad ingredients in a bowl, mix the dressing in lightly and chill for at least an hour before serving.

Scallop and Bacon Kebabs
SERVES 4

6 large shelled scallops
juice of ½ lemon
freshly ground black pepper
100 g (4 oz) button mushrooms

1 green pepper
6 rashers bacon
2 tablespoons olive oil

Remove the black sac from the scallops and cut each scallop in half, making sure the red coral remains intact with one of the slices. Sprinkle the scallops with lemon juice and black pepper. Remove the stalks from the mushrooms; remove the core and seeds of the green pepper and cut the flesh into 1.5 cm (½ in) squares. Blanch them for 5 minutes and drain well. Remove the bacon rinds and stretch the rashers using the back of a knife. Cut each one in half and wrap the bacon strips around the scallops. Thread them on to four skewers, alternating with the mushrooms and pieces of green pepper. Brush with olive oil and grill under a medium-hot grill for 8–10 minutes, turning frequently and basting with the pan juices.

Chilled Scallops with a Light Curry Sauce
SERVES 4

Just a hint of curry flavouring is required for this sauce – the taste should be subtle and not overpoweringly spicy.

6 scallops
150 ml (¼ pt) water
150 ml (¼ pt) dry white wine
1 slice onion
3 peppercorns
1 bay leaf

¼ teaspoon curry powder
1 teaspoon tomato purée
150 ml (¼ pt) mayonnaise
150 ml (¼ pt) double cream
1 lettuce
quarters of lemon

Prepare the scallops by separating the coral and discarding the black sac that circles them. Wash gently in cold water and pat dry with kitchen paper. Combine the water, wine, onion, peppercorns and bay leaf in a saucepan, bring to the boil and simmer gently for 5 minutes. Strain and return the liquid to a clean pan. Add the scallops and poach gently for 4 minutes. Leave to cool. Strain, reserving the liquid, cut the scallops into 0.5 cm (¼ in) thick slices and halve the corals. Dissolve the curry powder in 1 tablespoon of the liquid, blend in the tomato purée, add to the mayonnaise and mix well. Lightly whip the cream, mix in the curried mayonnaise and fold in the scallops. Chill before serving.

Fish

Boiled Mussels
SERVES 4

1.5 kg (3 lb) mussels
150 ml (¼ pt) water
150 ml (¼ pt) dry white wine
1 small onion

2 tablespoons finely chopped parsley
pinch thyme
6 peppercorns

Wash, scrape and remove the beards from the mussels. Place in a large wide pan. Combine the water and wine in another pan and bring to the boil. Peel and finely chop the onion. Scatter the onion, parsley and thyme over mussels, add the peppercorns and pour over the boiling liquid. Cover and boil for 5-6 minutes until the mussels have opened; discard any mussels that have not opened.

Brochette de Moules
SERVES 4

Plate 14, illustrated facing page 81.

1.5 kg (3 lb) mussels
  cooked according to the
  previous recipe
6 rashers streaky bacon
50 g (2 oz) cooked ham

1 egg, beaten
dried breadcrumbs
salt and freshly ground black pepper
butter
juice of 1 lemon

Drain the mussels and remove from their shells. Remove rinds from the bacon and cut it and the ham into 2.5 cm (1 in) squares. Skewer mussels, ham and bacon on four metal skewers, brush with the beaten egg and roll in the breadcrumbs. Season with salt and pepper and cook in butter until golden-brown on all sides. Sprinkle with lemon juice before serving.

Moules au Gratin
SERVES 4

1.5 kg (3 lb) mussels
  cooked according to Boiled
  Mussels above
40 g (1½ oz) butter
2 tablespoons flour
2 egg yolks

salt and freshly ground black pepper
1 tablespoon dry sherry
4 tablespoons fresh white breadcrumbs
50 g (2 oz) grated Emmenthal cheese
2 tablespoons melted butter
pinch cayenne pepper

Dry the mussels, remove empty shells and place the mussels in their half-shells in a flameproof baking dish. Reserve the liquid and juices. Melt the butter, add the flour and mix well. Gradually stir in the strained mussel liquid, beating continuously until the sauce is smooth and comes to the boil. Lower the heat and beat in the egg yolks one by one. Season with salt and pepper and stir in the sherry. Pour the sauce over the mussels. Combine the breadcrumbs and cheese and sprinkle this mixture on the sauce; pour over melted butter, sprinkle with a little cayenne and brown quickly under a hot grill.

Mussels à la Demi-Coquille
SERVES 4

2 shallots or 4 spring onions
1 green pepper
150 ml ($\frac{1}{4}$ pt) dry white wine
1.5 kg (3 lb) mussels
300 ml ($\frac{1}{2}$ pt) mayonnaise

1 crushed clove garlic
$\frac{1}{2}$ teaspoon Dijon mustard
1 teaspoon lemon juice
2 tablespoons finely chopped parlsey
3 crushed green peppercorns

Peel and very finely chop the shallots. Very finely chop the green pepper flesh. Combine the white wine, shallots and green pepper in a saucepan, bring to the boil and simmer for 5 minutes. Put the mussels into a large saucepan over a high heat, pour over the wine with vegetables, add parsley and cook for 5–6 minutes, shaking the plan until the mussels have opened. Remove mussels with a slotted spoon and strain the cooking liquid into a jug, reserving the shallots, pepper and parsley. Reduce the liquid to half over a high heat. Remove the top shells from the mussels and arrange on a serving dish. Scatter over the shallots, pepper and parsley. Add the crushed garlic, mustard, lemon juice and cooled cooking liquid to the mayonnaise with the crushed peppercorns. Mix well. Top each mussel with a little mayonnaise and serve well chilled.

Meat

Meat

Beef with Parsley and Anchovies
SERVES 4–5

It is always rather difficult to judge just how much parsley a recipe calls for, so in this recipe I have measured it after chopping. You will need to start off with quite a large bunch to get the required amount. In this recipe the combination of anchovies and beef is one that used to be extremely popular and which I find delicious. Serve the steak with new potatoes tossed in sour cream and sprinkle with a little extra finely chopped parsley just before serving, and with a crisp green salad made with crunchy cos lettuce.

700 g (1½ lb) topside of beef
1 clove garlic
4 anchovy fillets
2 tablespoons olive oil

25 g (1 oz) finely chopped parsley
150 ml (¼ pt) dry white wine
freshly ground black pepper

Cut the meat into slices 5 cm (2 in) thick. Beat it hard with a mallet to tenderise it. Peel and very finely chop the garlic. Drain and finely chop the anchovy fillets. Heat the oil in a heavy frying-pan, add the meat and cook over a high heat until the meat is browned on both sides. Add the garlic, anchovies and parsley, lower the heat and cook gently for 5 minutes. Add the wine, season with plenty of freshly ground black pepper and cover tightly. Continue to cook over a low heat for 30 minutes until the meat is thoroughly tender.

Grilled Skirt with Parsley and Anchovy Butter
SERVES 4

For lovers of a good steak who find they can no longer afford to buy best rump, entrecôte or fillet, best skirt is a sensation – succulent, tender and deliciously rich in flavour and juices.

50 g (2 oz) butter
3 anchovy fillets
2 tablespoons finely chopped parsley

freshly ground black pepper
700 g (1½ lb) best skirt
oil

Mash the butter until soft and mash the anchovy fillets. Combine the butter, parsley and anchovy, season with freshly ground black pepper and mix well. Shape into a thin sausage on a piece of foil, roll up tightly and refrigerate until firm. Pull off the skin from the skirt (it comes off cleanly and it is better to pull than to cut it). Cut the meat against the grain into 0.5 cm (¼ in) wide strips. Rub with oil, then beat the strips vigorously with a mallet or rolling-pin. Season with pepper but do not season with salt as this draws the juices from the meat. Grill the meat 1 cm (½ in) away from the highest possible heat for 2-3 minutes on each side. Cut the chilled butter into thin slices and top the steak.

Plate 15. Stir-Fried Shredded Beef

Plate 16. Bobotie

Meat

Stir-Fried Shredded Beef

SERVES 4–6

Plate 15, illustrated facing page 96.

225 g (8 oz) rump steak or
   topside of beef
2 cloves garlic
2.5 cm (1 in) fresh root ginger
3 stalks celery
3 carrots
4 spring onions
1 tablespoon dry sherry

3 teaspoons cornflour
1 tablespoon soy sauce
freshly ground black pepper
1 tablespoon sunflower oil
100 g (4 oz) fresh bean sprouts
2 tablespoons water
1 teaspoon caster sugar
3 tablespoons chicken stock

Chill the beef for 30 minutes in a deep-freeze to make it firm, then slice the meat into the thinnest possible slices across the grain. Cut the slices into very thin matchstick strips about 3 cm (1½ in) long. Peel and finely chop the garlic and ginger. Cut the celery and carrots into very thin slices. Cut the spring onions into 0.5 cm (¼ in) slices. Mix the sherry, cornflour and soy sauce in a bowl. Season with black pepper, add the meat, mix well and leave to stand for 15 minutes. Heat the sunflower oil until a haze rises from it, remove the beef from the marinade with a slotted spoon, add it to the oil and stir-fry over the highest possible heat for 30 seconds. Add the carrots, celery, bean sprouts, spring onions, water and any remaining marinade and stir for 2 minutes. Add the sugar and mix in the stock; stir until the sauce has thickened and is glossy. Check the seasoning and serve as soon as possible.

Stroganoff Salad

SERVES 4

3 tablespoons olive oil
1 tablespoon white wine vinegar
½ teaspoon Dijon mustard
salt and freshly ground black pepper
2 onions
18 black olives
225 g (8 oz) firm button mushrooms
275–350 g (10–12 oz) rare roast beef

300 ml (½ pt) sour cream
½ teaspoon paprika

Garnish
shredded lettuce
paprika
finely chopped parsley

Combine the olive oil, vinegar and mustard in a screw-top jar, season with salt and pepper and shake well to mix. Peel and thinly slice the onions and divide into rings. Halve and stone the black olives and rinse in cold water. Very thinly slice the mushrooms. Thinly slice the beef and cut it into neat julienne strips. Combine the onions, olives and mushrooms, pour over the mixed dressing, mix well and refrigerate for 30 minutes. Drain off the excess dressing (this can be used as a dressing for a green or mixed salad), season the sour cream with salt, freshly ground black pepper and paprika, add the onions, olives, mushrooms and beef and stir lightly with a fork to mix. Pile into a serving dish, surround with shredded lettuce and sprinkle with a little paprika and parsley.

Meat

Roast Entrecôte Steak Farmhouse Style
SERVES 4

Serve the cold meat with a creamy horseradish sauce, a selection of mustards and a choice of pickles. Buy the beef a few days before you plan to cook it and keep it lightly covered in the fridge.

2 rashers fat bacon
1 clove garlic
2 anchovy fillets
1.5–2 kg (3–5 lb) entrecôte steak

50 g (2 oz) butter
freshly ground black pepper
1 tablespoon brandy

Cut the bacon into very thin strips. Peel the garlic and cut into thin slivers. Chop the anchovy fillets and pound with the butter until very smooth. Using a very thin sharp knife, cut small slashes into the outside of the meat and push the garlic and bacon into these narrow pockets. Rub the anchovy butter over the sides of the meat not covered with fat. Season with pepper. Pour over the brandy and roast in a hot oven (220°C / 425°F / Reg 7) for 15 minutes per 450 g (1 lb) and 10 minutes extra, basting frequently. Remove the meat onto a serving dish and cool. When quite cold, cover lightly with foil and keep in the fridge until required. Strain the juices into a shallow pan and leave in a cold place for the fat to set. Carefully remove the fat and cut the rich jelly underneath into small cubes to use as a garnish for the meat.

Steak au Poivre
SERVES 4

One of my favourite steak recipes, and one I often ask for in restaurants. The sharp flavourings contrast well with the rich solidness of the meat. Serve with a crisp green salad and a bland vegetable such as creamed spinach.

2 tablespoons black peppercorns
4 rump or fillet steaks
1 teaspoon salt
50 g (2 oz) butter

1 teaspoon Worcestershire sauce
1 tablespoon lemon juice
2 tablespoons brandy

Place the peppercorns inside a polythene bag and crush them on a wooden board with a rolling pin. Firmly press them into each side of each steak. Heat a frying-pan without fat, sprinkle the bottom with salt and when it begins to brown, put in the steaks. Brown them quickly on both sides, lower the heat and cook until done to your liking. Heat together the butter, Worcestershire sauce and lemon juice and pour over the meat. Heat the brandy and when hot but not boiling, pour over the meat and ignite quickly. Bring it flaming to the table.

Meat

Beef Marikoff
SERVES 4

2 large onions
150 g (5 oz) button mushrooms
700 g (1½ lb) beef fillet
2 tablespoons flour

salt and freshly ground black pepper
65 g (2½ oz) butter
300 ml (½ pt) plain yoghourt
1 tablespoon tomato purée
pinch paprika

Peel and thinly slice the onions. Thinly slice the mushrooms. Cut the beef into 2.5 cm (1 in) strips and coat in the flour seasoned with salt and pepper. Heat 40 g (1½ oz) butter, add the onions and mushrooms and cook gently, without browning, until tender. Lift the onions and mushrooms from the pan with a slotted spoon and keep warm. Add the remaining butter to the pan juices and sauté the beef until tender and golden brown; arrange the meat on a serving dish and keep warm. Mix the yoghourt and tomato purée into the pan juices, add cooked onions and mushrooms and simmer gently for about 3 minutes. Season with salt, pepper and a little paprika. Pour the sauce over the meat.

Meat Pasties
SERVES 4

450 g (1 lb) self-raising flour
pinch salt
175 g (6 oz) lard
100 g (4 oz) chilled margarine
8 tablespoons iced water
450 g (1 lb) beef skirt
    from below the sirloin

5 potatoes
1 turnip
3 onions
freshly ground black pepper
milk

Sift the flour with a pinch of salt into a basin. Using two knives, cut the lard and margarine into the flour until the fat is the size of peas and coated with flour. Add the water and mix to a firm dough. Roll out into a rectangle on a well-floured board, dust lightly with flour, fold in three and turn the pastry half-way round so that the seams are on each side. Repeat the rolling and turn five more times, then chill the pastry for 30 minutes. Cut the meat into thin slivers. Peel and coarsely grate the potatoes and turnip. Peel and very finely chop the onions. Roll out the pastry to matchstick thickness and cut four 25 cm (10 in) diameter circles. Divide the potatoes between the centres of the circles and top with meat, onions and turnip. Season with salt and pepper, press the edges of the pastry, firmly together with thumb and forefinger and crimp the edges over, making a plump, tightly closed purse. Brush the pasties with milk and bake on a greased baking sheet in a very hot oven (230°C / 450°F / Reg 8) for 10 minutes, then lower the heat to 190°C / 375°F / Reg 5, and continue to cook for 35 minutes.

Meat

Kokony
SERVES 6

Kokony are Armenian beefburgers. They can also be made with minced lamb instead of beef.

450 g (1 lb) best beef skirt
1 green pepper
2 onions
6 cloves garlic
½ teaspoon cayenne pepper
¼ teaspoon ground coriander seed
¼ teaspoon ground cumin
2 tablespoons finely chopped parsley
3 tablespoons finely chopped
   celery leaves

1 tablespoon finely chopped mint
salt and freshly ground black pepper
1 egg white, beaten
6 tablespoons fine fresh white
   breadcrumbs
6 tablespoons sunflower oil
3 small pickled beetroot
450 g (1 lb) tomatoes
1 tablespoon tomato purée
150 ml (¼ pt) sour cream

Remove any gristle and finely chop the meat. Remove the core and seeds from the pepper and finely mince it. Peel and finely chop 1 onion. Peel and crush 4 cloves of garlic – all this can be done in a food processor. Combine the meat with the garlic, green pepper, onion, cayenne pepper, coriander, cumin, parsley, 1 tablespoon chopped celery leaves and the mint. Season with salt and pepper. Mix well and shape into six patties. Lightly coat the patties with beaten egg white and breadcrumbs. Heat the oil in a frying-pan, add the patties and cook over a high heat (be warned, the patties will spit, so protect yourself by covering them with a large saucepan lid) until golden brown on both sides. Remove the patties with a slotted spoon to a shallow baking dish. Peel and finely chop the remaining onion and garlic. Chop the beetroot. Cover the tomatoes with boiling water and leave for 2 minutes, drain and slide the skins off, then chop the tomatoes. Heat the juices in the pan, add the onion and garlic and cook over a medium heat until the onion is lightly brown. Add the tomatoes, purée, celery leaves and beetroot and season. Simmer the mixture for 20 minutes and stir in the sour cream. Pour the sauce over the patties and cook in a moderately hot oven (190°C / 375°F / Reg 5) for 30 minutes until the patties are cooked through.

Meat

Above Town Under-Roast

SERVES 4

A good combination of shin of beef and kidney with a crisp topping of potatoes.

900 g (2 lb) shin of beef
225 g (8 oz) ox kidney
450 g (1 lb) onions
2 large carrots
225 g (8 oz) swede

700 g (1½ lb) potatoes
seasoned flour
2 tablespoons dripping
750 ml (1¼ pts) stock

Remove any tough sinews and cut the meat into small dice. Cut out hard centre core from the kidney and cut the flesh into small pieces. Peel and roughly chop the onions. Peel and dice the carrots and swedes. Peel the potatoes and cut into pieces about the size of small eggs. Roll meat in seasoned flour until well coated. Melt the dripping in a flameproof casserole, add the beef and kidney and brown over a high heat on all sides. Remove the meat with a slotted spoon. Add the onions, carrots and swedes to the pan juices and cook over a low heat until the onions are soft and transparent. Add the meat, pour over the stock, bring to the boil, cover and simmer for 30 minutes. Place the potatoes on top of the stew – half in, half out of the stock. Do not replace the cover. Cook in a moderately slow oven (170°C / 325°F / Reg 3) for 2 hours, until the meat is cooked and the tops of the potatoes are crisp and golden brown.

Thursday Stew

SERVES 4

700 g (1½ lb) shin of beef
100g (4 oz) rashers streaky bacon
2 large onions
2 large carrots
flour
salt and freshly ground black pepper
1½ tablespoons dripping

100 g (4 oz) firm button mushrooms
pinch ground cloves
1 bay leaf
pinch thyme
450 ml (¾ pt) strong beef stock
grated rind of 1 lemon

Cut the beef into 2.5 cm (1 in) pieces. Remove rinds from the bacon and chop the rashers. Peel and quarter the onions; peel and chop the carrots. Coat the meat in seasoned flour. Melt the dripping in a heavy ovenproof casserole, add the bacon and meat and cook over a high heat, stirring every now and then until the meat is nicely browned on all sides. Add the vegetables, cloves, herbs, stock and lemon rind. Mix well, bring to the boil, cover and cook in a slow oven (150°C / 300°F / Reg 2) for about 3 hours or until the meat is tender.

Meat

Chili Con Carne

SERVES 8–10

900 g (2 lb) lean stewing beef
2 large onions
2 cloves garlic
700 g (1½ lb) ripe tomatoes
2 tablespoons sunflower oil
1 tablespoon flour
1 tablespoon tomato purée

salt and freshly ground black pepper
¼ teaspoon each ground oregano,
  sage, cumin and coriander
4 bay leaves
1 tablespoon chilli powder
150 ml (¼ pt) red wine
2 × 425 g (15 oz) tins red kidney beans

Coarsely mince the meat. Peel and finely chop the onions and garlic. Skin the tomatoes by covering with boiling water for 2 minutes, drain, peel and chop. Heat the oil in a heavy, large casserole. Add the onion and garlic and cook over a moderate heat, stirring until lightly brown. Add the meat and cook over a high heat until brown. Add the flour and stir until it has browned. Add the tomatoes and tomato purée, season with salt and pepper, mix in the herbs and spices. Add the wine and cook over a low heat without covering for 1½ hours, until the meat is fork-tender. Stir in the beans with their juice about 20 minutes before the end of cooking. Remove the bay leaves before serving.

Westminster Beef with Cardamom and Orange

SERVES 2

This dish has only 140 calories per serving.

225 g (8 oz) shin of beef
  with all the fat removed
2 onions
½ red pepper
3 cardamoms
1 tablespoon vegetable oil
200 ml (7 fl oz) consommé

thinly shredded rind and juice
  of 1 orange
salt and freshly ground black pepper

Garnish
finely chopped parsley

Cut the meat into thin slices against the grain and bash it out with a mallet. Peel and thinly slice the onions. Core the red pepper and thinly slice the flesh, having removed the seeds. Crush the cardamom seeds. Rub a heavy frying-pan with a smear of oil and heat through. Add the meat and sear on both sides. Remove the meat to an ovenproof dish. Add the tablespoon of oil to the juices in the pan, put in the onions and cook over a medium heat until they are soft and golden. Add the red pepper, cardamoms and consommé and stir for 3 minutes. Season the meat with salt and pepper, cover with the onions and red pepper. Pour over the liquid from the pan and the orange juice, top the meat and vegetables with the orange rind, cover tightly and cook in a slow (150°C / 300°F / Reg 2) for 3 hours. Serve the meat with the onions and red peppers over it, and pour over the juices. Sprinkle with finely chopped parsley and serve at once.

Meat

China Chilo
SERVES 6

700 (1½ lb) chuck steak
3 sprigs thyme
1 cucumber
1 lettuce
4 shallots or 2 onions

100 g (4 oz) butter
150 ml (¼ pt) strong stock or gravy
salt and freshly ground black pepper
350 g (12 oz) long-grain rice

Remove any skin or gristle from the meat but leave on any fat. Mince the meat finely. Trim the thyme leaves off the stalks. Peel and cut the cucumber into small dice. Clean and finely shred the lettuce leaves. Peel and finely chop the shallots. Melt the butter, add the onion and cook over a low heat until soft and transparent. Raise the heat, add the meat and brown over a fast flame, stirring occasionally, until the meat is a good dark colour. Add the cucumber, lettuce and thyme and cook for 2 minutes. Add the stock, mix well, season with salt and pepper, and simmer for an hour or until very tender. Put the rice into a saucepan with enough cold water to come 2.5 cm (1 in) over the top of the rice and add ½ teaspoon of salt. Bring to the boil, stirring occasionally. Cover tightly until the water has all been absorbed by the rice and the rice is tender and fluffy. Arrange the rice in a ring in a serving dish and spoon the mixture into the centre.

'I'm Only Here for the Beer' Casserole
SERVES 4

2 large onions
1 large clove garlic
1 green pepper
900 g (2 lb) lean stewing steak
2 tablespoons dripping or vegetable oil
1 tablespoon flour
300 ml (½ pt) strong stock
450 ml (¾ pt) brown ale

1 tablespoon tomato purée
bouquet garni
salt and freshly ground black pepper
¼ teaspoon nutmeg
pinch brown sugar
1 teaspoon white wine vinegar
4 slices white bread
Dijon mustard

Peel and thinly slice the onion. Crush the garlic. Remove the seeds and core from the green pepper and finely chop the flesh. Cut the steak into bite-sized cubes. Heat the dripping or oil in a heavy flameproof casserole, add the meat and brown quickly on all sides over a high heat. Remove the meat with a slotted spoon and add the onion, garlic and pepper to the juices in the pan. Cook until the onion is golden brown. Stir in the flour, mix well, add the meat and pour in the stock, ale and tomato purée. Add the bouquet garni, seasoning, nutmeg, sugar and vinegar, mix well and bring to the boil. Cover tightly and transfer to a moderately hot oven (190°C / 375°F / Reg 5) and cook for about 1½ hours, until the meat is fork-tender. Remove the crusts from the bread and cut each slice into 4 cm (1½ in) wide fingers. Spread the fingers lightly with mustard. Arrange them over the top of the casserole and return to the oven, uncovered, for 15 minutes, until the bread rises to the surface and is crisp and brown.

Meat

Maccaruna i Casa alla Filippino
SERVES 4

1 small onion
2 cloves garlic
1 large aubergine
225 g (8 oz) rump steak
3 tablespoons olive oil
225 g (8 oz) tin tomatoes
3 tablespoons red wine

1 tablespoon tomato purée
pinch oregano
salt and freshly ground black pepper
450 g (1 lb) short-cut macaroni
1 egg
1½ tablespoons grated Parmesan cheese
40 g (1½ oz) butter

Peel and finely chop the onion. Peel and very finely chop the garlic. Coarsely grate the aubergine and cut the meat into very small dice (do not mince). Heat the oil in a saucepan, add the onion and garlic and cook over a low heat until the onion is soft and transparent. Raise the heat, add the aubergine and stir until the oil has been absorbed. Rub a separate heavy frying-pan with a smear of oil and heat over a high heat. Add the meat and stir until the meat is well-browned. Add the meat to the aubergine and onion, mix in the tomatoes, adding the wine, tomato purée and oregano and seasoning with salt and pepper; cook over a medium heat, without a lid, stirring occasionally to prevent sticking, for about 30 minutes, until the sauce is reduced and the meat is fork-tender. Bring a large saucepan of water to the boil, add a good teaspoon of salt, throw in the macaroni, stir well and boil for 15–20 minutes, until the pasta is just tender. Beat the egg and Parmesan together. Drain the macaroni well, put into a serving bowl and add butter, egg and Parmesan; pour over the sauce and toss again so that some bits of sauce find their way into the macaroni. Serve at once.

Bobotie
SERVES 6–8

Plate 16, illustrated facing page 97.

Bobotie is a wonderful meat stretcher that is made on the lines of moussaka, but with curry undertones. Serve the dish with rice and a selection of curry side dishes and chutneys.

2 slices white bread with crusts removed
300 ml (½ pt) milk
2 onions
2 cloves garlic
450 g (1 lb) good stewing steak
450 g (1 lb) aubergines
2 tablespoons oil
2 tablespoons curry powder
juice of 1 lemon
1 tablespoon apricot jam
2 tablespoons peach chutney

1 tablespoon sugar
1 tablespoon white wine vinegar
400 g (14 oz) tin tomatoes
1½ tablespoons tomato purée
salt and freshly ground black pepper
pinch dried mixed herbs
2 eggs
pinch grated nutmeg
4 bay leaves
50 g (2 oz) flaked almonds

Soak the bread in the milk. Peel and finely chop the onions and garlic. Mince the meat. Coarsely grate the aubergines without peeling them. Heat the oil in a large, heavy frying-pan. Add the onions and garlic and cook them over a low heat until the onion is soft and transparent. Raise the heat and add the meat, stirring it over a high heat until the meat is well-browned. Add the aubergines and curry powder and stir over a medium heat for 3 minutes to release the flavours of the curry spices and soften the aubergines. Add the lemon juice, apricot jam, peach chutney, sugar and white wine vinegar, mix in the tomatoes and tomato purée and season with salt and pepper. Mix in the herbs and simmer for 3 minutes. Squeeze the excess milk out of the bread and add the bread to the meat, mixing well to break up the bread. Simmer for 5 minutes. Beat the eggs with the milk and season the custard with salt, pepper and nutmeg. Spoon the meat mixture into a shallow baking dish and pour over the custard. Press the bay leaves into the mixture sideways so that they stick up through the custard and sprinkle with the flaked almonds. Bake the dish in a moderate oven (180°C / 350°F / Reg 4) for about 40 minutes until the custard is set.

Maidenwell Goulash
SERVES 6

1 large onion
1 carrot
4 stalks celery
1 parsnip
450 g (1 lb) potatoes
900 g (2 lb) chuck steak or shin of beef
flour
salt and freshly ground black pepper
75 g (3 oz) lard or dripping

1 teaspoon paprika
2 tablespoons white wine vinegar
½ teaspoon dried mixed herbs
2 bay leaves
pinch ginger
2 beef stock cubes
600 ml (1 pt) water
150 ml (¼ pt) red wine
1 tablespoon tomato purée

Peel and roughly chop the onion and carrot. Thickly slice the celery. Peel and roughly chop the parsnip and potatoes. Cut the beef into small bite-sized pieces and coat with flour seasoned with salt and pepper. Heat the lard or dripping in a heavy saucepan. Add the onion and cook over a low heat, stirring, until the onion is soft and transparent. Raise the heat and add the meat, stirring until the meat is browned on all sides. Add the paprika and vinegar, mix well and stir in dried herbs, bay leaves, ginger, stock cubes, water and red wine. Bring to the boil and simmer for about 45 minutes. Add the carrot, celery, parsnip and potatoes, stirring in the tomato purée, and add more water if necessary to cover the ingredients. Cover tightly and continue to cook for 30–40 minutes until the meat and vegetables are absolutely tender. Check the seasoning, remove the bay leaves and serve as hot as possible.
NOTE: the gravy should be fairly thick; if it is not thick enough, mix a little flour to a smooth paste with a little gravy and stir it into the bubbling stew to thicken.

Meat

Chitty-Bag Stew
SERVES 4

Here sweet and sour are combined to make an inexpensive stew with an unusual taste.

700 (1½ lb) stewing steak
2 green peppers
1 onion
4 tablespoons olive oil
1½ tablespoons vinegar

3 teaspoons mustard
225 g (8 oz) tin apricots
150–300 ml (¼–½ pt) red wine
salt and freshly ground black pepper
few drops Worcestershire sauce

Cut the meat into 2.5 cm (1 in) cubes. Discard the cores and seeds of the green peppers and cut the flesh into thin strips. Peel and thinly slice the onion. Combine and heat in a flameproof casserole or stew pan the olive oil, vinegar and mustard. Add the meat and brown all sides over a high heat. Add the green peppers and onion and cook gently until the onion is transparent. Mix in the apricots and juice, pour over enough red wine to cover the meat, season with salt and pepper and add the Worcestershire sauce. Bring to the boil, cover and cook slowly for about 2 hours until the meat is tender.

Union Beef Stew with Dumplings
SERVES 4

550 g (1¼ lb) chuck steak
1 large onion
50 g (2 oz) dripping
2 tablespoons flour
2 teaspoons made English mustard
2 teaspoons horseradish sauce
600 ml (1 pt) stock
600 ml (1 pt) brown ale

1 teaspoon sugar
salt and freshly ground black pepper

Dumplings
100 g (4 oz) self-raising flour
50 g (2 oz) shredded suet
1½ teaspoons dried mixed herbs
water to mix

Cut the meat into 4 cm (1½ in) cubes. Peel and chop the onion. Heat the dripping in a heavy saucepan, add the onion and cook over a medium heat until transparent. Remove with a slotted spoon. Add the meat to the dripping and cook over a high heat, stirring frequently, until the meat is well browned on all sides. Sprinkle with the flour and mix well. Add the mustard and horseradish sauce and gradually blend in the stock, beer and sugar. Season with salt and pepper and transfer to a heavy casserole. Cover tightly and cook in a moderately slow oven (170°C / 325°F / Reg 3) for 1½ hours or until the meat is tender. To make the dumplings, sieve the self-raising flour into a bowl with a generous pinch of salt. Mix in the suet and herbs and make a well in the centre. Stir in enough water to make a pliable dough. Divide the mixture into eight and, using floured hands, roll into eight balls. Add the dumplings to the stew and continue to cook for a further 15–20 minutes.

Meat

Old English Casserole of Beef
SERVES 6

900 g (2 lb) shin of beef
4 large carrots
4 shallots, peeled
2 tablespoons dripping or
  vegetable oil
3 teaspoons mustard powder
600 ml (1 pt) good stock or
  water and 1 beef stock cube

1 teaspoon marjoram
salt and freshly ground black pepper
1 tablespoon grated fresh or
  dried horseradish
2 tablespoons brandy

Cut the beef into 2 cm ($\frac{3}{4}$ in) cubes. Peel the carrots and cut into same-sized cubes. Peel the shallots and leave whole. Melt the dripping in a heavy frying-pan, add the meat and cook over a high heat until well-browned on all sides. Remove with a slotted spoon. Add the carrots and shallots to the pan juices and cook over a low heat, stirring to prevent sticking, until the shallots are nicely golden coloured on all sides. Remove with a slotted spoon. Stir the mustard into the pan juices and blend in 450 ml ($\frac{3}{4}$ pt) of the stock. Add the marjoram and season with salt and pepper. Return the meat and vegetables to the pan, heat through and put into an ovenproof casserole. Add the remaining stock if necessary to cover the ingredients, cover tightly and cook in a moderately slow oven (170°C / 325°F / Reg 3) for 2–3 hours or until the meat is tender. Just before serving, stir in the horseradish and brandy.

Basic Minced Beef
SERVES 4

This recipe can be made in bulk and frozen for up to four months and used later for the basis of such dishes as spaghetti sauce, chili con carne or Spanish casserole, adding the different flavourings when reheating.

1 onion
1 tablespoon lard or dripping
450 g (1 lb) minced beef
1 tablespoon flour

300 ml ($\frac{1}{2}$ pt) good stock
2 teaspoons tomato purée
salt and freshly ground black pepper

Peel and very finely chop the onion. Heat the fat in a heavy saucepan, add the onion and cook over a high heat, stirring to prevent sticking. Add the meat and continue to cook over a high heat, stirring until the meat has browned. Sprinkle with the flour, mix well and stir in the stock and tomato purée. Season with salt and pepper, bring to the boil and simmer for 30 minutes until the meat is cooked. To reheat, turn the frozen mixture into a heavy saucepan and stir over a very low heat to prevent sticking, until thawed, then add flavouring ingredients, bring to the boil and cook as necessary.

Meat

Spanish Casserole
SERVES 4

Serve with a salad.

175 g (6 oz) long-grain rice
3 stalks celery
1 small green pepper
450 g (1 lb) basic minced beef
(see page 107)

$\frac{1}{4}$ teaspoon paprika
$\frac{1}{2}$ tin tomato soup

Cook the rice, rinse it in cold water and drain well. Chop the celery, core and remove the seeds from the green pepper and chop the flesh. Season the minced meat with paprika and place layers of meat, rice, celery and pepper in a lightly greased casserole, finishing with a layer of rice. Pour in the tomato soup and bake in a moderate oven (180°C / 350°F / Reg 4) for 30 minutes.

Cauliflower and Meat Pie
SERVES 6

1 large onion
2 rashers streaky bacon
225 g (8 oz) carrots
1 stalk celery
2 tablespoons olive oil
350 g (12 oz) minced lean beef
400 g (14 oz) tin tomatoes
2 teaspoons tomato purée
150 ml ($\frac{1}{4}$ pt) chicken stock

salt and freshly ground black pepper
1 teaspoon ground cumin
1 large cauliflower
40 g (1$\frac{1}{2}$ oz) butter
2 tablespoons flour
450 ml ($\frac{3}{4}$ pt) milk
50 g (2 oz) grated Parmesan cheese
pinch nutmeg
2 eggs

Peel and very finely chop the onion. Remove rinds and mince the bacon. Peel and grate the carrots. Very finely chop the celery. Heat the oil in a saucepan. Add the onion, bacon and meat and cook over a medium high heat, stirring, until the meat is lightly browned. Add the carrots, celery, tomatoes, tomato purée and chicken stock, season with salt and pepper and mix in the cumin. Bring to the boil and simmer gently for 45 minutes, tightly covered. Mix well to break up the tomatoes. Meanwhile, break up the cauliflower into florets and steam until it is just tender. Layer the cauliflower and meat sauce in a lightly buttered casserole dish. Melt the butter in a saucepan, add the flour and mix well. Gradually blend in the milk, stirring continually over a medium-high heat until the sauce comes to the boil and is thick and smooth. Add half the grated cheese and season the sauce with salt, pepper and a pinch of ground nutmeg. Beat the eggs and add them to the sauce, beating well to blend smoothly. Pour the sauce over the casserole, sprinkle with the remaining cheese and bake in a moderately hot oven (190°C / 375°F/ Reg 5) for 30 minutes, until the dish is heated through and the custard topping is golden brown.

Meat

Individual Colcannon Pies

SERVES 4

1 cabbage
1 onion
2 tablespoons vegetable oil
450 g (1 lb) cooked minced beef
1 tablespoon tomato purée
pinch each marjoram and oregano
2 bay leaves
salt and freshly ground black pepper
300 ml ($\frac{1}{2}$ pt) good stock

40 g (1$\frac{1}{2}$ oz) butter
1$\frac{1}{2}$ tablespoons flour
300 ml ($\frac{1}{2}$ pt) milk
75 g (3 oz) grated Cheddar cheese
pinch cayenne pepper
2 egg yolks
300 ml ($\frac{1}{2}$ pt) good stock
2 tomatoes, sliced

Wash and shred the cabbage and cook in a little boiling, salted water until just tender and drain well. Peel and very finely chop the onion. Heat the oil, add the onion and cook over a low heat until soft and transparent. Raise the heat, add the meat and cook, stirring, until the meat is well-browned. Stir in the tomato purée, add the herbs, season with salt and pepper and mix in the stock. Cook over a medium-high heat, stirring occasionally, until the meat mixture is richly flavoured and not too liquid. Melt the butter in a small saucepan. Add the flour and mix well. Gradually blend in the milk, stirring continually over a medium-high heat until the sauce comes to the boil and is thick and smooth. Beat in 50 g (2 oz) of the grated cheese, season with salt, pepper and a pinch of cayenne and stir until the cheese has melted. Remove from the heat and beat in the egg yolks. Place half the cabbage in the bottom of four lightly greased baking dishes. Cover with the meat mixture and the remaining cabbage. Top with the sliced tomatoes and then pour over the sauce. Sprinkle with the remaining cheese. Bake the pies in a moderately hot oven (190°C / 375°F / Reg 5) for about 20 minutes until the dishes are heated through and the topping is golden brown.

Meat

Leeks Bolognaise
SERVES 4

12 leeks
1 onion
50 g (2 oz) mushrooms
2 tablespoons olive oil
225 g (8 oz) minced lean beef

225 g (8 oz) tin tomatoes
salt and freshly ground black pepper
300 ml ($\frac{1}{2}$ pt) white sauce
50 g (2 oz) grated cheese

Trim, wash and drain the leeks and cook until just tender in boiling, salted water. Drain well and arrange in an ovenproof serving dish. Peel and finely chop the onion. Wash, dry and chop the mushrooms. Heat the oil, add the onion and cook for 2 minutes, add the meat and mushrooms and cook for a further 5 minutes. Mix in the tinned tomatoes, season with salt and pepper, cover and simmer until the meat is cooked, about 10–15 minutes. Spread the meat mixture over the leeks, cover with the white sauce and sprinkle with the grated cheese. Heat through and brown in a hot oven or under the grill.

Mexican Hamburgers
SERVES 4–6

Serve with baked potatoes and salad.

450 g (1 lb) chuck steak
450 g (1 lb) belly of pork
  with skin removed
1 onion
2 cloves garlic
1 green pepper

salt and freshly ground black pepper
3 tablespoons oil
400 g (14 oz) tin tomatoes
2 teaspoons chilli powder
pinch ground cumin
4 tablespoons water or red wine

Cut the meat into cubes. Peel and halve the onion. Peel the garlic. Remove the core and seeds from the green pepper. Slice all three. Finely chop the steak or chop in a food processor, and then finely chop the pork. Combine beef and pork in a bowl, season with pepper and mix well. Shape into eight 1 cm ($\frac{1}{2}$ in) thick hamburgers. Heat 1 teaspoon oil in a large, heavy frying-pan until a haze of heat rises. Add the hamburgers and cook quickly until brown and sealed on both sides. Remove the hamburgers and lower the heat. Add the remaining oil, heat through and add the onion, garlic and green pepper. Cook over a moderate heat, stirring, until the onion is soft. Pour off the excess oil, add the tomatoes, chilli and cumin and season with salt. Add the water or red wine, mix well, bring to the boil and simmer for 10 minutes. Place half the hamburgers in a shallow, ovenproof casserole, pour over half the sauce, cover with the remaining hamburgers and then with the remaining sauce. Cover tightly and cook in a slow oven (140°C / 275°F / Reg 1) for 1 hour or until the meat is cooked.

Meat

Welsh Baby Lamb with Redcurrant Tartlets and Mint Stuffing

SERVES 6

Plate 17, illustrated facing page 112.

Serve with new potatoes and some baby broad beans cooked with a little savory, and garnish with watercress.

225 g (8 oz) shortcrust pastry
6 tablespoons redcurrant jelly
1 Welsh leg of baby lamb
75 g (3 oz) butter, melted
salt and freshly ground black pepper

1 tablespoon dried thyme
75 g (3 oz) fresh white breadcrumbs
1 tablespoon finely chopped fresh mint
40 g (1½ oz) butter

Roll out the pastry thinly, use it to line six tartlet cases and prick the bottom of the cases. Fill them three-quarters full with redcurrant jelly and refrigerate until required. Roast the lamb in a hot oven (200°C / 400°F / Reg 6) for 25 minutes per 450 g (1 lb) and about 15 minutes extra, basting it regularly with the melted butter, seasoned with the salt, pepper and thyme. Leave it to stand for at least 15 minutes outside the oven before carving. Bake the tartlets in a hot oven (200°C / 400°F / Reg 6) for 10 minutes, reduce the heat to moderate (180°C / 350°F / Reg 4) and continue to cook for about 5 minutes until the pastry is golden brown. Make a mint stuffing by combining the mint and breadcrumbs into balls, seasoning them with salt and pepper and frying them in the 40 g (1½ oz) butter until crisp.

Milk Soaked Lamb

SERVES 4–5

700 g (1½ lb) lean lamb
pinch marjoram and oregano
1 teaspoon rosemary
2 bay leaves
150 ml (¼ pt) milk
salt and freshly ground black pepper

2 onions
2 tablespoons olive oil

Garnish
finely chopped parsley

Cut the lamb into 5 cm (2 in) cubes. Beat them slightly with a rolling pin and place them in a dish, packing them in tightly. Combine the herbs and the milk and season with salt and pepper. Pour the liquid over the lamb, cover and place in the fridge. Peel and thinly slice the onions. Heat the olive oil in a frying-pan, add the onions and cook until golden brown. Remove with a slotted spoon and keep warm. Drain off the milk and juice from the meat. Add the meat to the hot oil and fry over a high heat until the pieces are browned on both sides. Add the onions, pour over the liquid and simmer gently for 10–15 minutes until the meat is tender. Check the seasoning and sprinkle with a little finely chopped parsley.

Meat

Noisettes d'Agneau Espagnole

SERVES 6

1 onion
1 carrot
40 g (1½ oz) butter
25 g (1 oz) flour
450 ml (¾ pt) tomato juice
pinch oregano and basil

2 tablespoons tomato purée
salt and freshly ground black pepper
100 g (4 oz) lean ham
350 g (12 oz) broad egg noodles
3 tablespoons olive oil
6 noisettes of lamb

With this recipe you make the sauce first. Peel and finely chop the onion and carrot and cook the vegetables in 25 g (1 oz) butter until lightly browned. Add the flour, stirring over a medium high heat until that, too, is golden brown. Gradually blend in the tomato juice, stirring continually until the sauce comes to the boil. Add herbs and tomato purée, season and simmer for 30 minutes, stirring occasionally. Finely chop the ham and add to the pan. Cook the noodles in boiling salted water until tender (about 12 minutes), Meanwhile, heat the oil in a heavy frying-pan until smoking, add the noisettes and cook over a high heat for 4–6 minutes each side. Season with salt and freshly ground black pepper and keep warm. Reserve the juices in the pan. Heat 15 g (1 oz) butter with the pan juices until melted. Scrape the side of the pan with a wooden spoon to mix in all the residue. Put the noodles in a heated serving dish, top with the noisettes and spoon over the sauce.

Rond de Gigot aux Herbes

SERVES 4

With this dish I serve a rice and pea risotto and a watercress salad.

4 thick slices of lamb
salt and freshly ground black pepper
1½ tablespoons vegetable oil
1½ teaspoons mixed dried rosemary,
   thyme and powdered savory
50 g (2 oz) butter

1 tablespoon brandy
½ tablespoon flour
1 tablespoon tomato purée
1 tablespoon redcurrant jelly
150 ml (¼ pt) red wine
150 ml (¼ pt) good stock

Cut the slices from the thickest part of the leg, about 1 cm (½ in) thick and lightly beat them with a mallet, season them with salt and pepper and brush with ½ tablespoon oil. Sprinkle the herbs over both sides and press them into the flesh with the back of a wooden spoon. Heat the butter and remaining oil in a heavy frying-pan. Add the slices of lamb and cook over a high heat for 4–5 minutes each side; sprinkle with the brandy and set alight when it bubbles, shaking the pan until the flames die. Remove the slices to a heated serving dish with a slotted spoon and keep warm. Add the flour to the pan juices and stir until the flour is a hazelnut brown. Add the tomato purée and redcurrant jelly and mix well; gradually mix in the red wine and stock, stirring continually until the sauce is thick and smooth. Check the seasoning and simmer for 3 minutes. Strain through a fine sieve. Pour the sauce over the slices just before serving.

Plate 17. Welsh Baby Lamb with Redcurrant Tartlets and Mint Stuffing

Plate 18. Gigot d'Agneau Provençal

Meat

Lamb Shish Kebab
SERVES 4

Serve on a bed of rice with salad.

700 g (1½ lb) boned leg of lamb
1 onion
6 juniper berries
2 tablespoons olive oil
juice of ½ lemon

1 tablespoon finely chopped parsley
salt and freshly ground black pepper
4 rashers bacon
100 g (4 oz) firm button mushrooms

Cut the lamb into neat 2.5 cm (1 in) dice, discarding all fat. Peel and thinly slice the onion and crush the juniper berries with a pestle and mortar. Combine the olive oil, lemon juice, onion, parsley and juniper berries and season generously with salt and freshly ground black pepper. Add the meat and leave to marinate for at least 3 hours. Cut the bacon into 2.5 cm (1 in) wide strips and roll up neatly. Brush the mushrooms with a little of the marinade. Divide the meat, bacon and mushrooms into four portions and thread on skewers, leaving a small gap between each piece of meat. Grill under a hot flame for 6–8 minutes, turning frequently, until the meat is browned on all sides.

Marinated Leg of Lamb
SERVES 6

A recipe that is popular with those who like dishes with a rich gamey flavour. It has the advantage that, whereas plain roast lamb tends to be dreary when cold, the meat cooked in this delicious way is very good served cold with salads.

1 stalk celery
1 teaspoon thyme
1 bay leaf
1 small onion
2 cloves
1 leg lamb

olive oil
300 ml (½ pt) red wine
1 tablespoon sea salt
1 tablespoon crushed peppercorns
pinch allspice

Three days in advance, thinly slice the celery stalk, crush the thyme and bay leaf, peel the onion and stick the cloves into the onion. Rub the leg with as much olive oil as it will absorb. Place the leg in a dish (not metal). Combine the wine, with the other ingredients and pour them over the lamb. Marinate in the refrigerator for three days, turning the leg twice a day. On the day of cooking, wipe the lamb with a cloth and strain the marinade through a sieve. Place the lamb on a rack in a roasting pan, pour over the strained marinade and roast in a moderately slow oven (170°C / 325°F / Gas 3) for 20 minutes per 450 g (1 lb), basting frequently with the juices in the pan. Transfer the meat to a warm serving dish, strain the juices in the pan, leave them to settle for a couple of minutes and skim off any fat from the surface. Serve the sauce separately.

Meat

Gigot D'Agneau Provençal
SERVES 6

Plate 18, illustrated facing page 113.

A delicious savoury leg of lamb, stuffed with garlic sausage and roasted on a bed of aromatic vegetables. Ask your butcher to bone and trim the leg for stuffing. Serve with broccoli spears topped with crisply fried breadcrumbs and with sliced cooked potatoes, layered with a little melted butter and cream, seasoned with salt and a pinch of nutmeg and baked at the same time as the lamb.

1 leg of lamb
   (boned, with knuckle end removed)
   about 1.5 kg (3 lb) boned weight
salt
1 tablespoon green peppercorns
2 tablespoons finely chopped parsley
pinch dried oregano
1 piece garlic sausage about
   5cm (2 in) in diameter and
   23 cm (9 in) long

2 large onions
450 g (1 lb) carrots
50 g (2 oz) butter
225 g (8 oz) tin tomatoes
150 ml ($\frac{1}{4}$ pt) dry red wine
300 ml ($\frac{1}{2}$ pt) stock
pinch ground cumin
2 tablespoons vegetable oil
1 tablespoon tomato purée

Spread the lamb open, season the inside with salt and sprinkle over the crushed peppercorns, parsley and oregano. Remove the skin from the garlic sausage and place it in the centre of the lamb, roll up neatly and tie firmly with thin string. Peel and thinly slice the onions and divide into rings. Peel and dice the carrots. Heat the butter, add the onions and carrots and cook over a low heat, stirring until the onions are soft and transparent. Add the tomatoes, mix well and spread the vegetables over the base of a roasting tin. Place the lamb on the vegetables, pour over the wine mixed with the stock and cumin, and brush the top of the lamb with oil. Roast in a hot oven (200°C / 400°F / Reg 6) for an hour, basting occasionally with the cooking liquid. Transfer the vegetables with a slotted spoon to a serving dish and leave the lamb to settle for 10 minutes, before carving into thick slices. Arrange the slices on the vegetables, cover with foil and keep warm in a slow oven. Boil the gravy with the tomato purée to reduce by about one-third and pour over the meat and vegetables just before serving.

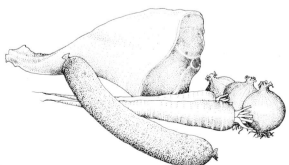

Meat

Marinated Lamb Kebabs
SERVES 4

Serve with a saffron-flavoured rice or with risotto.

700 g (1 ½ lb) boned leg of lamb
2 bay leaves
1 small onion
2 cloves garlic
1 teaspoon dried oregano
pinch cumin

¼ teaspoon finely grated lemon rind
juice of 1 lemon
3 tablespoons olive or sunflower oil
salt and freshly ground black pepper
2 small green peppers

Trim most of the fat from the lamb and cut the meat into 2 cm (¾ in) cubes. Crumble the bay leaves. Peel the onion and grate it finely. Crush the garlic. Combine the garlic, bay leaves, oregano, cumin, onion, lemon rind, lemon juice and oil and mix well. Season with salt and plenty of freshly ground black pepper. Put the meat into a bowl, pour over the marinade and leave covered at room temperature for at least 4 hours, turning the meat occasionally to make sure it is well-saturated. Cut the pepper flesh into squares the same size as the meat. Thread the meat and peppers onto skewers, brush the ingredients with any remaining marinade and grill under a high heat and close to the flame or element, turning the kebabs every now and then, for about 7 minutes, until the meat is crisp on the outside but still slightly pink in the middle.

Tender Lamb Cutlets
SERVES 2

The joy of this dish is that you have the meat, vegetables and gravy cooked together with the minimum of effort.

6 small lamb cutlets
2 small onions
350 g (12 oz) new potatoes
150 ml (¼ pt) good stock

salt and freshly ground black pepper
25 g (1 oz) butter
100 g (4 oz) frozen peas
2 teaspoons finely chopped mint

Ask your butcher to trim the cutlets, or trim off all excess fat and neatly cut off the meat from the top of the bones yourself. Peel and very thinly slice the onions and divide into rings. Peel the potatoes and cut them in half. Place the onions and potatoes in a lightly greased ovenproof dish and pour over the stock. Season with salt and pepper, cover and cook in a slow oven (150°C / 300°F / Reg 2) for 40 minutes. Melt the butter in a frying-pan, add the cutlets and cook over a high heat until brown on both sides. Cook the peas in boiling salt water for 5 minutes. Add the cutlets and peas to the onions and potatoes, sprinkle over the mint, and return to the oven for a further 20 minutes.

Meat

Piquant Lamb Cutlets
SERVES 4

Serve with a watercress and chicory salad.

8 small lamb cutlets
1 teaspoon Worcestershire sauce
1 teaspoon lemon juice

½ teaspoon rosemary
salt and freshly ground black pepper
40 g (1½ oz) butter

Buy small, lean, plump cutlets from the best end of neck of lamb. Remove any skin and excess fat and scrape the end of the bones to give a neat appearance. Combine Worcestershire sauce, lemon juice, rosemary and seasoning and rub the mixture well into both sides of the cutlets. Dot with butter and grill under a high heat for about 5 minutes on each side or until the chops are nicely browned on the outside but still pink on the inside.

Envelopes of Lamb with a Green Stuffing
SERVES 6

Plate 19, illustrated facing page 128.

700–900 g (1½–2 lb) shank end
   of lamb
salt and freshly ground black pepper
1 onion
15 g (½ oz) butter
100 g (4 oz) bacon
225 g (8 oz) sorrel or spinach

225 g (8 oz) sausage-meat
1 teaspoon finely grated lemon rind
50 g (2 oz) fresh white breadcrumbs
2 eggs
pinch dried mixed herbs
2 × 400 g (14 oz) packets
   frozen puff pastry

Using a sharp, pointed knife, cut the bone out of the leg of lamb. Lay the flesh out flat and beat it with a mallet or rolling pin. Season with pepper and roast it, fat side up, for about 15 minutes in a hot oven (220°C / 425°F / Reg 7). Peel and very finely chop the onion and soften it in melted butter for about 4 minutes. Finely mince the bacon. Blanch the sorrel in a little boiling salted water for 5 minutes and drain it well (if using spinach, add a teaspoon of lemon juice to the water). Chop the sorrel or spinach finely. Combine it with the onion, bacon, sausage-meat, lemon rind, breadcrumbs and 1 egg; add a pinch of dried mixed herbs, season with salt and pepper and mix well. Cut the meat into thin slices across the grain. Roll out one packet of puff pastry to a 45 cm (18 in) square and the other packet to a slightly larger square. Mark six squares on the first piece of pastry, divide the lamb between the squares and top with the stuffing. Dampen the pastry between the fillings, cover with the larger square of pastry and press down firmly between the parcels. Cut through with a knife and press the edges firmly together with the back of a fork. Make slits in the top of each parcel. Beat the remaining egg and brush each parcel. Bake in a hot oven (220°C / 425°F / Reg 7) for 10 minutes then lower the heat to moderate (180°C / 350°F / Reg 4) for a further 15 minutes until golden brown.

Meat

Hunter's Pie

SERVES 4

700 g (1½ lb) middle neck of lamb
225 g (8 oz) onions
700 g (1½ lb) potatoes
15 g (¼ oz) butter
2 tablespoons single cream

salt and white pepper
300 ml (½ pt) gravy

Garnish
2 tablespoons finely chopped parsley

Trim off any excess fat from the meat and render it down in a hot pan.
Strain and reserve 2 tablespoons of dripping. Cut up the meat. Peel and
chop the onions. Peel the potatoes and cook until tender in boiling salted
water, then mash them with the butter, cream and salt and pepper. Heat
the 2 tablespoons of dripping in a heavy frying-pan, add the onions and
cook over a medium heat until soft and golden. Raise the heat, add the
lamb, brown on all sides; lower the heat and cook gently for 30 minutes,
stirring occasionally to prevent burning. Remove the meat, draining off
the fat. Arrange half the mashed potatoes around the sides of a pie dish or
casserole, place the meat in the middle, season and cover with the
remaining mashed potatoes. Bake the dish in a moderate oven
(180°C / 350°F / Reg 4) for 30 minutes. Heat the gravy in a saucepan,
make a hole in the centre of the pie and pour in the gravy. Sprinkle with
parsley before serving.

Turkish Lamb Stew

SERVES 5–6

900 g (2 lb) lean lamb
1 green pepper, seeded and sliced
4 tomatoes, peeled and sliced
3 large onions, sliced
1 teaspoon chopped fennel or dill
1 teaspoon sage

2 bay leaves
salt and freshly ground black pepper
750 ml (1¼ pts) meat stock
4 potatoes, peeled and diced
2 cloves chopped garlic

Cut the lamb into 2.5 cm (1 in) cubes. Put all the ingredients except the
potatoes and garlic into a large saucepan. Cover and bring to the boil.
Skim the surface and remove any scum and simmer gently for 1¼ hours.
Add the garlic and diced potatoes and continue cooking for a further 45
minutes or until the meat is tender.

Greek Lamb with Lemon and Herbs

SERVES 5–6

900 g (2 lb) boned leg or
   shoulder of lamb
4 tablespoons olive oil
600 ml (1 pt) water
2 chicken stock cubes
1 tablespoon finely chopped parsley

pinch thyme
¼ teaspoon rosemary
pinch nutmeg
salt and freshly ground black pepper
juice of ½ lemon
2 egg yolks

Cut the lamb into neat 2.5 cm (1 in) cubes. Heat the oil until smoking, add the lamb and brown quickly on all sides. Heat the water and dissolve the stock cubes, pour the stock over the meat, bring back to the boil, lower the heat and simmer gently. Stir in the parsley, thyme, rosemary and nutmeg, season, stir well, cover and simmer for about 40 minutes, or until the meat is tender. Combine the lemon juice with the egg yolks and beat well until the yolks are smooth. Remove the meat from the heat and, stirring continually with a wooden spoon, gradually blend the yolk mixture with the cooking liquid. Heat through without boiling and serve at once.

Dill-Flavoured Fricassee of Lamb

SERVES 4

The flavour of dill goes well with lamb and makes a good alternative to the more usual additions of rosemary or mint. Serve with rice or potatoes.

1 large onion
1.2 kg (2½ lb) best end of neck of lamb
1 teaspoon dill seed
salt
6 black peppercorns
1 bay leaf
25 g (1 oz) butter

2 tablespoons flour
2 tablespoons finely chopped dill weed
juice of ½ lemon
1 egg yolk
4 tablespoons double cream
freshly ground black pepper

Peel and chop the onion. Cut the meat into pieces and put in a large saucepan with the bone and enough water to cover. Add the dill seed, the onion, a pinch of salt, the peppercorns and the bay leaf. Bring to the boil, skim off the scum from the surface, cover and simmer until the meat is tender – about an hour. Strain the liquid and discard dill seed, onions, peppercorns and bay leaf. Melt the butter in a large saucepan, add the flour, mix well and gradually blend in the reserved stock, stirring continually until the mixture is thick and smooth. Add the dill and lemon juice, blend in the egg yolk and cream and season with salt and pepper. Add the meat to the sauce and heat through without boiling.

Lamb Curry with Spinach

SERVES 4

700 g (1 ½ lb) boned shoulder
  of lamb
2 onions
2 cloves garlic
4 tomatoes
450 g (1 lb) picked over spinach

4 tablespoons sunflower oil
5 cm (2 in) cinnamon stick
6 cardamoms
1 tablespoon medium curry paste
3 teaspoons ground almonds
salt

Cut the lamb into small cubes. Peel and finely chop the onions; peel and crush the garlic. Peel the tomatoes, remove the cores and seeds and chop the flesh. Wash, drain and shred the spinach. Heat the oil. Add the onions, garlic and spices and cook until the onion is soft and transparent. Remove the ingredients with a slotted spoon. Raise the heat and add the meat; cook, stirring, until the meat is browned on all sides. Return the onions, garlic and spices to the pan with the meat, add the tomatoes, curry paste and ground almonds, mix well, season with salt and cook over a low heat for about 30 minutes or until the meat is really tender. If the mixture gets too dry, add a little water. Add the spinach, mix well, cover and simmer until the spinach is cooked.

Lamb Patties

SERVES 4–6

Serve with thickly sliced fried potatoes and slices of beetroot in vinegar.

450 g (1 lb) lamb cut from scrag end
1 large onion
1 tablespoon finely chopped parsley
2 small eggs, beaten

salt and freshly ground black pepper
dried breadcrumbs
3 tablespoons dripping, bacon fat
  or cooking oil

Put the lamb twice through the fine blades of a mincing machine with the onion. Add the parsley and eggs, season well with salt and freshly ground black pepper and mix well. Divide the mixture into quantities about equal to 2 tablespoons and shape them into roughly circular patties about 0.5 cm (¼ in) thick. Press the patties into the breadcrumbs. Heat the fat or oil in a frying-pan until smoking. Add the patties and cook over a high heat for about 3 minutes on each side until brown and cooked through. Drain on kitchen paper and keep warm while cooking the rest.

Meat

Spiced Roast Leg of Pork
SERVES 6

Buy your leg of pork on Wednesday for Sunday lunch and leave it, well spiced, in the refrigerator until you roast it to give the flavouring time to sink right into the meat. Serve the joint with apple sauce and a rich gravy made from the juices in the pan.

1.8 kg (4 lb) fillet end leg of pork
2 cloves garlic
1 tablespoon juniper berries
¼ teaspoon ground cumin, mace,
  rosemary

good pinch cayenne, ground sage
  and thyme
2 tablespoons coarse sea salt
freshly ground black pepper
2 tablespoons gin

Ask your butcher to score the skin of the pork. Crush garlic, grind juniper berries in a mortar. Combine all the ingredients and rub them into the skin and flesh of the joint, making sure all the surface is spiced. Leave the joint in the fridge for 3 days. Place the joint, skin side up, on a rack in a roasting tin. Roast without basting in a hot oven (220°C / 425°F / Reg 7) for 25 minutes per 450 g (1 lb) and 25 minutes extra. Leave the joint to settle for 10 minutes before carving. Carving is easier if the crackling is removed and served separately.

Pork Adobo
SERVES 6

A classic Filippino dish with both Spanish and Chinese overtones. The meat is very slowly cooked with a mixture of vinegar and soy sauce, onion and garlic, until it is fork-tender and almost all the liquid has evaporated. Serve it with rice and a green vegetable or salad.

1.1 kg (2½ lb) pork
1 head garlic
150 ml (¼ pt) cider vinegar
1 tablespoon soy sauce

freshly ground black pepper
600 ml (1 pt) water
1 tablespoon lard

Cut the meat into 4 cm (1½ in) cubes. Peel the garlic cloves and leave them whole. Place the pork in a heavy saucepan with the vinegar and garlic. Add the soy sauce, season with freshly ground black pepper and add the water. Bring to the boil, lower the heat, cover the pan tightly and simmer very slowly for about 1½ hours or until the meat is really tender and most of the liquid has evaporated. Separate the garlic from the meat pieces. Heat the lard in a heavy frying-pan, add the garlic and cook over a medium heat until lightly browned. Add the meat and brown on all sides. Pour in any remaining cooking liquid and simmer for 5 minutes.

Braised Loin of Pork with Vegetables

SERVES 6–8

1.1 kg (2½ lb) loin of pork
1 clove garlic
salt and freshly ground black pepper
½ teaspoon dried oregano
2 tablespoons sesame seeds
4 tablespoons olive or vegetable oil
1 large onion
175 g (6 oz) cabbage

350 g (12 oz) potatoes
225 g (8 oz) parsnips
½ teaspoon chopped fresh sage
½ teaspoon chopped fresh thyme
cider
2 tablespoons fresh orange juice
150 ml (¼ pt) single cream
1 tablespoon finely chopped parsley

Bone the loin and remove the skin. Reserve the bone and place the loin in a casserole dish. Score the fat with a sharp knife and rub it with the garlic clove. Season with salt and pepper and rub into the fat together with the oregano. Sprinkle with the sesame seeds and pour over 2 tablespoons oil. Roast in a hot oven (220°C / 425°F / Reg 7) for 20 minutes to seal in the juices. Peel and chop the onion. Shred the cabbage. Peel the potatoes and parsnips and cut them into 2½ cm (1 in) cubes. Remove the pork from the oven and surround with the vegetables. Place the bone from the loin on top of the vegetables, season with salt and pepper and sprinkle with the sage and thyme. Add enough cider to come halfway up the vegetables. Add the orange juice and drizzle over the remaining oil. Cover with two layers of foil, then the casserole lid and cook in a moderate oven (180°C / 350°F / Reg 4) for 1¼ hours, removing the cover and foil for the last 15 minutes of cooking time so that the vegetables and meat become golden on top. Transfer the pork to a serving dish and keep hot. Stir the cream into the vegetables, add the parsley and mix lightly. Arrange the vegetables around the pork and serve.

Noisettes de Porc aux Pruneaux

SERVES 4

8 prunes
200 ml (7 fl oz) dry white wine
450 g (1 lb) pork fillet
seasoned flour

50 g (2 oz) butter
2 tablespoons redcurrant jelly
150 ml (¼ pt) single cream
salt and freshly ground black pepper

Soak the prunes overnight in wine and remove stones. Cook the prunes in the wine for 30 minutes. Very thinly slice the pork fillet, place slices between two sheets greaseproof paper and flatten with a mallet. Dredge the slices in seasoned flour. Heat the butter until foaming in a heavy saucepan. Add the pork slices and cook over a high heat until golden brown; arrange on a heated serving dish. Drain the cooked prunes, reserving the liquid, arrange the prunes around the pork and keep warm while making the sauce. Put the prune liquid into a small heavy pan and boil until reduced by about a third. Add the redcurrant jelly and stir until it has melted. Reduce the heat, mix in the cream, season with salt and pepper and heat through without boiling. Pour the sauce over the pork slices and serve at once.

Pork à la Lecke

SERVES 4

700 g (1½ lb) pork fillet
flour seasoned with salt and pepper
225 g (8 oz) firm button mushrooms
300 ml (½ pt) dry white wine
15 g (½ oz) butter

1 tablespoon olive oil
2 tablespoons brandy
225 g (8 oz) long-grain rice
2 tablespoons finely chopped parsley
150 ml (¼ pt) double cream

Remove any fatty threads from the pork fillet, and slicing slightly diagonally, cut the fillets into 0.5 cm (¼ in) thick slices. Flatten these with a rolling pin and coat them in seasoned flour. Thinly slice the mushrooms. Bring the wine to the boil in a saucepan. Add the mushrooms and simmer for 5 minutes. Combine the butter and oil in a frying-pan and heat until foaming. Add the pork slices and cook over a high heat until the meat is browned on both sides. Pour over the brandy, heat through and set alight, shaking the pan until the flames die out. Add the mushrooms and wine to the pork, cover tightly and simmer for 15 minutes. Cook the rice in boiling, salted water for about 20 minutes until tender. Arrange around a heated serving dish. Remove the pork and mushrooms from the liquid with a slotted spoon and arrange them in the centre of the rice. Bring the liquid in the pan to the boil, lower the heat, stir in the parsley and cream, check the seasoning and cook over a low heat without boiling, stirring continually for about 2 minutes until the sauce thickens. Pour the sauce over the meat.

Fillet of Pork St John Parkes

SERVES 4

350 g (12 oz) parsnips
salt
juice of ½ lemon
8 firm ripe tomatoes
450 g (1 lb) pork fillet
freshly ground black pepper

pinch paprika
2 tablespoons olive oil
150 ml (¼ pt) strong stock

Garnish
½ teaspoon finely chopped fresh sage

Peel and thinly slice the parsnips. Pour over cold water to cover, season with salt and add the lemon juice. Bring to the boil, cover and simmer for 15 minutes. Drain well. Immerse the tomatoes in boiling water and leave for 2 minutes, then drain and peel the skins. Remove the cores and seeds and roughly chop the flesh. Trim any fat or gristle from the pork and cut the meat into 0.5 cm (¼ in) thick slices. Using a meat mallet or rolling pin, flatten the pork between sheets of dampened greaseproof paper until they have doubled in width. Season with salt, pepper and paprika. Heat the oil in a frying-pan and fry the meat until lightly browned on both sides. Drain on kitchen paper. Arrange the pork in an ovenproof dish and place the parsnips and tomatoes on top. Pour over the stock, cover tightly with foil and cook in a moderately hot oven (190°C / 375°F / Reg 5) for 30 minutes. Sprinkle with the fresh sage and serve.

Jellied Spiced Pork Country-Style

SERVES 4–6

1 large pork bone
1 large onion
1 bay leaf
300 ml (½ pt) chicken stock
8 black peppercorns
450 g (1 lb) pork fillet
¼ teaspoon ground cinnamon

¼ teaspoon ground ginger
1 teaspoon paprika
salt and freshly ground black pepper

Garnish
chopped beetroot or watercress

Ask the butcher to cut the bone into 4 or 5 pieces. Peel and roughly chop the onion and put into a large saucepan together with the bones, bay leaf, chicken stock and peppercorns. Bring to the boil, cover tightly and simmer for 30 minutes. Strain the stock and leave until cold, then remove the fat from the surface. Cut the pork into very small dice and put into a clean saucepan with the strained stock, spices and a generous seasoning of salt and freshly ground black pepper. Bring to the boil, skim any scum from the surface, cover and simmer for 1½ hours until the meat is fork tender. Transfer to a 900 ml (1½ pt) pudding basin and leave to cool. Cover the top with a plate, weight down (a large tin of fruit will do) and chill for at least 4 hours until set firm. Turn out the pork, garnish with chopped beetroot or watercress and serve cut in slices.

Stewed Pork with Red Wine

SERVES 6

Serve with sautéed potatoes and, if you like, some lightly boiled leeks or calabrese broccoli.

1.1 kg (2½ lb) boned shoulder or loin of pork
salt and freshly ground black pepper
5 coriander seeds

1 onion
pinch dried sage
dry red wine

Rub the meat with salt and pepper and leave in the fridge for at least 6 hours for the seasonings to penetrate the meat. Cut the meat into fairly large cubes. Crush the coriander seeds. Peel and chop the onion. Combine the meat in a casserole with the onion, coriander and a pinch of sage. Pour in just enough red wine to cover, bring to the boil and cook over a low heat, covered, for about 2 hours, until most of the liquid has been absorbed and the meat is really tender.

Pork Goulash

SERVES 4

An aromatic stew which makes a reasonably priced but satisfying main dish. The flavour of paprika, which is not hot like cayenne, should be quite in evidence.

700 g (1½ lb) boned shoulder of pork
3 large onions
40 g (1½ oz) butter
½ tablespoon paprika
1 tablespoon flour
450 ml (¾ pt) dry cider

about 450 ml (¾ pt) stock
1 tablespoon tomato purée
pinch sage and thyme
3 bay leaves
salt and freshly ground black pepper
700 g (1½ lb) potatoes

Cut the meat into 2.5 cm (1 in) cubes. Peel and thinly slice the onions. Melt the butter in a heavy saucepan, add the meat and cook until lightly browned on all sides. Add the onions and cook for a further 3 minutes until soft and golden. Sprinkle with the paprika and flour and mix well. Cook, stirring continuously, over a medium-high heat for a further 3 minutes and then stir in the cider and enough stock to ensure the meat is well covered. Add the tomato purée and herbs, season with salt and pepper, cover and simmer gently for an hour. Peel the potatoes and cut into 2.5 cm (1 in) cubes. Remove the bay leaves from the goulash, add the potatoes and enough additional stock to cover them and continue to simmer for a further 30–40 minutes, until the potatoes are cooked through and the meat is tender.

Meat

Pork Stuffed Peppers
SERVES 4

4 large green peppers
450 g (1 lb) pork belly
small bunch chives
1 sprig marjoram
50 g (2 oz) white bread with
   crust removed

2 eggs
salt and freshly ground black pepper
pinch grated nutmeg
100 g (4 oz) Gruyère cheese, sliced
150 ml (¼ pt) stock

Halve the green peppers and remove their seeds and cores. Remove the rind from the pork and cut the meat into 2.5 cm (1 in) cubes. Chop the chives and remove the stalk from the marjoram. Add the bread to the herbs and either grate coarsely or process until the bread is reduced to coarse crumbs. If using a food processor, add the meat and mix until it is the consistency of coarse sausage-meat, otherwise use the coarse blade of a mincer. Add the eggs, season with salt, pepper and the nutmeg and mix the ingredients together. Fill the peppers with the meat mixture and place in a lightly greased baking dish. Cover with the slices of cheese. Pour the stock around the peppers and cover loosely with foil. Cook in a moderate oven (180°C / 350°F / Reg 4) for 45 minutes until the peppers are tender and the meat is cooked through.

Pork and Onion Pudding
SERVES 4

Serve this dish with gravy and mashed potatoes.

225 g (8 oz) self-raising flour
pinch salt
100 g (4 oz) shredded suet
450 g (1 lb) lean pork belly
1 large potato

2 onions
½ teaspoon finely chopped fresh sage
4 tablespoons strong stock
salt and freshly ground black pepper

Mix the flour, salt and suet together in a bowl. Add just enough water to make a firm dough that can be shaped into a ball and come cleanly away from the sides of the bowl. Roll out two-thirds of the dough to about 0.5 cm (¼ in) thick and use it to line a lightly greased 1 litre (2 pt) pudding basin. Remove the rind and any bones from the pork and cut the meat into small dice. Peel and coarsely grate the potato. Peel and finely chop the onions. Combine the meat, potato and onions with the sage and stock, season with salt and pepper, mix well and pack into the basin. Roll out the remaining dough and cover the basin, pressing the pastry edges firmly together. Cover with two layers of greaseproof paper, then with foil and tie tightly with string. Put the basin into a large saucepan and pour in enough hot water to come three-quarters of the way up the sides of the basin. Boil for 2½ hours, adding more water if necessary.

Slow-Cooked Pork with Carrots and Parsley

SERVES 4

550 g (1¼ lb) pork belly, boned
450 g (1 lb) carrots
1 onion
50 g (2 oz) butter
3 tablespoons finely chopped parsley
salt and freshly ground black pepper

grated nutmeg
4 tablespoons stock

Garnish
sprigs parsley

Cut the pork into very thin strips. Peel and thinly slice the carrots. Peel and roughly chop the onion. Melt 25 g (1 oz) butter in a round casserole and arrange layers of onion, carrot and pork in the pan, sprinkling the layers with parsley and seasoning them with salt, pepper and nutmeg. Add the stock. Dot the remaining butter over the top and cover with a double thickness of foil, pressing down so that the ingredients are packed in well. Cover with a lid and cook over very gentle heat for 1½ hours. Invert the pan onto a serving plate so that the ingredients come out like a round cake, garnish with parsley and serve.

Pork Chops with Leeks and Cider

SERVES 4

2 cloves garlic
1 teaspoon fresh rosemary
salt and freshly ground black pepper
2 teaspoons made English mustard
4 pork chops

350 g (12 oz) small leeks
300 ml (½ pt) dry cider
4 tablespoons double cream
50 g (2 oz) fresh breadcrumbs
25 g (1 oz) grated Cheddar cheese

Peel the garlic and crush the cloves together with the rosemary and a generous seasoning of salt and pepper. Mix the mustard into the seasoning. Remove the excess fat from the pork chops and chop the fat finely. Rub the chops all over with the seasoning mixture. Heat the pork fat in a heavy-based frying-pan over medium heat until melted, about 5 minutes. Add the chops and cook over high heat until nicely browned on both sides. Arrange the chops in an ovenproof dish. Cut the leeks in half lengthwise and wash thoroughly. Arrange the leeks on top of the pork chops and pour over the cider and cream. Top with the breadcrumbs and cheese, cover with foil and cook in a moderate oven (180°C / 350°F / Reg 4) for 1 hour. Remove the foil for the last 10 minutes of cooking to brown the breadcrumb topping.

Meat

Pork Casserole with Runner Beans

SERVES 4

A filling country-style dish which has a wonderful aroma and is delicious to eat. Serve with a hot potato salad.

700 g (1½ lb) boned shoulder of pork
2 shallots
1 onion
1 clove garlic
1½ tablespoons vegetable oil
1 sprig thyme
3 bay leaves
salt and freshly ground black pepper

2 teaspoons paprika
pinch ground mixed spice
1 tablespoon flour
dry white wine
350 g (12 oz) runner beans
75 g (3 oz) stuffed green olives
1 green pepper

Cut the pork into 2.5 cm (1 in) cubes. Peel and chop the shallots and onion. Peel and finely chop the garlic. Heat the oil in a heavy casserole dish, add the pork and brown on all sides over a high heat. Add the shallots, onion, garlic, thyme and bay leaves. Season with salt and pepper and add the paprika and mixed spice. Stir over a low heat for 3 minutes. Add the flour and cook, stirring, until lightly browned. Stir in enough wine to cover the ingredients and continue to cook, stirring constantly, until the sauce comes to the boil. Cover tightly and simmer for 1 hour. Top and tail the beans and cut them into thin diagonal slices. Slice the stuffed olives. Remove the core and seeds from the green pepper and cut the flesh into thin slices. Degrease the casserole, add the beans, olives and green pepper and continue to simmer, tightly covered, for a further 30 minutes or until the meat is tender. Check seasoning and serve.

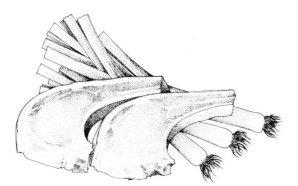

Meat

Pork, Apple and Vegetable Bake

SERVES 4

Here is a very tasty way to use up leftover Sunday roast pork.

2 cooking apples
1 large onion
2 carrots
1 tablespoon dripping

8 thin slices cold roast pork
1 tablespoon brown sugar
150 ml ($\frac{1}{4}$ pt) cider
salt and freshly ground black pepper

Peel, core and slice the apples. Peel and finely chop the onion and cut the carrots into matchstick strips. Heat the dripping in a frying-pan, add the onion and carrots and cook until the onion is soft, about 3 minutes. Using a slotted spoon, transfer the vegetables to a casserole dish. Fry the pork in the dripping until lightly browned on both sides. Arrange the meat on the vegetables, cover with the apple slices and season with salt and pepper. Sprinkle the brown sugar over the top and pour over the cider. Cook in a moderate oven (180°C / 350°F / Reg 4) for 35–40 minutes until the vegetables and apple are tender.

Leftover Meat and Cabbage Casserole

SERVES 4

1 cabbage
1 clove garlic
225-275 g (8–10 oz) cooked beef or lamb
1 tablespoon dripping
$\frac{1}{2}$ tablespoon flour

150 ml ($\frac{1}{4}$ pt) stock
3 tablespoons tomato purée
salt and freshly ground black pepper
3 tablespoons fresh white breadcrumbs
15 g ($\frac{1}{2}$ oz) butter, melted

Clean and shred the cabbage and cook in a little boiling salted water until just tender. Drain well. Crush the garlic. Mince the meat through the coarse blades of a mincer. Heat the dripping in a frying-pan, add the garlic and meat and cook over a medium high heat for 2 minutes. Sprinkle with the flour and mix well. Gradually blend in the stock and tomato purée. Season with salt and pepper, add the cabbage and cook over a low heat for 5 minutes. Transfer the mixture to a shallow baking dish, sprinkle with the breadcrumbs, pour over the melted butter and bake in a hot oven (220°C / 425°F / Reg 7) for about 15 minutes or until the breadcrumbs are crisp and golden brown.

Plate 19. Envelopes of Lamb with a Green Stuffing

Plate 20. Fegato Garbo e Dolce

Meat

Ham or Tongue with Whisky Sauce

SERVES 4

225 g (8 oz) carrots
1 small onion
50 g (2 oz) firm button mushrooms
75 g (3oz) butter
1½ × 400 g (14 oz) tins consommé
freshly ground black pepper
2 tablespoons whisky

pinch dried mixed herbs
225 ml (8 fl oz) double cream
1 tablespoon raisins
1 tablespoon finely chopped parsley
8 slices cooked ham or tongue
50 g (2 oz) fresh white breadcrumbs

Peel the carrots and cut into very small dice. Peel and very finely chop the onion. Chop the mushrooms. Melt 50 g (2 oz) of the butter in a saucepan, add the onion and carrots and cook over a very low heat, covered by a sheet of buttered greaseproof paper, until the carrots are soft (about 20 minutes). Meanwhile, make the sauce: boil the consommé in a saucepan over a high heat until it is reduced by half. Season with pepper, add the whisky and herbs and stir over a high heat for 2 minutes. Add the cream and continue to cook, stirring occasionally, until the sauce has reduced by another third and is syrupy. Add the mushrooms and raisins to the carrots and stir over a moderate heat until the mushrooms are just soft. Add the carrots, onion, mushrooms and raisins to the sauce, with the parsley, and heat through. Roll up the slices of ham or tongue neatly, place them in a greased baking dish, pour over the sauce and sprinkle with the breadcrumbs. Dot with the remaining butter and put under a medium grill for about 10 minutes, until the dish is heated through and the topping is golden brown.

Salt Pork and Potatoes

SERVES 4–6

A traditional half-meat, half-soup dish from Sweden that makes an inexpensive, hearty and nourishing family meal needing no additional vegetables. Serve it in wide soup plates with mustard on the side. This soup should be fairly thick, but the consistency will depend to some extent on the quality of the peas. If it becomes too thick, add more water.

225 g (8 oz) dried yellow peas
2.1 litres (3½ pts) water
450 g (1 lb) salt pork
2 onions

½ teaspoon ground ginger
1 teaspoon marjoram
salt and white pepper

Rinse the peas well in cold running water and put them in a large saucepan with water. Cover and leave in a cold place for a few hours. Then bring the peas quickly to the boil, remove from the heat and skim off any pea castings floating on top, then simmer, covered, for 2 hours. Cut the pork into 5 cm (2 in) squares. Peel and roughly chop the onion. Add the pork, onions, ginger, marjoram and seasoning to the peas, bring to the boil, cover and continue to simmer for a further hour or until the pork is really tender.

Meat

Home-made Spiced Sausages

MAKES ABOUT 3.4 kg (7½ lb)

The quantities given are designed for a big picnic or to freeze. Half can be made, but it isn't worth the effort. Sausage skins can now be bought commercially – ask a reliable grocer or butcher.

2.2 kg (5 lb) good stewing beef
450 g (1 lb) lean pork
700 g (1½ lb) pork fat
1 tablespoon coriander seeds
freshly ground black pepper

¾ teaspoon grated nutmeg
¼ teaspoon each dried sage and thyme
1½ tablespoons rock salt
1 scant tablespoon allspice
150 ml (¼ pt) vinegar

Pass the beef and lean pork twice through a coarse blade of a mincer, and the pork fat once. Heat a small frying-pan and roast coriander seeds over a high heat for 4 minutes, then grind them with a pestle and mortar. Combine the meat and fat in a large bowl and sprinkle with spices, herbs and seasoning, pour in the vinegar and mix with the hands until well-blended. Fill into continuous sausage skins, cut off the length you require and twist into links, storing the rest in the deep freeze until required. Cook the sausages over a high heat, after pricking the skins here and there with a sharp fork, until a shining, rich brown.

Sausageburgers with Mash and Browned Onion Rings

SERVES 4

Serve with a home-made tomato sauce.

700 g (1½ lb) potatoes
2 onions
2 tablespoons vegetable oil
450 g (1 lb) good sausage-meat
1 clove garlic, crushed
2 tablespoons finely chopped parsley

pinch chilli powder and paprika
pinch dried sage
salt and freshly ground black pepper
25 g (1 oz) butter
2 tablespoons single cream

Cook the potatoes until tender. Meanwhile, peel and thinly slice the onions and divide them into rings. Heat the oil in a large heavy frying-pan and cook the onions over a low to medium heat, stirring frequently, until the onion rings become a dark, nutty brown (this can take quite some time). Combine the sausage-meat with the garlic, parsley, spices and sage and season the mixure with salt and pepper. Mix well and shape into four patties on a well-floured board. Grill under a hot grill for about 5 minutes on each side until sizzling and well browned. Drain the potatoes well and mash smoothly with the butter, cream, salt and pepper. Shape the potatoes on the edge of a shallow serving dish. Arrange the onions, drained of excess oil, in the centre. Place the sausageburgers on the onions and serve.

Meat

Sausage and Cabbage Casserole
SERVES 4

Serve with mashed potatoes.

8 herb-seasoned sausages
1 green cabbage
1.1 litres (2 pts) water
2 sprigs parsley
1 sprig thyme

1 bay leaf
4 rashers lean bacon
salt and freshly ground black pepper
pinch grated nutmeg
450 ml ($\frac{3}{4}$ pt) beef stock

Grill or fry sausages over a low heat until well-browned. Reserve the fat they exude. Roughly chop the cabbage. Bring the water to the boil, add the cabbage, bacon and herbs, bring back to the boil and cook for 10 minutes. Drain well, remove herbs and leave to cool. Remove rinds from the bacon and roughly chop the rashers. Combine the bacon and cabbage, pour over a little sausage dripping and season with salt, pepper and a little nutmeg. Arrange half the cabbage and bacon in a lightly greased baking dish, cover with the sausages and top with the remaining cabbage and bacon mixture. Pour over the stock and bake in a moderate oven (180°C / 350°F / Reg 4) for 30 minutes.

Black Pudding and Tater Pie
SERVES 4

Serve with a home-made tomato sauce and Dijon mustard.

1 small firm cabbage
2 onions
4 rashers streaky bacon
1 black pudding
1 large potato

50 g (2 oz) dripping
salt and freshly ground black pepper
150 ml ($\frac{1}{4}$ pt) good stock
25 g (1 oz) melted butter

Remove the core from the cabbage and shred the leaves. Peel and thinly slice the onions into rings. Remove the bacon rinds and roughly chop the rashers. Cut the black pudding into 1 cm ($\frac{1}{2}$ in) slices. Peel and thinly slice the potato. Melt the dripping in a large frying-pan. Add the bacon and onions and cook over a low heat until the onions are soft and transparent. Add the cabbage, season with salt and pepper and stir for 3 minutes. Arrange alternate layers of cabbage mixture and black pudding in a lightly greased casserole, beginning and ending with a layer of cabbage. Pour over the stock, top with overlapping slices of potato and brush with the melted butter. Bake in a moderate oven (180°C / 350°F / Reg 4) for 45 minutes.

Paprika's Toad-in-the-Hole
SERVES 4

Serve with shredded cabbage cooked in a little dry white wine, doused liberally with melted butter and seasoned with salt and freshly ground black pepper.

8 large top-quality pork sausages
50 g (2 oz) ham
100 g (4 oz) flour
2 eggs
300 ml (½ pt) milk

salt and freshly ground black pepper
pinch paprika
pinch each dried sage and thyme
1 tablespoon finely chopped parsley
40 g (1½ oz) lard or dripping

Fry the sausages until cooked and brown. Very finely chop or mince the ham. Combine the flour with the eggs, milk and seasoning and beat until smooth. Add the paprika, herbs and ham and mix well. In a hot oven (200°C / 400°F / Reg 6), heat the lard or dripping in an ovenproof serving dish until a haze rises from the fat. Arrange the sausages in the dish and pour over the batter. Cook in a hot oven for about 40 minutes, until the batter has risen and is golden brown and crisp.

Saucisses au Vin Blanc
SERVES 6

Serve with sautéed potatoes and shredded cabbage lightly cooked in butter and well seasoned with salt and freshly ground black pepper.

700 g (1½ lb) pork sausages
1 large onion
25 g (1 oz) butter
1 tablespoon flour

1 teaspoon Dijon mustard
600 ml (1 pt) dry white wine
pinch mixed dried thyme and marjoram
salt and freshly ground black pepper

Cook the sausages over a moderately low heat in a dry frying-pan until they are nicely browned on all sides. Drain off excess fat. Peel and finely chop the onion. Melt the butter in a saucepan. Add the onion and cook over a low heat until soft and transparent. Add the flour and mustard and mix well. Gradually add the wine, stirring continually over a medium-high heat until the sauce is thick and smooth. Add the herbs, season with salt and pepper and simmer the sauce for 20 minutes. Add the sausages to the sauce and continue to simmer for a further 5 minutes.

Meat

Calf's Liver with Avocado
SERVES 6

4 avocados
flour
salt and freshly ground black pepper
1.1 kg (2½ lb) calf's liver,
    thinly sliced

6 tablespoons clarified butter
3 tablespoons butter
lemon juice
fresh parsley or chervil
100 ml (4 fl oz) medium-dry sherry

Halve the avocados, remove the stones, peel and slice the flesh into lengthwise segments. Mix the flour with salt and pepper. Dip the liver into the flour and shake off the excess. Similarly dip the avocado slices. Heat the clarified butter in a frying-pan and sauté the liver for a couple of minutes on each side. Do the same with the avocados, but only for about a minute on each side. Place the liver on a serving platter and put the avocado slices on top. Pour off the cooking butter from the pan. Add fresh butter and melt it quickly. Add the lemon juice, chopped parsley or chervil and the sherry, mix together and pour over the liver and avocado. NOTE: To clarify butter, heat it in a saucepan until foaming and strain through muslin.

Fegato Garbo e Dolce
SERVES 6

Plate 20, illustrated facing page 129.

Wafer-thin slices of calf's liver served with a sweet-and-sour sauce. Accompany with noodles tossed in butter and a little Parmesan cheese.

900 g (2 lb) calf's liver in 1 piece
1 large egg
salt and freshly ground black pepper
flour
fine dry breadcrumbs
100 g (4 oz) butter

juice of 1 large lemon
1½ teaspoons sugar

Garnish
sprigs fresh tarragon

Using a very sharp knife, cut the liver against the grain into slices as thin as those of really thinly cut streaky bacon. Beat the egg with a little salt. Lightly flour the slices, dip them in beaten egg and coat with breadcrumbs. Heat the butter in a heavy frying-pan until it foams, add the slices of liver and cook them over a high heat until they are browned on both sides. Remove the liver to a heated serving dish and keep warm. Add the lemon and sugar to the pan juices and stir over a low heat until the sugar has dissolved. Season with pepper, pour the sauce over the liver and serve as quickly as possible.

Meat

Liver Venetian Style
SERVES 4

700 g (1½ lb) well-chilled liver
450 g (1 lb) onions
½ tablespoon olive oil
40 g (1½ oz) butter
salt and freshly ground black pepper

2 tablespoons dry vermouth

Garnish
2 tablespoons finely chopped parsley,
celery leaves or spring onion tops

Cut the liver into very thin slices, against the grain, with a really sharp knife. Peel and thinly slice the onions and divide into rings. Heat the oil and butter in a large, heavy frying-pan, add the onions and cook over a low heat, stirring occasionally, until the onions are soft, tender and yellow. Raise the heat to high, push the onions to one side and fry the liver for about 5 minutes, until it is brown on both sides. Season with salt and pepper, pour over the vermouth, sprinkle with parsley and serve.

Liver and Leek Casserole
SERVES 4

2 rashers lean bacon
700 g (1½ lb) lamb's liver
4 leeks
4 ripe tomatoes

celery salt
freshly ground black pepper
pinch dried mixed herbs

Finely chop the bacon; thinly slice the liver; wash, dry and finely slice the leeks. Peel the tomatoes and chop very finely, reserving all their juices. Cook the bacon for a few minutes, over a medium heat, without adding any extra fat. Add the liver and brown over a high flame. Combine the bacon, liver and leeks in an ovenproof casserole, season with celery salt and pepper and sprinkle with a little mixed herbs. Spread with the tomatoes, cover the casserole tightly and bake in a moderate oven (180°C / 350°F / Reg 4) for 35–40 mintues, until the liver is tender.

Liver and Bacon Hot-Pot
SERVES 5–6

700 g (1½ lb) lamb's liver
flour seasoned with salt and pepper
2 onions
4 carrots
6 rashers streaky bacon

900 g (2 lb) potatoes
2 tablespoons olive oil or
25 g (1 oz) butter
2 beef stock cubes
2 tablespoons tomato ketchup

Cut the liver into thin slices and coat well with seasoned flour. Peel and roughly chop the onions and carrots. Remove the rinds and cut the bacon into 5 cm (2 in) pieces. Peel and slice the potatoes. Heat the oil or butter, add the bacon and fry for 3 minutes over a medium heat. Add the liver and cook over a high heat until it is browned on all sides. Add the vegetables and pour in enough water to cover; bring to the boil, add stock cubes and tomato ketchup. Stir well, cover and simmer gently for about an hour until the meat and vegetables are tender.

Pig's Trotters and Parsley Sauce

SERVES 4

4 pig's trotters
1 onion
1 carrot
1 stalk celery
6 black peppercorns
salt
15 g ($\frac{1}{2}$ oz) butter
1 tablespoon flour

300 ml ($\frac{1}{2}$ pt) milk
2 tablespoons finely chopped
  parsley
1 teaspoon lemon juice
white pepper

Garnish
sprigs parsley

Wash the trotters and wrap them in muslin. Place them in a large pan and cover with cold water. Peel and roughly chop the onion and carrot and chop the celery. Add the vegetables and black peppercorns to the pan and season with salt. Bring to the boil, cover and simmer for 2–2$\frac{1}{2}$ hours. Remove the trotters from the pan, unwrap and arrange on a heated serving dish; keep hot. (The stock can be used to make soup.) Melt the butter in a saucepan, stir in the flour and gradually add the milk. Cook over a medium heat, stirring, until the sauce is thick and smooth. Add the parsley and lemon juice and season with salt and white pepper. Bring to the boil, then pour the sauce over the trotters, garnish with parsley sprigs and serve.

Calves' Brains with Onions and Mushrooms

SERVES 4

450 g (1 lb) calves' brains
salt
8 very small onions
100 g (4 oz) firm button mushrooms
25 g (1 oz) butter
1 tablespoon flour

300 ml ($\frac{1}{2}$ pt) hot chicken stock
freshly ground black pepper
2 egg yolks
$\frac{1}{2}$ tablespoon lemon juice
1 tablespoon finely chopped parsley

Wash the brains and soak them in warm water for 1 hour, then drain and remove the arteries and membranes. Plunge into boiling salted water and cook for 15 minutes, then rinse in cold water, drain well and leave to cool. Cut the brains into bite-sized pieces. Peel the onions and thinly slice the mushrooms. Blanch the mushrooms in boiling salted water for 3 minutes and drain well. Melt the butter in a saucepan and stir in the flour. Gradually blend in the chicken stock and stir constantly over a medium heat until the sauce has thickened. Add the onions and mushrooms and season with salt and pepper. Simmer gently for 30 minutes, then add the brains and cook for a further 15 minutes until the brains are tender. Using a slotted spoon, transfer the brains, onions and mushrooms to a heated serving dish. Beat the egg yolks with the lemon juice and add a little of the hot sauce. Mix until smooth and then add the remaining sauce, stirring all the time over a low heat until the sauce is thick and smooth. Stir in the parsley, check seasoning and pour the sauce over the brains and vegetables. Serve at once.

Maidenwell Sweetbreads

SEVES 4

450 g (1 lb) sweetbreads
100 g (4 oz) ham
1 green pepper
salt
40 g (1½ oz) butter
1 tablespoon olive oil
1 tablespoon flour
150 ml (¼ pt) milk

150 ml (¼ pt) chicken stock
freshly ground black pepper
2 egg yolks
2 tablespoons finely crushed
  water biscuits
40 g (1½ oz) finely grated
  Cheddar cheese

Clean the sweetbreads thoroughly. Divide them into 2.5 cm (1 in) pieces. Chop the ham. Remove the core and seeds of the green pepper and chop the flesh. Blanch the pepper in boiling salted water for 5 minutes and drain well. Heat 25 g (1 oz) butter with the oil in a saucepan, add the sweetbreads and cook over a medium heat for 3 minutes. Remove with a slotted spoon and keep warm. Blend the flour into the pan juices and gradually add the milk and stock, stirring constantly until the sauce is thick and smooth. Return the sweetbreads to the pan, add the ham and green pepper and season with salt and pepper. Cover and simmer for 15 minutes. Beat the egg yolks and stir in a little of the sauce. Blend with the remaining sauce and cook gently, stirring until the mixture is slightly thickened and shiny. Transfer to a baking dish and top with the biscuit crumbs mixed with the grated cheese. Brown quickly under a hot grill and serve at once.

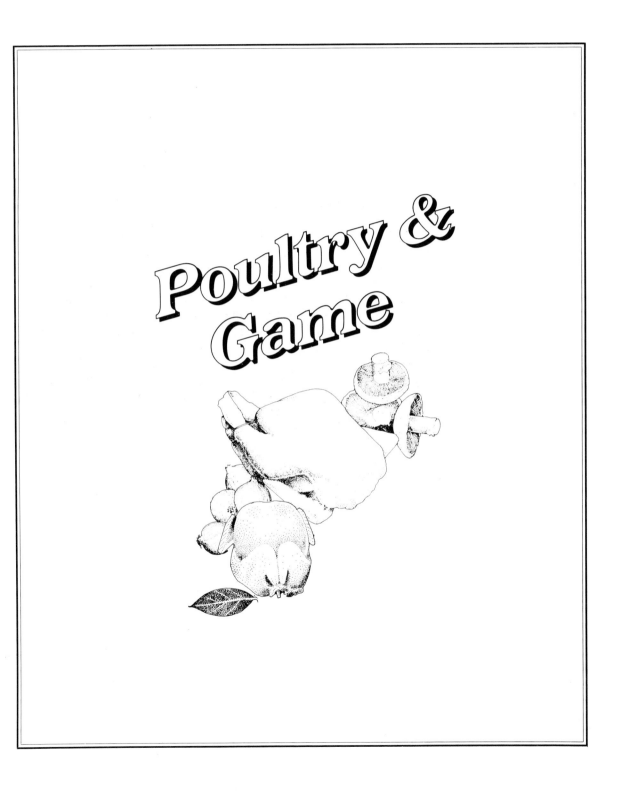

Poultry & Game

Poultry & Game

Golden Glazed Chicken

SERVES 6

A special French treatment that keeps the chicken deliciously moist.

1 chicken liver
2 tablespoons brandy (optional)
50 g (2 oz) fresh breadcrumbs
100 g (4 oz) butter, softened
1 clove garlic, minced
4 spring onions, finely chopped
1 tablespoon finely chopped parsley

1 tablespoon finely chopped chives
pinch thyme
salt and freshly ground black pepper
1 large roasting chicken
2 tablespoons oil
300 ml ($\frac{1}{2}$ pt) chicken stock

Finely chop the chicken liver, add the brandy and mash well with a fork. Add the breadcrumbs, 75 g (3 oz) butter, garlic, spring onion and herbs, season with salt and pepper and mix to a paste. Turn the chicken breast-side up. Loosen the skin around the tail end, using a small sharp knife. Rub a little oil on your fingers and gently insert them under the skin of the breast, pushing gently until all the skin has been separated. Using a spatula, spread the butter stuffing very thinly and evenly under skin. Spread any remaining stuffing inside the bird. Brown the bird all over in the remaining butter and the oil, place in a casserole, pour in the chicken stock, cover and cook in a moderately hot oven (190°C / 375°F / Reg 5) for about an hour, basting occasionally, and leaving the bird uncovered for the last 10 minutes of cooking time to brown and crisp the skin. Serve hot with a gravy made from the juices in the pan, or leave the chicken to cool and serve cold.

Smothered Poussins

SERVES 4

Serve with sautéed potatoes and a green vegetable or salad.

2 poussins or spring chickens
2 cloves garlic
100 g (4 oz) cottage cheese
1 tablespoon green peppercorns
  in brine, strained

75 g (3 oz) butter
1 teaspoon dried mixed herbs
salt and a pinch paprika

Halve the chickens along the breast and backbone using a pair of kitchen scissors. Peel and finely chop the garlic. Add the cottage cheese, peppercorns, butter, herbs and seasoning and blend until the mixture is reduced to a smooth paste. Spread the chickens with the cheese paste on the skin sides and lay them cut side down in a roasting dish. Roast in a hot oven (200°C / 400°F / Reg 6) for 40 minutes, basting frequently with the pan juices. When the chicken halves are cooked, remove to a warm serving dish and spoon over the juices from the pan.

Scrumpy Chicken

SERVES 4–6

1 roasting chicken with giblets
½ packet sage and onion stuffing
1 apple
25 g (1 oz) butter
100 g (4 oz) sausage-meat

finely grated rind of 1 lemon
salt and freshly ground black pepper
300 ml (½ pt) dry cider
pinch tarragon

Prepare the chicken for roasting. Make up the stuffing according to the directions on the packet. Finely chop the chicken liver and heart. Peel and grate the apple. Heat half the butter in a small pan. Add the chicken liver and heart and the sausage-meat. Cook for 5 minutes over a medium heat, stirring frequently to break up the sausage-meat. Mix in the stuffing, grated apple and finely grated rind of the lemon. Season with salt and pepper. Stuff the chicken with this mixture. Rub the remaining butter over the chicken and sprinkle with salt and pepper. Place the bird in a roasting tin with the neck and gizzard and roast in the normal way. Halfway through the cooking time, pour over the cider and a pinch of tarragon. Baste frequently until the bird is cooked. Serve with the strained juices from the pan.

Courgette-Stuffed Pot-Roasted Chicken

SERVES 6

1 roasting chicken
50 g (2 oz) softened butter
1 teaspoon chopped parsley
pinch dried mixed herbs
1 clove garlic, crushed
salt and freshly ground black pepper
3 courgettes

3 carrots
1 celeriac root or 4 stalks celery
3 leeks
chicken stock
700 g (1½ lb) potatoes
3 tablespoons vegetable oil
1 tablespoon soy sauce

With a sharp, pointed knife, ease the skin away from the flesh at the cavity-end of the breast then, with the fingers, force the skin of the breast and the tops of the legs away from the flesh without splitting the skin. Combine the butter, herbs, garlic, salt and pepper and insert between the skin and breast meat, gently spreading it around. Coarsely grate the courgettes, season with salt and pepper and stuff the bird with them. Coarsely chop the carrots and celeriac. Thickly slice the leeks. Place the chicken in a casserole and surround with the vegetables. Pour in enough stock to cover 2.5 cm (1 in) of the chicken and vegetables. Cover really tightly and cook in a moderately hot oven (190°C / 375°F / Reg 5) for about 1½ hours until almost tender. Meanwhile, peel the potatoes, cook until tender and cut into fairly thick slices. Uncover the chicken, arrange the potatoes over the vegetables, brush the oil over the breast, the tops of the legs and the potatoes, and brush the breasts with soy sauce. Return to a hot oven (200°C / 400°F / Reg 6) for 15 minutes to brown.

Whole Casseroled Chicken

SERVES 6

Serve with rice or potatoes.

½ packet sage and onion stuffing
2 rashers bacon
1 roasting chicken, medium to large
    with giblets
1 tablespoon finely chopped parsley
salt and freshly ground black pepper
8 carrots

8 small parsnips
12 shallots
1 bouquet garni
150 ml (¼ pt) dry white wine
25 g (1 oz) butter, melted
juice of ½ lemon

Make up the stuffing according to the instructions given on the packet. Add the bacon and chicken liver cut into small pieces and the parsley. Season with salt and pepper and stuff the chicken with this mixture. Place the chicken in the centre of a flameproof casserole or very heavy saucepan and surround it with the vegetables, bouquet garni, chicken neck, gizzard and heart. Pour in the white wine and enough water to cover the vegetables, season with salt and pepper, bring to the boil, cover tightly and simmer for about 1½ hours. Check once in a while to see if a little more water is needed. Remove bouquet garni, chicken neck, gizzard and heart, place the chicken in a heated serving dish, surround with the vegetables and pour over the melted butter mixed with the lemon juice.

Chicken with Cider

SERVES 4

Serve with plain boiled rice.

4 chicken legs and thighs
1 large carrot
1 onion
celery leaves
1 chicken stock cube
750 ml (1¼ pts) water

4 rashers bacon with rinds removed
4 stalks celery
100 g (4 oz) firm button mushrooms
flour
salt and freshly ground black pepper
150 ml (¼ pt) dry cider

Remove all the meat from the chicken portions and cut it into thin strips. Peel and chop the carrot and onion. Put the chicken bones, carrot, celery leaves, chopped onion and crumbled stock cube in a pan with the water and cook for 30 minutes to extract the flavour from the bones. Strain the stock. Cut the bacon into thin strips. Finely chop the celery and mushrooms. Cook the bacon over a lower heat until the fat has run from it. Coat the chicken in flour seasoned with a little salt and pepper. Add the chicken to the bacon and cook over a high heat, stirring, until the chicken is lightly browned. Add the cider and 600 ml (1 pt) stock, season with salt and pepper and stir over a medium heat until the sauce is thickened and smooth. Add the celery and mushrooms and simmer for about 15 minutes until the celery and chicken are tender.

Chicken Breasts on a Bed of Shredded Vegetables

SERVES 4

make it again

A glorious, quickly made dish that stretches two chicken breasts into four luscious servings.

2 chicken breasts
flour
salt and freshly ground black pepper
paprika
2 carrots
1 onion
2 cloves garlic
1 green pepper

2 tomatoes
4 stalks celery
50 g (2 oz) mushrooms
15 g ($\frac{1}{2}$ oz) butter
50 g (2 oz) ham
4 tablespoons oil
4 tablespoons dry white wine
50 g (2 oz) Gruyère cheese

Remove the skins from the breasts. Pull off the thin fillets from underneath the breasts and slice the remainder in two, horizontally. Place all the pieces of breast between two sheets of greaseproof paper and then flatten them with a rolling pin or mallet until they are wafer-thin. Coat the breasts in flour seasoned with salt, pepper and a little paprika. Peel and coarsely grate the carrots. Peel and very thinly slice the onion. Peel and finely chop the garlic. Thinly slice the green pepper flesh. Skin the tomatoes, remove the cores and seeds and chop the flesh. Trim the celery stalks and cut them into thin matchstick lengths. Thinly slice the mushrooms and soften them in the butter over a medium heat. Mince the ham. Heat the oil in a large frying-pan and add the chicken breasts, cooking over a high heat until they are golden brown on both sides. Remove the breasts with a slotted spoon and drain on kitchen paper. Add the carrots, onion, garlic, celery and green pepper to the oil and cook over a medium heat, stirring until the vegetables have softened (about 5 minutes). Add the tomatoes, season with salt and pepper, pour over the wine and press down the vegetables with the back of a spoon. Place the chicken breasts on the vegetables, cover with the mushrooms and a layer of ham, and top with the grated cheese. Sprinkle with a little paprika, cover and simmer for about 6 minutes to finish cooking the chicken.

Quantock Chicken

SERVES 4–5

1 green pepper
100 g (4 oz) mushrooms
1 onion
1.5 kg (3 lb) chicken, jointed

just under 300 ml ($\frac{1}{2}$ pt) dry cider
salt and freshly ground black pepper
150 ml ($\frac{1}{4}$ pt) plain yoghourt
1 tablespoon finely chopped parsley

Remove the core and seeds from the green pepper and chop the flesh. Halve the mushrooms. Peel and chop the onion. Put the chicken, green pepper, onion, mushrooms and cider in an ovenproof casserole. Season with salt and pepper. Cook in a moderate oven (180°C / 350°F / Reg 4) for 1$\frac{1}{2}$ hours. Remove the lid, pour on the yoghourt and sprinkle with parsley just before serving.

143

Poultry & Game

Chicken à la Bonne Femme

SERVES 4

4 leeks
4 small carrots
225 g (8 oz) firm button mushrooms
25 g (1 oz) butter
4 chicken portions
600 ml (1 pt) stock or stock and
   cider mixed

75 g (3 oz) frozen peas
3 tablespoons tomato purée
salt and freshly ground black pepper
pinch dried mixed herbs
4 tablespoons single cream

Wash and clean the leeks, dry well and slice thinly. Peel and dice the carrots. Thinly slice the mushrooms. Melt the butter in a frying-pan. Add the chicken and brown the pieces all over on a high heat. Lower the heat and add the leeks and carrots and cook, stirring, for 4 minutes. Add the mushrooms and cook for 2 minutes. Add the stock, bring to the boil, cover and simmer for about 10 minutes or until the chicken is tender. Mix in the peas and tomato purée, season with salt and pepper, add the herbs and simmer until the peas are just tender. Stir in the cream and serve.

Golden Bird

SERVES 4

Plate 21, illustrated facing page 152.

Called Golden Bird because the chicken is cooked to a sun-coloured tenderness in a mixture of turmeric and yoghourt and has the exciting taste of the East without being too fiery. Serve with a mixed green salad and rice cooked with a little powdered saffron.

300 ml ($\frac{1}{2}$ pt) plain yoghourt
2 teaspoons turmeric
2 cloves crushed garlic
1.5 kg (3 lb) chicken
2 large onions

1 green pepper
50 g (2 oz) butter
4 cloves
pinch ground cinnamon
1 tablespoon chopped mango chutney

Combine the yoghourt, turmeric and crushed garlic, pour onto the chicken and leave to marinate for at least 4 hours. Drain the chicken and reserve all the juices. Peel and thinly slice the onions. Remove the core and seeds from the green pepper and cut it into thin strips. Heat the butter in a casserole, add the onions and pepper and cook until the onions are golden brown. Add the chicken and cook for 10 minutes. Pour over the marinade and add the cloves, cinnamon and chutney. Cover and cook in a moderate oven (180°C / 350°F / Reg 4) for 1½ hours until tender.

144

Chicken in Lemon and Tarragon Sauce with Rice

SERVES 4

Serve with a salad or green vegetables.

350 g (12 oz) cooked chicken
50 g (2 oz) ham
175 g (6 oz) firm button mushrooms
50 g (2 oz) butter
2 teaspoons dried tarragon
2 teaspoons lemon juice
225 g (8 oz) long-grain rice
900 ml (1 ½ pt) water
1 chicken stock cube

1 small onion or shallot
25 g (1 oz) flour
300 ml (½ pt) milk
salt and freshly ground pepper
     (preferably white peppercorns)

Garnish
finely chopped parsley

Chop or thinly slice the chicken. Cut the ham into thin strips. Thinly slice the mushrooms. Melt 15 g (½ oz) of the butter, add the mushrooms and cook over a low heat for 3 minutes until the butter has been absorbed (the flame should be really low so that the mushrooms do not lose their juice and discolour). Add the tarragon to the lemon juice and leave to steep. Put the rice into a heavy saucepan, add water and stock cube, bring to the boil, stirring occasionally, then simmer uncovered for about 25–30 mintues until all the liquid has been absorbed and the rice is tender but still nutty in texture. Peel and finely chop the onion, sauté in 15 g (½ oz) butter until soft and transparent, and mix into the rice. Turn into a serving dish, shape into a ring and keep warm. Melt the remaining butter in a saucepan, add flour and mix well. Gradually blend in the milk, stirring continually over a medium heat until the sauce is thick and smooth. Add the chicken, ham, mushrooms, lemon juice and tarragon, season with salt and pepper and simmer for 2 minutes. Spoon the chicken into the rice ring and garnish with chopped parsley.

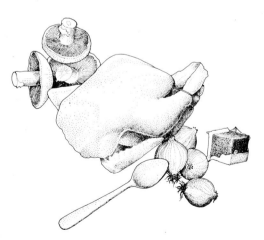

145

Stir-Fried Chicken with Green Pepper and Walnuts

SERVES 4–6

350 g (12 oz) chicken breasts
1 egg white
1 tablespoon cornflour
1 tablespoon dry sherry
1 tablespoon soy sauce
salt and white pepper
1 fresh red chilli pepper
  or ½ dried chilli
2 cloves garlic

2 small green peppers
3 spring onions
1 small leek
oil for frying
100 g (4 oz) shelled walnuts
2 teaspoons brown sugar
½ tablespoon white wine vinegar
1 tablespoon ginger wine

Remove the chicken skin and cut the breasts into thin horizontal slices. Place the slices between two sheets of greaseproof paper and beat them with a rolling pin until wafer-thin. Cut the slices into thin matchstick strips against the grain. Mix the egg white with the cornflour and sherry into a smooth paste. Add the soy sauce, season with salt and pepper, mix well; add the chicken pieces and toss with a fork to coat the chicken with the sauce. Remove the seeds from the chilli pepper and finely chop the flesh. Peel and finely chop the garlic. Remove the core and seeds from the green peppers and cut the flesh into thin strips. Trim the spring onions and cut into thin strips lengthwise. Trim the leek and slice thinly. Heat some oil in a wok or large heavy pan, add the walnuts and cook over a high heat for about 3 minutes, stirring, until the walnuts are crisp, then remove with a slotted spoon and keep warm. Add the chilli, garlic, leek and peppers to the oil in the pan and cook, stirring all the time over a high heat for 2 minutes. Add the chicken and spring onions and stir-fry until the chicken is opaque. Add the sugar, vinegar, ginger wine and walnuts and toss over a high heat for 1 minute. Check seasoning.

Chicken Curry

SERVES 4

3 onions
2 cloves garlic
4 tablespoons sunflower oil
1½ tablespoons hot curry paste
2 tablespoons tomato purée

1 small chicken, jointed
1 tablespoon desiccated coconut
juice of ½ lemon
salt

Peel and finely chop the onion. Peel and crush the garlic. Heat the oil, add the onion and garlic and cook until the onion is soft, golden and transparent. Add the curry paste and tomato purée and cook for 4 minutes. Add the chicken, mix well, cover tightly and simmer for about 30 minutes until the chicken is tender. If the mixture becomes dry, add a little water. Stir in the desiccated coconut, which will absorb any oil, and the lemon juice, and season with salt.

Malay Chicken Satay
SERVES 4

700 g (1½ lb) chicken breasts
2.5 cm (1 in) piece fresh ginger root
1 onion
2 cloves garlic
1 teaspoon coriander seeds
3 tablespoons peanuts
salt and freshly ground black pepper
pinch cayenne pepper
1 tablespoon honey
3 tablespoons lemon juice
1 tablespoon brown sugar
2 tablespoons soy sauce

Satay Sauce
2 onions
100 g (4 oz) roasted peanuts
pinch chilli powder
2 tablespoons vegetable oil
150 ml (¼ pt) water
1 teaspoon brown sugar
1 tablespoon soy sauce
juice of ½ lemon
salt

Very thinly slice the chicken breasts and then cut into strips about 1 × 2.5 cm (½ × 1 in). Mince the ginger root; peel and very finely chop the onion. Crush the garlic and coriander seeds. Finely chop or mince the peanuts. Combine all the ingredients, add the chicken and marinate for at least 3 hours. Thread the chicken strips on long skewers, putting 2 or 3 on each one and leaving at least 10 cm (4 in) clear at one end. Grill over a hot fire, turning once or twice until the chicken is cooked, brown and slightly crisp around the edges. Dip into the Satay sauce to eat.

Sauce
Peel and chop 1 onion. Peel and chop the second onion and combine with the peanuts and chilli powder in a liquidiser. Process until the mixture is reduced to a paste. Heat the oil. Add the chopped onion and cook over a medium heat until soft and golden. Add the paste and stir for 3 minutes. Gradually blend in the water, stirring all the time. Add the sugar and cook for 5 minutes. Mix in the soy sauce and lemon juice and season if necessary with a little salt. Serve the sauce hot or warm. It can be made in advance and reheated.

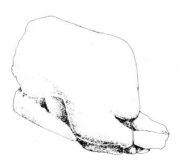

Sweet and Sour Chicken with Almonds

SERVES 4–6

Serve with plain boiled rice.

1 roasting chicken with giblets
1 large onion
3 carrots
2 stalks celery
3 tablespoons olive oil
1 tablespoon cornflour
3 tablespoons sherry

2 tablespoons soy sauce
1 tablespoon sugar
150 ml ($\frac{1}{4}$ pt) stock
salt and freshly ground black pepper
100 g (4 oz) split blanched almonds
25 g (1 oz) butter

Use a sharp knife to joint the chicken and cut all the flesh from the bones. Remove the skin and combine the skin, carcass and giblets to make a clear stock. Cut the chicken flesh into neat 2.5 cm (1 in) pieces, peel and thinly slice the onion, peel and thinly slice the carrots and celery stalks. Heat the olive oil in a large frying-pan, add the chicken and cook over a medium heat until the pieces of meat are golden brown on all sides. Lower the heat and continue to cook gently until the chicken is just tender. Add the vegetables and cook, stirring continually, for a further 10 minutes. Combine the cornflour, sherry, soy sauce and sugar and mix until smooth. Pour the sauce over the chicken and vegetables, blend in well, bring to the boil and continue stirring until the sauce is thick, smooth and shiny. Blend in the stock, season and transfer to a warm serving dish. Fry the almonds in melted butter until golden brown, drain, and mix into the chicken at the last minute.

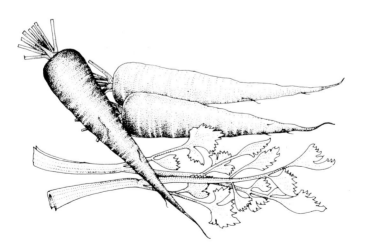

Chicken Puff Pie

SERVES 6

Serve with a salad.

2 large onions
2 stalks celery with leaves
1.5 kg (3 lb) roasting chicken
1 chicken stock cube
2 bay leaves
salt and freshly ground black pepper
40 g (1½ oz) butter

3 tablespoons flour
150 ml (¼ pt) milk
2 tablespoons grated Parmesan cheese
450 g (1 lb) frozen puff pastry, thawed
melted butter

Peel and finely chop the onions and chop the celery. Place the chicken in a pan with the onions and enough water to cover. Add the stock cube to the water with the bay leaves, chopped celery stalks and leaves. Bring to the boil, season with salt and pepper and simmer gently for about an hour until the chicken is just tender. Strain the liquid and reserve. Leave the chicken to cool, remove the flesh, discarding the skin and bones, dice and combine with the onions and celery, discarding the bay leaves. Remove as much fat as possible from the stock. Pour the stock into a saucepan and cook over a high heat, boiling until it is reduced by about half. Melt the butter in a saucepan, add the flour and mix well. Gradually add the milk and 450 ml (¾ pt) stock, stirring continually, over a high heat until the sauce is thick and smooth; simmer, stirring, for 5 minutes. Add the chicken, onions and celery, mix in the cheese and season with nutmeg, salt and pepper. Check the seasoning and leave to cool a little. Roll out the pastry on a well-floured board to a thin sheet large enough to line and top a pie dish. Line the pie dish with half the pastry and brush with melted butter. Fill the dish with the chicken mixture and cover with the remaining pastry, pressing the two edges of the pastry firmly together. Brush the top of the pie generously with melted butter and score pastry with a criss-cross pattern. Bake in a hot oven (200°C / 400°F / Reg 6) for 5 minutes, lower the heat to moderate (180°C / 350°F / Reg 4) and continue to cook for a further 30 minutes until the pastry is risen and golden brown and nicely crisp. Give another brush with melted butter halfway through cooking time.

Chicken Petelana

SERVES 10

You can sprinkle the top with cheese and brown under the grill for a few minutes before serving. Serve with rice and salad.

1 large (2½ kg/5 lb) or 2 small,
  cooked chickens
450 g (1 lb) small button mushrooms
40 g (1½ oz) butter
4 tablespoons finely chopped parsley
350 g (12 oz) cooked peas
5-6 tinned artichoke hearts
450 g (1 lb) cooked sliced carrots
225 g (8 oz) cooked sliced turnip

100 g (4 oz) butter
4 tablespoons flour
600 ml (1 pt) strong chicken stock
300 ml (½ pt) dry white wine
150 ml (¼ pt) dry sherry
300 ml (½ pt) single cream
salt and freshly ground black pepper
pinch cayenne pepper
2 green peppers

Cut the cooked chicken into thin slices. Sauté the mushrooms in 40 g (1½ oz) butter until the butter has been absorbed. Fill a large casserole with alternate layers of chicken, parsley and vegetables. Melt 100 g (4 oz) butter, add 4 tablespoons of flour and mix well. Add the stock, stirring over a medium-high heat until the sauce is thick and smooth. Add the white wine and sherry and mix well. Lower the heat and stir in the cream, season with salt, pepper and a pinch of cayenne and cook, without boiling, for 5 minutes. Pour the sauce over the chicken and vegetables, shaking the dish so that it sinks through. Cut the peppers into thin strips and blanch for 3 minutes. Drain well and arrange the peppers in a lattice pattern over the dish. Cover tightly with foil and bake in a moderate oven (180°C / 350°F / Reg 4) for 30–45 minutes.

Lemon and Tarragon Cold Roast Chicken

SERVES 6

1.5 kg (3 lb) roasting chicken
salt and freshly ground black pepper
juice of 1 lemon
40 g (1½ oz) softened butter
2 tablespoons sunflower oil

2 teaspoons dried tarragon
2 teaspoons soy sauce

Garnish
watercress

Rub the chicken all over with salt and pepper and then rub the lemon juice well into the skin. Then rub in the softened butter, oil and tarragon and season again with a little more salt and pepper. Stuff the squeezed lemon skins into the cavity of the bird and place in a roasting pan. Cover the top of the bird with foil, pour in 0.5 cm (¼ in) water into the pan and roast in a moderately hot oven (190°C / 375°F / Reg 5) for 45 minutes. Remove the foil, baste well with the juice from the pan and brush with the soy sauce. Roast for another 30 minutes, basting frequently, until the bird is a good golden brown and the skin is crisp. Leave to cool, chill and then cut off the drumsticks and wings and very thinly carve the breast and thighs. Arrange the meat on an oval platter and garnish with watercress.

Sozzled Chicken

SERVES 4

A dish to cheer you up!

1 roasting chicken
salt and freshly ground black pepper
pinch cayenne pepper
3 tablespoons olive oil
1 large onion
2 cloves garlic
300 ml ($\frac{1}{2}$ pt) stock

150 ml ($\frac{1}{4}$ pt) dry white wine
50 g (2 oz) ground almonds
2 egg yolks
2 tablespoons brandy

Garnish
1 tablespoon finely chopped parsley

Divide the chicken into eight pieces and season with salt, pepper and cayenne. Heat the olive oil until smoking in a large heavy frying-pan. Add the chicken and cook over a high heat until golden brown on all sides. Peel and finely chop the onion, peel and crush the garlic. Add both to the chicken and cook over a medium-low heat for 5 minutes, stirring to prevent sticking. Pour in the stock and wine, season with salt and simmer for 30 minutes or until the chicken is tender. Combine the ground almonds, egg yolks and brandy, mixing to a smooth paste. With a slotted spoon, remove the chicken pieces and onion to a heated serving dish and keep warm. Blend the paste into the pan juices and mix well. Cook gently for 10 minutes without boiling. Pour the sauce over the chicken and sprinkle with finely chopped parsley.

Braised Chicken in Lemon Sauce

SERVES 6

50 g (2 oz) butter
    plus extra for greasing
4 rashers bacon
1 chicken cut into serving pieces
    by the butcher
bunch parsley
salt and freshly ground black pepper

pinch grated nutmeg
4 tablespoons cold water
juice of 1 lemon
1 tablespoon flour
300 ml ($\frac{1}{2}$ pt) milk
150 ml ($\frac{1}{4}$ pt) sour cream

Grease a casserole dish with a little butter. Line it with bacon rashers (rinds removed). Place the chicken on the bacon with the bunch of parsley. Sprinkle with a little salt and pepper and the nutmeg. Pour in the cold water and half the lemon juice. Cover and cook in a moderately hot oven (190°C / 375°F / Reg 5) for 1–1$\frac{3}{4}$ hours, until the chicken pieces are tender. Arrange them in the centre of a large serving dish, discarding the parsley and bacon. Melt the butter in a saucepan, add the flour and mix well over a medium heat. Gradually add the milk, stirring continuously until the sauce is thick and smooth. Bring to the boil, remove from the heat, stir in the sour cream and remaining lemon juice. Pour the sauce over the chicken, and serve at once.

Chicken Fricassee

SERVES 4

Serve on slices of toast with the crusts removed.

550 g (1¼ lb) cooked chicken breast
4 small onions
4 small carrots
150 ml (¼ pt) chicken stock
25 g (1 oz) butter

25 g (1 oz) flour
4 small egg yolks
4 tablespoons single cream
1 teaspoon lemon juice
1 tablespoon finely chopped parsley

Very finely chop the chicken. Peel and very finely chop the onions. Peel the carrots and cut into small dice. Cook the chopped onion and carrot in the chicken stock until the carrot is tender. Strain off the stock and reserve. Melt the butter in a saucepan, stir in the flour and cook for 1 minute. Gradually add the stock and continue cooking, stirring for a further 2–3 minutes. Beat the egg yolks and cream together and add to the sauce stirring all the time. Cook over a medium heat until the sauce is thick and smooth. Add the chicken, lemon juice and vegetables to the sauce together with the parsley, stir over a low heat without boiling, until heated through.

Chicken Galantine

SERVES 10

A perfect picnic dish, this chicken galantine cuts like a dream and is full of surprises. A good butcher, given reasonable notice, should bone a chicken for you, leaving in the drumsticks and the second joint of the wings, so you end up with a kind of open-ended bag.

1 chicken, boned, with carcass and skin
225 g (8 oz) fat ham
50 g (2 oz) pistachio nuts
1 small green chilli pepper
2 cloves garlic (optional)
225 g (8 oz) pork sausage-meat
225 g (8 oz) minced pie veal
2 eggs, beaten

2 tablespoons finely chopped parsley
pinch dried mixed herbs
4 tablespoons brandy
salt and freshly ground black pepper
pinch cayenne and mace
4 tablespoons vegetable oil
2 tablespoons soy sauce

Remove any loose meat from the chicken and chop the flesh finely. Cut the ham and fat into very small dice. Chop pistachio nuts. Remove the seeds and very finely chop the chilli flesh. Crush the garlic. Combine the chicken flesh, sausage-meat, veal, ham, eggs, parsley, mixed herbs, pistachio nuts, chilli, garlic and brandy, season with salt, pepper and a little cayenne and mace and mix really well. Sew up the neck end of the chicken with a needle and stout thread. Pack the stuffing into the chicken carcass, retaining the chicken shape. Brush the chicken with a mixture of oil and soy sauce and roast it in a hot oven (220°C / 425°F / Reg 7) for 70 minutes, basting every now and then. Leave to cool, pack tightly in foil to consolidate and chill in refrigerator for at least 4 hours before carving into thin slices.

Plate 21. Golden Bird

Plate 22. Jellied Chicken and Bacon

Plate 23. Roast Quail

Plate 24. Aubergine Stuffed Tomatoes

Chicken with Tuna Mayonnaise

SERVES 6

1 carrot
1 onion
1 lemon
1.5 kg (3 lb) chicken
2 bay leaves
salt and freshly ground black pepper
150 ml ($\frac{1}{4}$ pt) dry white wine
1 stock cube
1 celeriac

2 teaspoons lemon juice
3 stalks celery
6 sprigs parsley
200 g (7 oz) tin tuna
3 anchovy fillets
300 ml ($\frac{1}{2}$ pt) mayonnaise
2 tablespoons double cream

Garnish
sliced pimiento-stuffed olives

Peel and roughly chop the carrot. Wash and quarter the onion without peeling. Quarter the lemon. Place the carrot, onion and lemon in a saucepan. Add the chicken and bay leaves, season with salt and pepper, add the wine and stock cube and pour in enough water to cover. Bring to the boil, cover tightly and simmer over a low heat for about an hour until the chicken is tender. Remove from the heat, leave for about 5 minutes and then remove the chicken and leave it to get completely cold. (The stock will make excellent soup). Peel the celeriac, cut it into thin slices and then into matchstick strips, dropping the strips as soon as they are cut into cold water to which the lemon juice has been added. Drain the celeriac and plunge it immediately into boiling, salted water and boil for about 4 minutes until just tender but still crisp. Cut the celery into neat matchstick strips. Finely chop the parsley. Drain the tuna and anchovies and pound them with the parsley to a paste in a mortar. Add the tuna mixture to the mayonnaise, mix in the cream and beat until smooth. Season lightly. Carve the chicken into very thin slices and arrange it with the celeriac and celery in a serving dish. Spoon over the tuna mayonnaise and garnish with slices of stuffed olive.

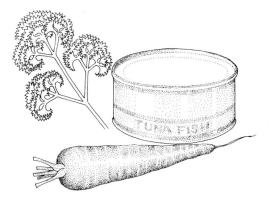

Poultry & Game

Jellied Chicken and Bacon
SERVES 6

Plate 22, illustrated between pages 152 and 153.

Serve with a garnish of salad vegetables and herbs.

900 g (2 lb) bacon in a piece
2 cloves
1 tablespoon brown sugar
2 tablespoons white wine vinegar
1 onion

1 small boiling fowl
bouquet garni
1 tablespoon sherry
salt and freshly ground black pepper

Soak the bacon if it is very salty, cover it with water, add the cloves, brown sugar and vinegar and bring slowly to the boil. Skim the surface of scum, cover and simmer gently for 1½–2 hours, until tender. Meanwhile, remove the outer skin from the onion and leave on the inner brown one; cut into quarters. Place the boiling fowl in a large pan with the onion and bouquet garni. Add sherry and just enough boiling water to cover. Season with a little salt and pepper, bring to the boil and simmer slowly for about 1½ hours, until the chicken is tender throughout. Strain the chicken liquid through a very fine sieve. Cut the chicken and bacon into thin slices while still warm and pack tightly in a bowl in alternate layers. Remove all possible fat from the chicken stock, first with a spoon, then with kitchen paper. Pour enough stock over the meat to cover it and top with a plate and heavy weight. Cool and leave to set in the fridge for at least 10 hours. Dip the mould into hot water and turn out.

Paprika Cranberry Venison's Turkey Pot Pies
SERVES 8

1 onion
1 green pepper
175 g (6 oz) firm button mushrooms
1 cauliflower
350 g (12 oz) cooked turkey
200 g (7 oz) tin tuna
400 g (14 oz) tin tomatoes
700 g (1 ½ lb) potatoes
100 g (4 oz) fresh white breadcrumbs
40 g (1 ½ oz) grated cheese

50 g (2 oz) butter
2 tablespoons flour
150 ml (¼ pt) milk
150 ml (¼ pt) dry cider
pinch dried mixed herbs
salt and freshly ground black pepper
pinch cayenne pepper
few drops Worcestershire sauce
40 g (1¼ oz) melted butter

Peel and chop the onion. Remove the core and seeds of the pepper and chop the flesh. Slice the button mushrooms. Steam the cauliflower until just tender and divide into florets. Roughly chop the turkey. Drain and flake the tuna. Drain the juice from the tomatoes and roughly chop the flesh. Peel the potatoes, boil them until just tender, then break them up with a fork (they do not need to be mashed). Combine the breadcrumbs with the cheese. Melt 15 g (½ oz) butter in a frying-pan. Add the onion and pepper and cook over a low heat until the onion is soft and transparent. Add the mushrooms and cook for a further 3 minutes. Melt 25 g (1 oz) of the butter in a large saucepan. Add the flour and mix well.

Gradually blend in the milk and cider, stirring continually until the sauce is thick and smooth. Add the onions, pepper, mushrooms, cauliflower, tomatoes, mixed herbs, turkey and tuna to the sauce and mix lightly. Season with salt, pepper and cayenne and a few drops Worcestershire sauce. Divide between eight pots (I use soup pots). Cover with the potatoes and then with the breadcrumb and cheese mixture. Dribble a little melted butter over the top and bake in a moderately hot oven (190°C / 375°F / Reg 5) for about 20 minutes until heated through and the topping is golden brown.

Festus Turkey

SERVES 6–8

225–450 g (½–1 lb) cooked turkey
1 fennel bulb or 4 large stalks celery
2 onions
225 g (8 oz) pasta shells
5 hard-boiled eggs
2 tablespoons finely chopped
  parsley or celery leaves

300 ml (½ pt) mayonnaise
salt and freshly ground black pepper
pinch grated nutmeg
fresh white breadcrumbs
butter

Very finely chop or mince the turkey. Trim the fennel and roughly chop. Peel and roughly chop the onions. Add the pasta, fennel and onions to a large pan half-filled with boiling salted water and boil until the pasta is tender and the vegetables are tender but still crisp (about 20 minutes). Drain well. Peel and roughly chop the hard-boiled eggs. Combine the turkey, eggs, parsley, pasta and vegetables in a bowl. Add the mayonnaise, season with salt, pepper and a pinch of nutmeg and mix well. Turn into a baking dish, cover with a thin layer of crumbs and dot with butter. Heat through in a hot oven (200°C / 400°F / Reg 6) for about 15 minutes until the top is crisp and golden brown.

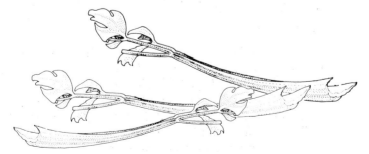

Rubicund Duck

SERVES 10

2 large ducks
rock salt
freshly ground black pepper
175 g (6 oz) jar stuffed olives
1 head celery
2 crisp eating apples
thinly peeled rind of 2 oranges
6 tablespoons redcurrant jelly
2 tablespoons dry English mustard

150 ml ($\frac{1}{4}$ pt) port or madeira
6 tablespoons red wine
2 tablespoons orange juice
1 tablespoon lemon juice
pinch each black pepper, cayenne
    pepper, and ginger

Garnish
watercress

Rub ducks well with rock salt and pepper. Place them on a rack in a baking dish and roast in a moderately hot (190°C / 375°F / Reg 5) oven for about 1$\frac{1}{2}$ hours, without basting, until cooked. Cover with foil if the skins brown too quickly. Leave the birds on the rack to cool. Remove all the skin and scrape any remaining fat from the flesh. Cut the skin into thin strips and fry over a high heat until crackling crisp. Drain on crumpled kitchen paper. Remove all meat from bones and dice. Rinse the olives in cold water, drain and slice thinly. Clean and thinly slice the celery. Peel and dice the apples. Remove all membranes from the orange rind, cut into thin shreds and blanch shreds for 2 minutes in boiling water. Dissolve the redcurrant jelly over a low heat and blend in the mustard. Add wines, fruit juices, spices and rind. Mix well, taste for seasoning and cool. Toss the duck, olives, celery and apple in the mixture and arrange on a serving dish. Surround with watercress and sprinkle over the crisp skin before serving. Serve accompanied by a green salad.

Pigeon and Orange Casserole

SERVES 4

$\frac{1}{2}$ teaspoon salt
1 teaspoon black pepper
4 plump pigeons, plucked and drawn
12 shallots
4 large carrots

50 g (2 oz) butter
2 tablespoons flour
2 heaped tablespoons marmalade
stock

Fry the salt and pepper without fat until the salt is lightly browned, which gives the seasoning a very special taste. Cool and rub the seasoning into the prepared birds. Peel the shallots and roughly chop the carrots. Heat the butter in a heavy, flameproof casserole and cook the pigeons over a high heat until browned on all sides. Remove the pigeons, add the shallots and carrots and cook for 3 minutes. Return the pigeons to the casserole, sprinkle with flour, mix in the marmalade and add enough stock to cover. Bring to the boil, cover and cook in a moderate oven (180°C / 350°F / Reg 4) for 1$\frac{1}{2}$ hours or until the birds are tender.

Braised Pigeons

SERVES 4

Borrowed from oriental cooking, the plum sauce gives this dish a marvellous piquancy.

4 pigeons
4 tablespoons flour
salt and freshly ground black pepper
2 onions
4 parsnips
4 large carrots
1 tablespoon olive oil

40 g (1½ oz) butter
1 orange
4 rashers bacon
150 ml (¼ pt) red wine
300 ml (½ pt) good stock
150 ml (¼ pt) plum sauce

Dip the pigeons into hot water then coat them in 2 tablespoons flour seasoned with salt and pepper. Peel and chop the onions. Peel and roughly chop the parsnips and carrots. Heat the oil and butter in a frying-pan, add the pigeons and brown well on all sides over a high heat. With a slotted spoon, remove the pigeons then stuff each one with a quarter of an orange. Wrap the pigeons in the bacon rashers from which the rinds have been removed. Add the vegetables to the pan juices and cook over a low heat until the onions are soft and transparent. Using a slotted spoon, spread the vegetables over the bottom of a casserole dish. Add the remaining flour to the pan and stir over a moderately high heat until the flour is lightly browned. Gradually add the wine and stock, stirring continuously. Cook until the sauce is thick and smooth. Season with salt and pepper. Place the pigeons on top of the vegetables, pour over the sauce, cover tightly and cook over a low heat for about 1–2 hours, depending on how old the pigeons are. Arrange the pigeons on a serving dish. Using a slotted spoon, arrange the vegetables around the pigeons and keep hot. Add the plum sauce to the juices and bring to the boil. Strain the sauce over the pigeons and serve at once.

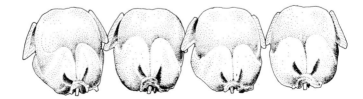

Poultry & Game

Roast Quail

SERVES 6

Plate 23, illustrated
between pages 152 and 153.

In his *Physiologie du Goût* Brillat-Savarin declared, 'The quail is the sweetest and nicest of game birds. It is an act of ignorance to serve it in any way except roasted', a sentiment with which I am totally in accord. Serve these roasted gems with a few new potatoes and leaf spinach, and you have a perfect summer main course.

6 quail
salt and freshly ground black pepper
225 g (8 oz) seedless green grapes
40 g (1½ oz) butter, melted
6 thin rashers streaky bacon, halved
6 round slices of white bread

1 glass red wine

Garnish
fresh coriander
seedless green grapes

Season the inside of the birds with salt and pepper and fill them with the grapes. Place the birds in a baking tin, brush with melted butter and top each with 2 strips of bacon. Roast the birds for 5 minutes in a very hot oven (230°C / 450°F / Reg 8), reduce the heat to 180°C / 350°F / Reg 4, and roast, basting frequently with the juices in the pan, for a further 15 minutes. Crisply fry the bread and place the birds on them. Accompany with a rich gravy made from the juices in the pan with the addition of some red wine. Garnish with coriander and grapes.

Pheasant à la Normande

SERVES 2

65 g (2½ oz) butter
1 tablespoon olive oil
1 large pheasant
½ lemon
1 sprig rosemary

celery salt and freshly ground
    black pepper
3 large Cox's apples
pinch cinnamon
4 tablespoons double cream
1 wineglass Calvados or dry cider

Heat 25 g (1 oz) butter with the oil in a large frying-pan. Add the pheasant and brown quickly on all sides. Remove the bird from the pan and pour the juices into the cavity, stuffing it with the half lemon and rosemary. Season the bird with celery salt and pepper. Peel, core and thickly slice the apples. Cook gently in the remaining butter in a clean pan for 3 minutes. Arrange a layer of apples at the bottom of a casserole, sprinkle with cinnamon and put the pheasant on top, surrounding with the remaining apples. Reserve 2 tablespoons cream, pouring the rest over the pheasant with the Calvados or cider. Cover with foil and cook in a moderate oven (180°C / 350°F / Reg 4) for about an hour, until the bird is tender. Carve and arrange the pieces on a heated serving dish. Add the remaining cream to the apple mixture, check the seasoning and heat through. Surround the pheasant with the apple sauce.

Poultry & Game

Rabbit in Sour Cream and Herbs
SERVES 4

2 tablespoons flour
salt and freshly ground black
    pepper
1 rabbit, cleaned and jointed
3 onions

25 g (1 oz) butter
1 tablespoon olive oil
150 ml ($\frac{1}{4}$ pt) chicken stock
pinch each tarragon and thyme
150 ml ($\frac{1}{4}$ pt) sour cream

Season the flour with salt and pepper and lightly coat the rabbit pieces with the flour. Peel and thinly slice the onions. Heat the butter and oil in a frying-pan, add the rabbit and quickly brown all over. Drain the joints on kitchen paper and transfer to a casserole. Arrange the onion slices over the rabbit and pour over the stock. Add the herbs, cover with a layer of foil and a tight-fitting lid and cook in a slow oven (150°C / 300°F / Reg 2) for 1$\frac{1}{2}$ hours until tender. Stir in the sour cream and serve.

Rabbit and Bacon Casserole
SERVES 4

1 plump rabbit
8 shallots
3 cloves garlic
175 g (6 oz) green bacon in one piece
50 g (2 oz) butter
1 tablespoon brandy
2 tablespoons flour

600 ml (1 pt) red cooking wine
pinch mace
bouquet garni
1 tablespoon finely chopped parsley
salt and freshly ground black pepper
225 g (8 oz) firm button mushrooms
1 green pepper or 2 stalks celery

Ask your butcher to cut the rabbit into joints or take off the legs and split the back into four pieces. Peel the shallots and leave them whole. Crush the garlic. Remove the rind from the bacon and cut into 1 cm ($\frac{1}{2}$ in) cubes. Heat the butter in a large frying-pan or heavy iron casserole. Add the bacon and cook over a medium heat until the bacon is crisp. Remove it with a slotted spoon and add the rabbit joints. Cook over a high heat until browned on all sides. Pour over the brandy, heat for 30 seconds and set alight. When the flames have died down, sprinkle with the flour, mix well and gradually blend in the wine. Return the bacon to the pan, add the shallots, garlic, mace, bouquet garni, parsley and seasoning, pour in the wine, cover and cook over a low heat for 1 hour. Thinly slice the mushrooms, deseed the pepper and finely chop the flesh. Add them to the rabbit and cook for a further 20 minutes. Remove the bouquet garni and check the seasoning.

Vegetables & Salads

Vegetables & Salads

Tomato Hanny
SERVES 4

An old-fashioned but useful dish to serve with a main course – delicious with fried sausages and bacon.

75 g (3 oz) brown breadcrumbs
100 g (4 oz) grated cheese
450 g (1 lb) tomatoes, sliced
salt and freshly ground black pepper

50 g (2 oz) butter
150 ml ($\frac{1}{4}$ pt) milk
2 tablespoons cream
paprika

Grease a baking dish and cover the bottom with half the breadcrumbs and half the grated cheese. Cover with the sliced tomatoes, season with salt and pepper and dot with butter. Pour over the milk mixed with the cream and top with the remaining breadcrumbs and cheese. Sprinkle with a little paprika and bake in a moderately hot oven (200°C / 400°F / Reg 6) for about 20 minutes. Brown quickly under the grill before serving.

Aubergine Stuffed Tomatoes
SERVES 4

Plate 24, illustrated facing page 152.

8 beefsteak tomatoes
1 large aubergine
salt
3 tablespoons vegetable oil
   plus a little extra
2 cloves garlic, crushed

pinch oregano
salt and freshly ground black pepper
25 g (1 oz) fresh white breadcrumbs

Garnish
fresh dill

Halve the tomatoes and, using a teaspoon, carefully scoop out the centres without splitting the skins (the tomato pulp makes a valuable addition to soups). Slice the aubergine, sprinkle the slices with salt and leave them to stand in a colander for 20 minutes. Wipe off the excess moisture and fry the slices in the oil until soft. Drain off the excess liquid, finely chop the aubergines, mix in the crushed garlic and oregano and season with salt and freshly ground black pepper. Stuff the tomatoes with the aubergine mixture, sprinkle with the breadcrumbs and drizzle with a little oil. Bake in a moderate oven (180°C / 350°F / Reg 4) for 20 minutes. Before serving, garnish with fresh dill.

Provençal Tomatoes
SERVES 4–6

8 ripe tomatoes
2 cloves garlic
4 anchovy fillets
3 tablespoons olive oil

$\frac{1}{2}$ tablespoon finely chopped parsley
1 teaspoon lemon juice
salt and freshly ground black pepper

Halve the tomatoes and arrange them, cut side up, in a greased baking dish. Crush the garlic; drain and very finely chop the anchovy fillets. Mix together the olive oil, garlic, anchovies, parsley and lemon juice and season with a little salt and plenty of pepper. Spread this mixture over the surface of the tomatoes and grill under a high heat until slightly browned.

Vegetables & Salads

Kallitow
SERVES 4–6

1 large onion
1 clove garlic
700 g (1½ lb) courgettes
½ red pepper
50 g (2 oz) split blanched almonds

50 g (2 oz) butter
1 tablespoon finely chopped parsley
squeeze lemon juice
salt and freshly ground black pepper

Peel and finely chop the onion and crush the garlic. Wipe the courgettes with a damp cloth and cut into neat dice. Finely chop the red pepper. Roast the almonds in a moderately hot (190°C / 375°F / Reg 5) oven for a few minutes until brown. Heat the butter, add the onion and garlic and cook over a low heat without browning until the onion is transparent. Add the red pepper and courgettes and cook for 15 minutes, shaking occasionally, until the courgettes are tender and crisp. Add the almonds, parsley and lemon juice, season with salt and black pepper, turn onto a warm plate and serve at once.

Courgettes and Mushrooms à la Grecque
SERVES 6

6 courgettes
100 g (4 oz) firm button mushrooms
2 cloves garlic
3 tablespoons olive oil
1 tablespoon white wine vinegar
½ teaspoon tarragon

½ teaspoon oregano
salt and freshly ground black pepper

Garnish
1 tablespoon finely chopped chives

Cut the courgettes into 1 cm (½ in) slices. Wash the mushrooms, dry well with kitchen paper and cut into thin slices. Crush the garlic. Put all the ingredients except the chives in a saucepan, bring gently to the boil, lower the heat and simmer for 10–15 minutes until the courgettes are tender but still on the crunchy side. Season with a little salt and black pepper. Transfer to a shallow serving dish, cool and chill for at least an hour before serving. Then sprinkle with chopped chives.

Mushroom Fritters
SERVES 6

100 g (4 oz) small button mushrooms
2 eggs, separated
100 g (4 oz) flour

150 ml (¼ pt) milk
salt and freshly ground black pepper
oil for deep-frying

Remove the stalks from the mushrooms and keep for a cream of mushroom soup. Combine the egg yolks, flour and milk and beat until smooth; season with salt and pepper. Whisk the egg whites until stiff and fold them into the batter mixture. Dip the mushroom caps in the batter and deep-fry them in very hot oil until they are golden brown and well puffed out. Drain the fritters on crumpled kitchen paper and keep each batch warm while the rest are being cooked.

163

Mushrooms with Sour Cream

SERVES 4

225 g (8 oz) firm button mushrooms
1 small onion
50 g (2 oz) butter

150 ml (¼ pt) sour cream
salt and freshly ground black pepper

Slice the mushrooms. Peel and finely chop the onion. Heat the butter in a saucepan, add the onion and cook over a low heat without browning until soft and transparent. Add the mushrooms and cook for 3 minutes. Mix in the sour cream, season with salt and pepper and heat through without boiling. Serve at once.

Mushrooms with Mint and Tomatoes

SERVES 4

450 g (1 lb) small, firm button
   mushrooms
4 spring onions
1 clove garlic
4 large, ripe tomatoes
12 mint leaves

4 tablespoons olive oil
1½ teaspoons lemon juice
salt and freshly ground black pepper
25 g (1 oz) freshly grated coarse
   white breadcrumbs
15 g (½ oz) butter

Leave the mushrooms whole if they are very small; if larger than large marbles, cut into thick slices. Trim and finely chop the spring onions, both bulb and green parts. Very finely chop the garlic. Cover the tomatoes with boiling water for 2 minutes, drain and slide the skins off. Halve the tomatoes, cut out the cores, discard the seeds and chop the flesh. Finely chop the mint. Heat the oil in a saucepan. Add the onion and garlic and cook over a low heat for 2 minutes. Add the mushrooms and tomatoes, lemon juice and finely chopped mint. Season with salt and freshly ground black pepper, cover and cook over a medium heat for 15 minutes, shaking the pan every now and then to prevent sticking. Turn into a warm serving dish. Fry the breadcrumbs in the butter until golden brown and sprinkle them over the dish just before serving.

Stewed Green Peppers and Celery
SERVES 4

4 green peppers
2 cloves garlic
1 head celery
150 ml ($\frac{1}{4}$ pt) olive or sunflower oil

400 g (14 oz) tin tomatoes
salt and freshly ground black pepper
$\frac{1}{2}$ teaspoon dried oregano

Remove the cores and seeds from the peppers and cut the flesh into thin rings. Peel and chop the garlic. Trim the celery stalks, reserve the leaves and thinly slice the stalks. Heat the oil in a heavy pan. Add the garlic and cook over a high heat until it turns brown. Discard the garlic, add the peppers and celery to the oil and cook over a low heat for 15 minutes. Chop the tomatoes and add them to the pan with the juice from the tin. Season with salt and pepper, add the oregano and cook uncovered over a medium heat for about 25 minutes until the tomatoes have become a thick sauce. Finely chop the celery leaves, turn the vegetables into a dish and sprinkle with the celery leaves.

Onion Goulash
SERVES 4

2 onions
1 cabbage
350 g (12 oz) tomatoes or
    400 g (14 oz) tin tomatoes

2 tablespoons olive oil or good dripping
salt and freshly ground black pepper
$2\frac{1}{2}$ teaspoons paprika

Peel and thinly slice the onions. Very thinly shred the cabbage. Peel the tomatoes by dipping them in boiling water for 2 minutes, and cut them into fairly small cubes. Heat the oil or dripping in a heavy pan, add the onions and cabbage and cook over a medium heat, stirring occasionally to prevent burning, until the onions are soft and golden brown. Add the tomatoes. Season with salt and pepper and add the paprika, cover and simmer for 20 minutes.

Arabian Beans
SERVES 4

Plate 25, illustrated
facing page 176.

225 g (8 oz) whole or sliced frozen
    green beans
40 g ($1\frac{1}{2}$ oz) split blanched almonds
salt

15 g ($\frac{1}{2}$ oz) butter
225 g (8 oz) tin tomatoes
freshly ground black pepper
pinch cayenne pepper

Cook the beans until tender according to the instructions on the packet. Drain well. Sprinkle the almonds with a little salt and fry in butter over a low heat until golden brown, then drain on crumpled kitchen paper to remove excess fat. Heat the tinned tomatoes, add the cooked beans, mix well and season with salt, pepper and a pinch of cayenne. Pour the vegetables into a serving dish and scatter over the almonds.

Fèvesà la Poulette

SERVES 4

The perfect accompaniment to a piece of boiled bacon or gammon.

900 g (2 lb) broad beans
300 ml ($\frac{1}{2}$ pt) chicken stock
1 teaspoon sugar
salt and white pepper
bouquet garni of thyme, sage, savory and parsley

1 egg yolk
150 ml ($\frac{1}{4}$ pt) double cream

Garnish
1 tablespoon chopped parsley

Shell the beans and cook them in boiling stock, to which sugar, a pinch of salt and bouquet garni have been added, until tender. Drain off and reserve the stock, and skin the beans if necessary. Beat the egg yolk with the cream until smooth. Add a little stock, beating all the time, and blend in the remaining stock. Heat the sauce over a low heat, stirring continually until it thickens and reaches simmering point – do not allow to boil. Add the beans and season with salt and white pepper. Top with chopped parsley and serve at once.

Pease Pudding

SERVES 6

450 g (1 lb) split yellow peas
1 large onion
1 potato
$\frac{1}{2}$ tablespoon sunflower oil
1 chicken stock cube

pinch dried mixed herbs
salt and freshly ground black pepper
40 g (1$\frac{1}{2}$ oz) butter
1 egg

Soak the peas in plenty of cold water for 4 hours. Peel and finely chop the onion. Peel and dice the potato. Heat the oil in a saucepan, add the onion and cook over a low heat until the onion is soft and transparent. Add the peas, potato and liquid the peas were soaked in, together with enough water to come about 2.5 cm (1 in) above the vegetables. Mix in the stock cube and herbs, season with salt and pepper, bring to the boil and cook for about an hour, until all the ingredients are mushy. (A pressure cooker saves time.) Remove from the heat, strain off any excess liquid and purée the ingredients. Add the butter and stir until it has melted. Beat the egg, add that to the purée and beat well to mix in the egg. Check the seasoning, turn into a greased pudding basin and cover with foil. Steam in enough boiling water to come half-way up the side of the basin, for an hour, until set. Turn out and cut into slices or leave until cold, and then slice and fry. Serve with bacon and eggs.

Provençal Peas

SERVES 6

1 small onion
50 g (2 oz) ham
outside leaves of 1 cos lettuce

25 g (1 oz) butter
salt and freshly ground black pepper
450 g (1 lb) frozen petits pois

Peel and finely chop the onion. Finely chop the ham. Wash and shred the lettuce leaves. Melt the butter in a saucepan, add the onion and cook until soft. Add the ham, lettuce and seasoning, mix well and cook over a medium heat for 5 minutes. Stir in the frozen petits pois, cover and cook until the peas are just tender, about 2–4 minutes.

Runner Beans with Cream and Savory

SERVES 4

450 g (1 lb) runner beans
salt
150 ml (¼ pt) single cream

1 teaspoon finely chopped savory
freshly ground black pepper

String and slice the beans and cook them in boiling salted water until just tender. Drain well. Combine the cream and savory and season with salt and pepper. Add to the beans, toss lightly and heat through.

Braised Fennel Italian Style

SERVES 4

4 fennel
75 g (3 oz) unsalted butter

salt and freshly ground black pepper
3 tablespoons Parmesan cheese

Trim off any roots from the fennel and cut each one in half lengthwise. Simmer them for 5 minutes in boiling, salted water, then drain well. Melt the butter in an ovenproof dish, dip each fennel piece in butter, turning to coat it thoroughly, and arrange it in the dish. Sprinkle with salt and pepper and the cheese, and bake the dish uncovered in a moderate oven (180°C / 350°F / Reg 4) for about 45 minutes or until the fennel is tender. Watch the topping carefully and don't let it become too dark. Cover the dish with foil when the cheese is golden enough, if the fennel pieces require a little more cooking.

Banana Curry

SERVES 4

This makes an effective side dish to serve with any meat or poultry curry. Use under-ripe bananas that have a slight tinge of green to their skins.

4 bananas
1 tablespoon vegetable oil
$\frac{1}{2}$ teaspoon turmeric
$\frac{1}{2}$ teaspoon caraway seeds

$\frac{1}{2}$ teaspoon salt
$\frac{1}{4}$ teaspoon chilli powder
1 teaspoon garam masala
3 tablespoons plain yoghourt

Peel the bananas, cut into 2 cm ($\frac{3}{4}$ in) slices. Heat the oil in a heavy saucepan. Add the turmeric and caraway seeds and cook over a low heat for 1 minute. Add the bananas, salt and chilli powder and continue to cook for 5 minutes. Sprinkle with garam masala, add yoghourt, stir gently without breaking up the bananas and simmer uncovered for a further 5 minutes until tender.

Spring Cabbage with Cream

SERVES 4

2 spring cabbages
salt
15 g ($\frac{1}{2}$ oz) butter

5 tablespoons double cream
$\frac{1}{4}$ teaspoon grated nutmeg
freshly ground black pepper

Remove the tough outer leaves and centre cores of the cabbages and shred the leaves. Cook the cabbages in 1 cm ($\frac{1}{2}$ in) boiling salted water until just tender but still crisp, about 7 minutes. Drain well. Melt the butter in a saucepan, add the cabbage and toss lightly over a low heat until the butter is absorbed. Add the cream and nutmeg and season with salt and pepper.

East Anglian Red Cabbage
SERVES 6

This vegetable dish makes an excellent accompaniment to pork or game.

40 g (1½ oz) butter	5 tablespoons red wine vinegar
1 small red cabbage	5 tablespoons water
1 onion	2 tablespoons brown sugar
2 cooking apples	salt and freshly ground black pepper

Grease a baking dish with 15 g (½ oz) butter. Halve the cabbage, cut out the core and shred the leaves. Peel and finely chop the onion. Peel, core and thinly slice the apples. Arrange layers of cabbage, onion and apple in the casserole, sprinkling each layer with a little vinegar, water and sugar and some salt and pepper. Finish with a layer of cabbage and dot with the remaining butter. Cover tightly with foil and bake in a slow oven (150°C / 300°F / Reg 2) for 2 hours.

Curried Cauliflower
SERVES 4

One of the nicest ways of serving cauliflower.

2 large and 1 small onion	1 teaspoon salt
1 clove garlic	300 ml (½ pt) water
300 ml (½ pt) plain yoghourt	
1 teaspoon sugar	**Garnish**
1 cauliflower	¼ teaspoon ground cinnamon
4 tablespoons vegetable oil	¼ teaspoon ground coriander

Peel and grate the small onion. Crush the garlic. Combine the yoghourt with the grated onion, garlic and sugar and mix well. Add the cauliflower divided into florets, and toss lightly so that the marinade can soak into the florets. Leave in a cool place for 2 hours, mixing lightly after the first hour. Peel and finely chop the remaining onions. Heat the oil in a heavy saucepan. Add the onions and cook over a medium-high heat until the onions are lightly brown. Add the cauliflower and marinade, season with salt and add the water. Simmer (do not boil) for about 10 minutes until the cauliflower is tender but still crisp. Combine the ground coriander with the cinnamon. Turn the cauliflower into a serving dish. Pour over the sauce and sprinkle with cinnamon and coriander.

Cauliflower with Watercress

SERVES 4

Plate 25, illustrated facing page 176.

This dish is equally delicious if you substitute carrots for the cauliflower.

1 cauliflower
2 bunches watercress
1 small onion
2 thin rashers lean bacon
25 g (1 oz) butter
1 teaspoon lemon juice

150 ml (¼ pt) single cream
salt, pepper, pinch grated nutmeg

Garnish
thinly sliced tinned pimiento

Trim the cauliflower and divide into florets. Cook in salted water until tender and drain well. Cut off the leaves and the top 5 cm (2 in) of the watercress stalks. Peel and very finely chop the onion. Remove rinds and very finely chop the bacon rashers. Heat the butter in a saucepan, add onion and bacon and cook over a low heat without browning until the onion is soft and transparent. Add the watercress and lemon juice, cover and cook for a further 3 minutes. Add the cream, season with salt, pepper and nutmeg and cook without boiling for 3 minutes more. Gently stir in the cauliflower, heat through and transfer to a heated serving dish. Garnish with pimiento.

Spinach with Onion Flakes

SERVES 4

450 g (1 lb) fresh spinach
2 tablespoons finely chopped onion
1 tablespoon olive oil

juice of 1 lemon
salt and freshly ground black pepper

Wash the spinach and remove the tough stalks. Shake well and cook without additional water for 10 minutes or until tender. Spread the chopped onion on a lightly oiled baking sheet and cook in a moderately hot oven (190°C / 375°F / Reg 5) for 5–8 minutes until crisp and golden brown. Add the olive oil and lemon juice to the spinach, season with salt and pepper and toss lightly. Arrange in a serving dish and top with the browned onions.

170

Vegetables & Salads

Sorrel or Spinach the Roman Way
SERVES 4–6

700 g (1½ lb) fresh sorrel or spinach
2 teaspoons Dijon mustard
4 tablespoons olive oil

1 tablespoon white wine vinegar
salt and freshly ground black pepper

Wash the sorrel or spinach and remove the tough stalks. Shake well and put the leaves into a saucepan. Cook in the water clinging to the leaves for 10 minutes or until just tender. Drain well. Mix the mustard with the oil and vinegar. Return the leaves to the pan, add the vinaigrette, season with salt and pepper and toss over a medium heat to heat through.

Oven-Fried Parsnips with Shallots
SERVES 4–6

450 g (1 lb) parsnips
1 tablespoon lemon juice
salt and freshly ground black pepper
12 shallots or pickling onions

olive or vegetable oil

Garnish
finely chopped parsley

Peel the parsnips and cut them lengthwise into thin slices. Marinate in the lemon juice, seasoned with salt and pepper for 30 minutes, drain well and pat dry on kitchen paper. Peel the shallots. Heat about 1 cm (½ in) oil in a shallow baking dish, put in the vegetables and cook in a hot oven (200°C / 400°F / Reg 6) for about 30 minutes until golden brown. Drain off the oil and arrange the vegetables in a serving dish; sprinkle with a little finely chopped parsley and serve at once.

Parsnip Cakes
SERVES 4

700 g (1½ lb) parsnips
juice of ½ lemon
salt and freshly ground black pepper

breadcrumbs, for coating
lard or dripping, for frying

Peel and roughly chop the parsnips and cover with cold water. Add the lemon juice, bring to the boil and simmer until the parsnips are soft. Drain off the water, season with salt and pepper and mash until smooth. Leave until cold then shape into cakes about 8 cm (3 in) across and 0.5 cm (¼ in) thick. Press the cakes into breadcrumbs and fry in hot lard or dripping until golden brown and crisp on each side.

Fluffy Mashed Swedes
SERVES 4

450 g (1 lb) swedes
25 g (1 oz) butter
3 tablespoons single cream
salt and freshly ground black pepper

1 teaspoon lemon juice
1 tablespoon very finely chopped
  parsley
pinch nutmeg

Remove the peel in quite thick strips (the outer layer of the swede tends to be tough in all but the very young roots) and cut the flesh into dice. Bring to the boil in salted water and cook for about 30 minutes until soft but not mushy. Drain well and mash with a fork or potato masher until smooth. Add the butter, cream, seasoning, lemon juice, parsley and nutmeg and beat with a fork until the mixture is smooth and fluffy. Pile into a serving dish and heat through in a moderately slow oven (170°C / 325°F / Reg 3).

Turnip Cooked with Onion in Stock
SERVES 4

1 turnip
1 large onion
1 tablespoon dripping

300 ml ($\frac{1}{2}$ pt) rich stock
salt and freshly ground black pepper
2 tablespoons finely chopped parsley

Peel the turnip and cut it into 0.5 cm ($\frac{1}{4}$ in) thick slices. Cut the slices into sticks about 1 cm ($\frac{1}{2}$ in) wide. Peel and thinly slice the onion and separate the slices into rings. Heat the dripping in a heavy pan. Add the onion rings and cook over a medium low heat until the onion is soft and transparent. Add the turnip, mix well and continue to cook, stirring every now and then, for about 5 minutes until all the fat has been absorbed. Pour over the stock, season with salt and pepper and bring to the boil. Cover and simmer gently for about 40 minutes until most of the stock has been absorbed and the turnip slices are almost transparent and rather waxy. Gently drain off any excess stock. Arrange the onion and turnip on a heated serving dish and sprinkle over the chopped parsley just before serving.

Bulgarian Carrots
SERVES 4

450 g (1 lb) new carrots
salt
2 cloves garlic
1 tablespoon finely chopped
  parsley or chives

150 ml ($\frac{1}{4}$ pt) plain yoghourt
freshly ground black pepper

Wash and scrub the carrots and cut them into matchstick strips. Cook in boiling salted water until just tender but still slightly crisp. Drain well. Squeeze the garlic through a garlic press. Mix the garlic and parsley or chives into the yoghourt, then add to the carrots and season with salt and pepper. Heat through without boiling.

Vegetables & Salads

Somerset Carrots

SERVES 4

If you find the sweetness of carrots does not appeal to you, then try this way of cooking them with cider vinegar. It makes an excellent accompaniment to a dish of lamb or pork.

700 g (1½ lb) carrots
4 spring onions
3 juniper berries

3 bay leaves
3 tablespoons cider vinegar
salt and freshly ground black pepper

Peel the carrots (add the peelings to your stock pot) and cut them into 2.5 cm (1 in) dice. Remove the green parts from the spring onions and finely chop the white bulbs. Crush the juniper berries with a fork. Put the carrots in a shallow saucepan with the onions, bay leaves and juniper berries. Cover with cold water, add the cider vinegar and season with salt and pepper. Bring to the boil and cook over a high heat without covering, until the liquid has been absorbed into the carrots and they are tender but still retain their texture. Remove the bay leaves and sprinkle over finely sliced spring onion tops before serving.

Potatoes Cooked in Milk

SERVES 4

This goes well with all bacon and pork dishes. Use firm, slightly waxy potatoes, and you can add some diced apple half-way through the cooking time.

700 g (1½ lb) potatoes
600 ml (1 pt) milk
salt and freshly ground black pepper

Garnish
2 tablespoons very finely chopped
 parsley or chives

Peel and dice the potatoes. Put them into a heavy-bottomed saucepan, add most of the milk and cook over a low heat, stirring occasionally, until the potatoes are tender and the milk has been absorbed (add a little more milk if necessary). Season with salt and pepper and sprinkle over the parsley or chives before serving.

Potato Kephtides

SERVES 4

The most usual form of *kephtides* are made from meat – a sort of highly spiced hamburger grilled over charcoal. But this recipe is based on cold mashed potatoes and is marvellous served with crisply fried bacon, sausage, or topped with a fried egg.

225 g (8 oz) tomatoes
4 spring onions
450 g (1 lb) mashed potatoes

40 g (1½ oz) flour
salt and freshly ground black pepper
dripping or olive oil

Peel and finely chop the tomatoes. Very finely chop the spring onions. Mix the potatoes with the tomatoes, flour and spring onions and season generously with salt and pepper. (If the mashed potatoes were not made with butter, add 15 g/½ oz melted butter as well.) Chill for a few minutes in the fridge, and then shape, with well-floured hands, into eight flat cakes about 0.5 cm (¼ in) thick. Place the cakes on a baking sheet that has been well greased with dripping or oil and brush over the tops with more oil or melted dripping. Bake the cakes in a hot oven (200°C / 400°F / Reg 6) for 15 minutes, until they are crisp and a light golden colour on top. Slide them off the baking sheet with a fish slice so that they do not break up.

Hasselback Potatoes

SERVES 6

12 potatoes
salt
40 g (1½ oz) butter, melted

4 tablespoons grated Cheddar cheese
1 tablespoon dried breadcrumbs

Peel the potatoes and trim into neat oval shapes. Cut into 0.5 cm (¼ in) thick slices to within about 1 cm (½ in) of the bottom, so that the slices remain together like the leaves of a book (a good way to do this is to place each potato against the edge of a thin chopping board and cut through the potato until the blade of your knife is level with the board). Put the potatoes, cut side up, in a baking tin, sprinkle them with salt and brush them with melted butter. Bake the potatoes in a hot oven (220°C / 425°F / Reg 7) for 25 minutes, basting occasionally. Sprinkle with the cheese and dried breadcrumbs and continue to bake for a further 20 minutes without basting until golden brown.

Vegetables & Salads

Potato Curry
SERVES 6

700 g (1½ lb) potatoes
sunflower oil for frying
1 large onion
225 g (8 oz) firm, ripe tomatoes
1 clove garlic
1 tablespoon fenugreek seeds
2 teaspoons ground coriander seeds

2 teaspoons turmeric
2 teaspoons ground ginger
pinch chilli powder
salt
150 ml (¼ pt) yoghourt
300 ml (½ pt) water
2 teaspoons tomato purée

Peel the potatoes, cut them into very thin chips and fry in very hot deep oil until crisp and golden. Drain well. Peel and slice the onion. Quarter the tomatoes. Peel and crush the garlic. Heat 1 tablespoon oil in a heavy frying-pan. When it gives off a haze, add the fenugreek seeds and stir for a minute to release the aroma of the seeds. Add the onion and stir until golden brown. Add the spices and garlic, season with salt and mix in the tomatoes, fried potatoes, yoghourt, water and tomato purée. Bring to the boil and simmer for 10 minutes, stirring to prevent sticking.

Pisto
SERVES 6

Plate 26, illustrated facing page 177.

When new potatoes are past their first flush of deliciousness, this Spanish dish makes a good alternative to plain boiled or mashed potatoes.

2 large onions
2 cloves garlic
2 red or green peppers
3 large ripe tomatoes
4 courgettes

225–350 g (8–12 oz) cooked potatoes
4 tablespoons olive oil
salt and freshly ground black pepper
1 tablespoon very finely chopped parsley
pinch oregano

Peel and thinly slice the onions and divide them into rings. Crush the garlic. Remove the cores and seeds of the peppers and cut the flesh into thin strips. Cover the tomatoes with boiling water, leave to stand for 2 minutes and slide the skins off. Roughly chop the flesh. Cut the courgettes in half and the potatoes into bite-sized pieces. Heat the oil in a frying-pan. Add the onion rings and garlic and cook over a low heat until the onion is transparent and pale yellow. Add the peppers and cook for a further 10 minutes until soft. Add the courgettes and tomatoes, season with salt and pepper, cover and simmer for 20 minutes. Add the potatoes, parsley and oregano, stir gently and cook for a further 10 minutes.

Special Baked Potatoes

SERVES 4

4 potatoes for baking
sunflower oil

coarse sea salt
freshly ground black pepper

Scrub the potatoes and cut in half lengthwise. Place cut side down in a baking dish and cut the rounded side into thin slices almost through to the cut side. Brush generously with sunflower oil and season with salt and pepper. Bake in a hot oven (200°C / 400°F / Reg 6) for about 45 minutes until crisp, golden and tender.

Potatoes and Bacon

SERVES 6

900 g (2 lb) new potatoes
50 g (2 oz) lard
2 rashers fat bacon, diced
40 g (1½ oz) flour
600 ml (1 pt) tomato juice

salt and freshly ground black pepper
1–2 teaspoons sugar

Garnish
2 tablespoons finely chopped parsley

Scrub the potatoes and cook them in their skins in boiling, salted water until tender. Drain, cool, peel and thickly slice. Heat the lard in a pan or casserole, add the bacon and lightly fry until the fat runs and the bacon begins to crisp. Add the flour, stir well into the fat, then little by little add the tomato juice, stirring all the while. The sauce should be of medium thickness, therefore a little warm water may be required. Add salt, pepper and sugar and bring gently to the boil. Add the sliced potatoes, mix gently, lower the heat and simmer until the potatoes are heated through. Sprinkle with parsley and serve.

Risotto al Funghi

SERVES 4

1 onion
225 g (8 oz) button mushrooms
100 g (4 oz) butter
150 ml (¼ pt) wine

350 g (12 oz) long-grain rice
1.2 litres (2 pts) stock
50 g (2 oz) grated Parmesan cheese
salt and freshly ground black pepper

Peel and finely chop the onion. Thickly slice the mushrooms. Melt half the butter in a heavy pan, add the onion and cook without browning until soft and transparent. Add the mushrooms, pour over the wine, stir well and cook for a further 3 minutes until the wine is absorbed. Add the rice; cook until it is lightly coloured and then stir in a cupful of stock. Cook over a low heat until the liquid is absorbed, then gradually add the rest of the stock, cooking the risotto for about 20 minutes, until the rice is cooked but not mushy. Stir in the remaining butter and the cheese and season with salt and pepper. Leave to stand 2 or 3 minutes before serving to enable the flavour of the cheese to penetrate the rice.

Plate 25. Cauliflower with Watercress, Arabian Beans

Plate 26. Pisto

Rice Pilaf

SERVES 4

1 onion
1 clove garlic
1 small green pepper
50 g (2 oz) dried apricots
1 tablespoon mango chutney
40 g (1½ oz) butter
1 tablespoon sunflower oil
50 g (2 oz) sultanas

350 g (12 oz) long-grain rice
salt and freshly ground black pepper
pinch each ground coriander and cumin
1 chicken stock cube

Garnish
25 g (1 oz) flaked almonds

Peel and finely chop the onion and garlic. Remove the core and seeds of the pepper and finely chop the flesh. Chop the apricots and chutney. Heat 25 g (1 oz) of the butter with the oil in a saucepan. Add the onion and garlic and cook over a low heat until the onion is soft and transparent. Add the pepper, apricots, chutney, sultanas and rice and stir over a medium heat until the rice becomes opaque. Add enough water to come 1 cm (½ in) over the ingredients, season with salt, pepper, coriander and cumin and mix in the stock cube, stirring until it is dissolved. Bring to the boil and cover tightly. Lower the heat to simmering and cook for 20 minutes. Stir well, remove from the heat, cover again and leave to stand for 10 minutes, by which time the liquid should have been absorbed and the rice should be tender. Fry the almonds in the remaining butter until crisp and golden. Turn the hot rice into a serving dish and garnish with the almonds.

Spanish Rice

SERVES 5–6

Serve with stews, pork, poultry or fish.

2 onions
1 large green pepper
400 g (14 oz) tin tomatoes
6 tablespoons olive oil
350 g (12 oz) long-grain rice

600 ml (1 pt) chicken stock
pinch oregano
pinch chilli powder
salt

Peel and finely chop the onions. Remove the core and seeds of the pepper and finely chop the pepper. Chop the tomatoes (I do this in the tin with a pair of kitchen scissors). Heat the oil in a heavy saucepan, add the onions and pepper and cook over a low heat for about 3 minutes, stirring to prevent browning. Add the rice and cook until the rice absorbs most of the oil and is transparent and not brown. Add tomatoes, stock, oregano chilli powder and salt, mix well and bring to the boil. Cover tightly and simmer for about 30 minutes, until the rice is tender and the liquid absorbed. Stir about once every 10 minutes or so to prevent sticking, adding a little water if the mixture becomes too dry before the rice is cooked. Some chopped parsley or grated cheese can be sprinkled over the surface of the rice before serving.

Vegetables & Salads

Spring Salad
SERVES 4

An unusual, refreshing salad that goes well with roast meat or poultry, grills or fish dishes. Add the dressing at the last minute as the watercress absorbs the liquid and tends to go limp.

2 generous bunches watercress
25 g (1 oz) slivered blanched almonds
4 firm, ripe tomatoes
2 hard-boiled eggs
2 fillets anchovy
pinch tarragon

small pinch aniseed
2 tablespoons olive oil
1 tablespoon tomato juice
½ tablespoon white wine vinegar
freshly ground black pepper

Cut off the leaves off the watercress. Roast the almonds in a hot oven for 1–2 minutes until golden brown. Cover the tomatoes with boiling water and leave for 2 minutes, remove the skins and cut the tomatoes into thin slices. Coarsely chop the hard-boiled eggs and arrange alternate rows of egg, watercress and tomato in a shallow dish. Sprinkle with almonds. Soak the anchovies in a little milk to remove excess salt, squeeze out and pat dry on kitchen paper. Pound the anchovies to a smooth paste with the tarragon and aniseed. Gradually blend in the olive oil, then mix in the tomato juice and wine vinegar. Season the dressing with freshly ground black pepper and pour it over the salad.

Spring Salad with Herb Vinaigrette
SERVES 4

Arrange *thin slices of tomato, very thin slices of leeks, matchsticks of celery* and *grated Cheddar cheese* in a serving bowl and pour over the following dressing just before serving:

1 teaspoon mixed tarragon, chervil
  and basil or dried mixed herbs
2 tablespoons white wine vinegar
½ teaspoon dry English mustard
salt and freshly ground black pepper

3 tablespoons olive oil
1 teaspoon finely chopped capers
1 teaspoon finely chopped parsley
1 teaspoon finely chopped chives
1 hard-boiled egg

If you use dried mixed herbs, soak them in a little warm water for 5 minutes and drain well. Add the vinegar to the mustard and mix until smooth. Season with salt and pepper. Blend in the olive oil and mix well. Add the capers and herbs. Finely chop the hard-boiled egg and lightly mix it into the dressing just before pouring it over the salad.

Vegetables & Salads

Spring Salad with Anchovy Vinaigrette
SERVES 4

Arrange *thinly sliced chicory, fresh grapefruit segements, chopped watercress, cottage cheese* and *black olives* in a serving dish and pour over the following dressing just before serving:

2 anchovy fillets	*1 tablespoon white wine vinegar*
a little milk	*3 tablespoons olive oil*
¼ teaspoon dry English mustard	*freshly ground black pepper*

Drain the oil from the anchovy fillets and soak them in a little milk for 5 minutes to remove excess salt. Squeeze out the milk and pound or mash the fillets to a paste. Blend in the mustard and gradually mix in the white wine vinegar. Add the olive oil, whipping with a fork until the ingredients are well amalgamated. Season with pepper.

Spring Salad with Yoghourt and Lemon Dressing
SERVES 4

Arrange *thin sticks of peeled cucumber, thin slices of celery, peeled and chopped firm tomatoes, chopped green pepper* and *wafer-thin rings of raw onion* in groups on a serving plate, and serve with the following dressing:

4 tablespoons plain yoghourt	*1 teaspoon lemon juice*
1 teaspoon Dijon mustard	*2 teaspoons water*
pinch celery salt	*1 rasher lean bacon*
freshly ground black pepper	

Combine the yoghourt, mustard, celery salt, pepper, lemon juice and water and mix well. Fry the bacon without extra fat until crisp, drain on kitchen paper and crumble. Leave to cool and then mix into the dressing. Chill before serving.

Crisp Slaw
SERVES 4

1 small white cabbage	*1 tablespoon finely chopped chives*
2 carrots	*1 tablespoon finely chopped parsley*
1 cooking apple	*3 tablespoons single cream*
1 tablespoon raisins	*1 tablespoon white wine vinegar*
1 tablespoon chopped walnuts	*salt and freshly ground black pepper*

Finely shred the cabbage. Peel and coarsely grate the carrots and apple. Combine the cabbage, carrots and apple with the raisins, walnuts, chives and parsley and mix immediately with a dressing made by combining the cream and vinegar and then season with salt and pepper.

Salad of Carrots and Spring Onions

SERVES 4

225 g (8 oz) carrots
2 spring onions
3 black olives
juice of 2 oranges and ½ lemon
1 tablespoon olive or sunflower oil

salt and white pepper
pinch ground ginger

Garnish
1 tablespoon finely chopped parsley

Peel and coarsely grate the carrots. Trim and finely chop the spring onions into a bowl of cold water and chill in the fridge for 30 minutes to crisp them. Drain well. Cut the black olives off their stones in small flakes. Combine the orange and lemon juice with the oil, season with salt, pepper and ginger and mix well. Pour the dressing over the carrots, spring onions and olives, toss lightly, put into four bowls and sprinkle over the chopped parsley.

Avocado and Spinach Salad

SERVES 4

700 g (1½ lb) spinach
3 rashers streaky bacon
50 g (2 oz) firm button mushrooms
2 tomatoes

150 ml (¼ pt) plain yoghourt
2 tablespoons lemon juice
salt and freshly ground black pepper
2 large ripe avocados

Wash and pick over the spinach, discarding the tough stalks and discoloured leaves. Dry well and roughly chop the leaves. Cook the bacon over a medium heat without extra fat until crisp and lightly browned. Drain on kitchen paper, then crumple finely. Thinly slice the mushrooms. Place the spinach, bacon, and mushrooms in a bowl. Cover the tomatoes with boiling water and leave for 2 minutes, drain well and slide the skins off. Halve the tomatoes, scoop out the cores and seeds and finely chop the flesh. Combine the tomato flesh, yoghourt, lemon juice and seasoning in a screw-top jar and shake well to mix. Peel the avocados, cut in half, remove the stones and slice the flesh. Add to the bowl and pour the dressing over the salad ingredients. Toss lightly with a fork and serve.

Vegetables & Salads

Chinese Leaves Salad
SERVES 4

450 g (1 lb) Chinese leaves
1 small onion
1 small red or green pepper
2 small eating apples
50 g (2 oz) sultanas or seedless raisins

4 tablespoons mayonnaise

Garnish
50 g (2 oz) flaked almonds

Use only the tender heart of the Chinese leaves for a salad, reserving the coarser outer leaves and also the base of the inner leaves for cooking. Slice the heart crosswise into fine shreds. Peel and finely chop the onion. Remove the stalk from the pepper, then halve it and scoop out the seeds and white ribs from the inside. Cut the flesh into fine strips. Core and chop the apples (unpeeled) into small cubes. Mix the Chinese leaves with the onion, pepper, apples and sultanas. Toast the almond flakes on a piece of foil under the grill, tossing and turning them all the time to get them an even golden-brown colour. This takes less than a minute, so stand by the grill all the time. Stir in the mayonnaise, lifting and turning the leaves to coat them evenly. Serve in a large bowl and garnish with the toasted almonds.

Tomato Salad with Fresh Basil
SERVES 4

A wonderful spring or summer salad which can be served as a light first course or as an accompaniment to a main course of fish or chicken.

4 large or 6 small firm, ripe tomatoes
1 small onion
4 anchovy fillets
milk
50 g (2 oz) mozzarella cheese

2 sprigs fresh basil
3 tablespoons olive oil
1 tablespoon white wine vinegar
½ teaspoon Dijon mustard
salt and freshly ground black pepper

Peel the tomatoes by dropping them in boiling water for 2 minutes and then sliding off the skins. Cut the tomatoes into thin slices and arrange them in a shallow serving dish. Peel the onion, cut it into thin slices and divide into rings. Drain off the oil from the anchovies, soak them in milk for 5 minutes to remove excess salt and cut each one in half lengthwise. Cut the cheese into matchstick strips about 2.5 cm (1 in) long. Chop the basil as gently as possible to avoid bruising the leaves. Arrange the onion rings, anchovy fillets and cheese over the tomatoes and sprinkle with basil. Combine the olive oil, vinegar and mustard in a screw-top jar, season with salt and pepper and shake to mix well. Pour the dressing over the salad and refrigerate before serving.

Vegetables & Salads

Spinach, Mushroom and Bacon Salad

SERVES 4

This delicious summer salad can also be served as a starter.

450 g (1 lb) young spinach
100 g (4 oz) firm button mushrooms
4 rashers lean bacon

juice of 1 lemon
1 teaspoon made English mustard
salt and freshly ground black pepper

Strip the tender leaves off the stalks (reserve the coarser leaves and stalks for soup) and wash in ice-cold water to clean and freshen. Pat gently dry on kitchen paper or in a clean cloth. Thinly slice the mushrooms and blanch in boiling acidulated water for 2 minutes. Drain and cool. Grill the bacon rashers until crisp, drain well on kitchen paper, cool, then crumble into pieces. Arrange the spinach and mushrooms in a serving dish. Combine the lemon juice and mustard, mix well and season with salt and pepper. Mix in the bacon and pour the dressing over the spinach. Chill well before serving.

Bacon and Dandelion Salad

SERVES 4

450 g (1 lb) young dandelion leaves
225 g (8 oz) rashers streaky bacon
1 clove garlic

1 sprig mint
2 tablespoons red wine vinegar
freshly ground black pepper

Choose young plants and trim off any tough outer leaves; wash under cold running water. Dry the dandelion leaves. Remove the rind from the bacon and cut the rashers into 1 cm ($\frac{1}{2}$ in) wide strips. Peel and finely chop the garlic. Finely chop the mint. Cook the bacon over a medium-high heat for 5 minutes without extra fat. Add the garlic and continue to cook over a low heat for a further 5 minutes without browning. Add the mint, vinegar and dandelion leaves and season with freshly ground black pepper. Continue to cook over a low heat stirring gently with a wooden spoon until the dandelion leaves are wilted and just soft – about 2 minutes. Serve at once or leave to cool.

Tomato, Egg and Leek Salad

SERVES 4

4–6 tomatoes
green tops of 2 large leeks
2 hard-boiled eggs
3 tablespoons olive oil

1 tablespoon white wine vinegar
salt and freshly ground black pepper
1 tablespoon finely chopped parsley

Immerse the tomatoes in boiling water for 2 minutes, remove skins and slice thinly. Wash the leeks, removing outer leaves, and very thinly slice their green tops. Combine the tomatoes and leeks in a serving dish. Chop the hard-boiled eggs and sprinkle them over the tomatoes and leeks. Combine the olive oil and vinegar, season with salt and pepper, add finely chopped parsley and mix well. Pour the dressing over the salad and chill before serving.

Grated Carrots with Spinach, Bacon and Mushrooms

SERVES 4

Plate 27, illustrated facing page 192.

450 g (1 lb) new carrots
1.1 kg (2½ lb) fresh spinach
40 g (1½ oz) butter
1 tablespoon finely chopped parsley
1 tablespoon finely chopped chives
salt and freshly ground black pepper
2 rashers streaky bacon

50 g (2 oz) firm button mushrooms
2 tablespoons olive oil
1 teaspoon white wine vinegar

Garnish
finely chopped parsley

Wash or scrape the carrots and grate coarsely. Pick over the spinach, removing coarse leaves and wash thoroughly. Melt the butter in a small saucepan, add the carrots and cook over a low heat, shaking to prevent sticking, until they are just tender – about 5 minutes. Add the parsley and chives, season with salt and pepper and keep warm. Heat 1 cm (½ in) salted water in a large saucepan until boiling. Add the spinach and cook over a high heat for about 6 minutes, until just tender. Drain well and roughly chop with kitchen scissors. Fry the bacon without extra fat until crisp and drain on kitchen paper. Thinly slice the mushrooms and fry for 2 minutes in bacon fat. Add them and any residual bacon fat to the spinach with the oil and vinegar, season with freshly ground black pepper and toss lightly. Remove the rinds and crumble the bacon into small pieces. Arrange the spinach and mushrooms in a ring on a serving dish, pile the carrots in the centre and garnish with parsley.

Watercress with Tomatoes and Hard-Boiled Eggs

SERVES 4

2 bunches watercress
8 small firm tomatoes
4 hard-boiled eggs
50 g (2 oz) Gorgonzola or other blue cheese

4 tablespoons olive oil
4 teaspoons lemon juice
salt and freshly ground black pepper

Wash and dry the watercress and cut off any tough stems. Cover the tomatoes with boiling water for 2 minutes and slide the skins off. Cut into thick slices. Peel and coarsely chop the hard-boiled eggs. Arrange them in the centre of a platter and surround with the watercress topped with overlapping layers of tomatoes. Crush the blue cheese with a fork and mix it with the oil and lemon juice. Season with salt and pepper and spoon the sauce over the egg.

Jacqueline's Salad
SERVES 4

1 iceberg lettuce heart
1 bunch watercress
1 bunch radishes
1 clove garlic
3 tablespoons olive oil

1 teaspoon Dijon mustard
1 tablespoon white wine vinegar
salt and freshly ground black pepper
50 g (2 oz) shelled walnuts

Roughly shred the lettuce and remove the watercress stalks. Trim and thickly slice the radishes. Rub a wooden bowl with a clove of garlic, discard the garlic and combine the olive oil, mustard and vinegar in the bowl. Season with salt and pepper and mix well. Add the salad ingredients and toss lightly just before serving.

Red Pepper and Fennel Salad
SERVES 4

1 large red pepper
1 small fennel
1 shallot
3 tablespoons olive oil

1 tablespoon white wine vinegar
1 teaspoon Dijon mustard
salt and freshly ground black pepper

Remove the core and seeds of the pepper and cut the flesh into thin strips. Remove any tough outer layers of the fennel and trim off any green leaves. Cut the fennel into small strips. Peel the shallot, cut into thin slices and divide into rings. Combine the pepper, fennel and shallot in a salad bowl. Put the olive oil, vinegar and mustard into a screw-top jar, season with salt and freshly ground black pepper. Shake to mix well. Pour the dressing over the salad and chill for 30 minutes before serving.

Cool Cauliflower Salad
SERVES 4

This is a sophisticated salad, too much for children, but greatly enjoyed by adults.

1 cauliflower
4 anchovies
9 black olives

4 spring onions
1 tablespoon chopped tinned pimiento
French dressing made without salt

Divide the cauliflower head into florets and cook in boiling, salted water for 8 minutes only. Drain and finely chop the anchovies, stone the olives, thinly slice the spring onions, including the green tops, and combine all these ingredients along with the pimiento in a bowl. Pour over the French dressing, toss lightly and serve.

Vegetables & Salads

Winter Salad
SERVES 4

My favourite of the chicory salads, and one that goes well with chicken, fish or game.

4 heads of chicory
1 large orange
12 black olives
2 thin rashers of bacon
3 tablespoons olive oil
1 tablespoon white wine vinegar

¼ teaspoon Dijon mustard
½ teaspoon caster sugar
salt and freshly ground black pepper
pinch aniseed
pinch tarragon

Trim off the outer leaves of the chicory and cut off 1 cm (½ in) of the stem. Peel and remove the pith and membrane from the orange. Cut into very thin slices and cut each slice into four. Halve and stone the olives. Fry the bacon rashers over a medium heat without extra fat until crisp. Drain well, remove the rind and crumble the rashers. Combine the oil, vinegar, mustard, sugar, seasoning and herbs in a screw-top jar and shake well. Cut the chicory into thin slices, combine with the other ingredients, pour over the dressing and toss lightly before serving.

Deauville Salad
SERVES 4

1 lettuce
50 g (2 oz) ham
100 g (4 oz) frozen peas
2 tomatoes
2 crisp eating apples
2 stalks celery
¼ teaspoon dried tarragon
1 teaspoon lemon juice

150 ml (¼ pt) mayonnaise
2 tablespoons double or single cream
few drops Tabasco sauce
2 tablespoons chopped tinned
  pimiento

Garnish
2 sliced hard-boiled eggs

Wash and dry the lettuce and arrange the leaves in a shallow serving dish. Chop the meat. Cook the frozen peas, drain and leave to cool. Cover the tomatoes with boiling water, leave for 2 minutes and then slide off skins and remove core and seeds. Chop the tomato flesh. Peel, core and dice the apples; chop the celery. Soak the tarragon in the lemon juice for a few minutes to soften the leaves. Combine the mayonnaise, cream and tarragon with lemon juice and mix in a few drops of Tabasco sauce. Add the ham, tomatoes, pimiento, apples, peas and celery and mix lightly. Pile the salad onto the lettuce leaves and garnish with hard-boiled egg.

Vegetables & Salads

Red Cabbage, Celery, Walnut and Cheese Salad

SERVES 4

1 small red cabbage
8 stalks celery
8 walnuts
175 g (6 oz) Cheddar cheese
150 ml ($\frac{1}{4}$ pt) plain yoghourt

3 teaspoons lemon juice
4 teaspoons tomato purée
salt and freshly ground black pepper
pinch each celery salt and curry powder

Very thinly shred the cabbage. Remove the leaves from the celery stalks, cut them into 5 cm (2 in) lengths and then into very thin matchsticks. Roughly chop the walnuts. Cut the cheese into thin slices and then into matchsticks. Combine the yoghourt and lemon juice, add the tomato purée and seasonings and mix well. Combine the cabbage, celery and walnuts, add the dressing and toss lightly. Arrange the salad on a plate and top with the cheese sticks.

Waldorf Salad

SERVES 4

If you have some left-over chicken, ham or tongue, some of this cut into small dice will turn this salad into a good lunch dish.

4 eating apples (Cox's, Newtons or
    Granny Smiths are all good)
juice of $\frac{1}{2}$ lemon
1 head celery
6 walnuts

200 ml (7 fl oz) home-made
    mayonnaise
2 tablespoons double cream
salt and white pepper

Peel and core the apples and cut the flesh into small dice. Sprinkle with lemon juice to prevent them going brown. Trim off the leaves and any tough fibres from the celery and chop the stalks. Shell the walnuts and chop. Combine the mayonnaise with the cream, season with salt and pepper, add the apples, celery and walnuts and toss lightly to mix. Pile into a serving dish and serve chilled.

Grapefruit Salad

SERVES 4

2 grapefruit
1 green pepper
2 tablespoons finely chopped mint
finely grated rind of 1 orange

150 ml ($\frac{1}{4}$ pt) plain yoghourt
celery salt
freshly ground black pepper
dash of Tabasco sauce

Peel the grapefruit, remove all the pith and membranes and cut out the fruit segments over a bowl to reserve all the juice. Discard the core and seeds of the green pepper and cut the flesh into very thin strips. Combine the grapefruit segments and juice, chopped mint, orange rind, green pepper and yoghourt, season with celery salt, pepper and a dash of Tabasco sauce, and mix well. Serve chilled.

Orange and Onion Salad
SERVES 4

3 oranges
1 lemon
1 onion

6 black olives
salt and pinch cayenne pepper
2 tablespoons olive oil

Using a sharp knife, remove the skin and all the membrane from the orange. Cut the orange into very thin slices and remove the pips. Cut the skin and membrane from the lemon and cut into segments. Arrange the orange slices and lemon segments in four bowls. Peel the onion and cut it into thin slices, divide the slices into rings and place them on top of the fruit. Halve the black olives and remove the stones. Place the olives on top of the onions and sprinkle with salt and cayenne pepper. Pour over the oil and chill in the fridge for 30 minutes before serving.

Potato Salad with Garlic Sausage and Apple
SERVES 4

A delicious first or light main course. The flavour of the potatoes is made extra special by the addition of some consommé. A little curry powder or paste can be added to the vinaigrette.

900 g (2 lb) new potatoes
150 ml (¼ pt) hot tinned consommé
3 tablespoons olive oil
1 tablespoon white wine vinegar
1 teaspoon Dijon mustard
2 tablespoons finely chopped
    spring onions

2 tablespoons finely chopped parsley
salt and freshly ground black pepper
100 g (4 oz) garlic sausage
2 crisp eating apples

Garnish
finely chopped parsley

Scrape the potatoes and boil in salted water until just tender but still firm, drain well, slice into a bowl and pour over the hot consommé. Cover with a cloth and leave to stand for 15 minutes. Combine the oil, vinegar and mustard with the spring onions and parsley, season with salt and pepper and mix well. Pour the vinaigrette over the potatoes and toss lightly to mix. Remove the skin from the garlic sausage and cut into the same-sized slices as the potatoes. Peel, core and dice the apples. Add the sausage and apple to the potatoes, toss lightly, turn into a serving dish, sprinkle with a little extra chopped parsley and chill well before serving.

Hot Potato Salad with Anchovies
SERVES 4

An unusual way of serving potatoes which goes particularly well with chicken or fish dishes.

900 g (2 lb) potatoes
3 spring onions
4 anchovy fillets

1 tablespoon finely chopped parsley
freshly ground black pepper
300 ml (½ pt) mayonnaise

Peel the potatoes and cut into small, even dice. Finely chop the spring onions. Drain and finely chop the anchovies. Cook the potatoes in boiling, salted water until just tender and drain well. Turn into a saucepan, mix in the spring onions, half the parsley and the anchovies, add a generous grinding of black pepper and fold in the mayonnaise. Heat through, turn into a serving dish and sprinkle with the remaining parsley. Serve at once.

Dandelion Salad Niçoise
SERVES 4

450 g (1 lb) young
  dandelion leaves
100 g (4 oz) tin tuna fish
2 hard-boiled eggs
1 small onion

12 black olives
½ green pepper
8 anchovy fillets
vinaigrette dressing

Pick over, wash and dry the dandelion leaves. Drain the tuna and break into chunks with a fork. Quarter the hard-boiled eggs. Peel and thinly slice the onion and divide into rings. Halve and stone the olives. Remove the seeds and core of the green pepper and cut the flesh into thin strips. Arrange all the ingredients attractively in a salad dish, pour over the dressing and toss lightly before serving.

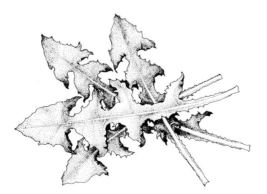

Courgette and New Potato Salad
SERVES 4

In summer there are baby courgettes which cry out to be eaten raw and this makes them the perfect partners to a salad of sweet new potatoes.

450 g (1 lb) new potatoes
225 g (8 oz) baby courgettes
2 spring onions
150 ml ($\frac{1}{4}$ pt) mayonnaise
2 tablespoons single cream

salt and freshly ground black pepper

Garnish
2 tablespoons finely chopped parsley

Scrub the potatoes and boil in salted water until just tender; cool and cut into small dice. Wash the courgettes in cold running water, cut off the stalks and dice the flesh. Chop the spring onions. Combine the potatoes, courgettes and onions and pour over the mayonnaise mixed with cream. Season with a little salt and pepper and toss lightly. Refrigerate for at least 30 minutes and sprinkle with parsley just before serving.

Blue Cheese Saladette
SERVES 4

1 cucumber
175 g (6 oz) blue Cheshire cheese
150 ml ($\frac{1}{4}$ pt) double cream
salt and freshly ground black pepper
pinch cayenne pepper
700 g (1$\frac{1}{2}$ lb) cooked new potatoes
2 frankfurter sausages

2 tomatoes
1 tablespoon Dijon mustard
150 ml ($\frac{1}{4}$ pt) mayonnaise
1 tablespoon finely chopped
   spring onions
1 bunch watercress
2 tablespoons vinaigrette dressing

Remove the top and bottom of the cucumber and cut the cucumber into eight thick pieces. Remove the centres with an apple corer. Mash the cheese until smooth, lightly whip the cream, combine the cheese and cream, season with salt, pepper and cayenne and mix lightly together. Dice the potatoes and frankfurters. Cover the tomatoes with boiling water and leave for 2 minutes, drain and slide the skins off. Remove the cores and seeds and chop their flesh. Mix the mustard with the mayonnaise, add the potatoes, frankfurters, tomatoes and spring onions and mix lightly. Remove the watercress stalks and toss the leaves lightly in the vinaigrette dressing. Arrange the watercress in the centre of a serving dish and surround with a circle of potato mixture. Place the cucumber pieces on the watercress and, using a piping bag with a medium nozzle, pipe the cheese into the centre of the cucumbers, finishing with a swirl of the mixture on top of each piece. Serve chilled.

Vegetables & Salads

Pasta Salad

SERVES 6

450 g (1 lb) pasta shells
  or spirals
200 ml (7 fl oz) mayonnaise
2 tablespoons double cream
salt and freshly ground black pepper
few drops Worcestershire and Tabasco
  sauces

175 g (6 oz) ham in one piece
1 small green pepper
175 g (6 oz) cooked peas
175 g (6 oz) cooked French beans

Garnish
1 tablespoon finely chopped chives

Cook the pasta in plenty of boiling, salted water until just tender and drain well. Combine the mayonnaise with the cream and flavour with a little salt, pepper, Worcestershire sauce and Tabasco. Add the warm pasta and toss lightly. Leave to cool. Cut the ham into small dice. Remove the core and seeds of the green pepper and chop the flesh. Add the ham, peas, beans and pepper to the pasta, mix well, check the seasoning, pile into a serving dish and sprinkle with the chopped chives.

Crabmeat and Rice Salad

SERVES 4

4 large cooked crab claws
2 cloves garlic
300 ml (½ pt) home-made mayonnaise
pinch mace
4 small firm tomatoes

1 small onion
1 green pepper
225 g (8 oz) long-grain rice
salt and freshly ground black pepper

Crack the claws (I do this by wrapping them in a clean cloth and tapping with a hammer), remove all the meat and chop it coarsely. Squeeze the garlic through a garlic press or crush with a fork and mix with the mayonnaise and mace. Peel and chop the tomatoes, finely chop the onion and green pepper. Cook the rice in boiling salted water until just tender. Drain, rinse through with cold water and drain again. Mix the rice with the mayonnaise, fold in the crab, tomato, onion and pepper and season.

Red Bean and Tongue Salad

SERVES 2

425 g (15 oz) tin red kidney beans
50 g (2 oz) cooked tongue
2 stalks celery
1½ tablespoons olive oil
½ tablespoon white wine vinegar

¼ teaspoon Dijon mustard
salt and freshly ground black pepper
1 tablespoon finely chopped green
  pepper
1 teaspoon finely chopped parsley

Drain off all the liquid from the beans. Cut the tongue into thin matchstick strips and chop the celery. Combine the olive oil, vinegar and Dijon mustard. Mix well and season with salt and pepper; put all the ingredients into a bowl, pour over the dressing and toss well. Transfer to a small earthenware container, cover tightly with foil and keep in the fridge until required.

Finclaire Salad
SERVES 4

A good buffet, quick lunch or supper dish. Serve with hot jacket potatoes or hot French bread and butter.

1 kipper
225–275 g (8–10 oz) cooked chicken
4 stalks celery
1 small green pepper
1 teaspoon horseradish sauce
3 tablespoons mayonnaise
2 tablespoons sour cream
salt and freshly ground black pepper

pinch cayenne pepper
1 teaspoon grated raw onion
1 bunch watercress

Garnish
8 halved and stoned
*   black olives (optional)*

Place the kipper tail end up in a jug and pour enough boiling water over to reach the tail. Leave for 5 minutes, drain off the water, remove the skin and bones and flake the flesh. Chop the chicken meat. Remove the leaves and any coarse fibres from the sides of the celery stalks and chop the flesh. Remove the core and seeds from the pepper and finely chop the flesh. Combine the horseradish, mayonnaise and sour cream and season with salt, pepper and a pinch of cayenne. Add the chicken, kipper, onion, celery and pepper and mix lightly. Remove any coarse stalks from the watercress, arrange the leaves at the edge of a serving dish and pile the salad in the centre. Garnish with halved and stoned black olives.

Midsummer Meat Salad
SERVES 4

A salad of new potatoes in mayonnaise goes very well with this dish.

450 g (1 lb) cooked beef, lamb or pork
4 ripe tomatoes
1 large clove garlic
1 tablespoon finely chopped parsley
1 tablespoon finely chopped fresh chervil
*   or basil or $\frac{1}{4}$ teaspoon dried mixed*
*   herbs soaked in a little warm water*

4 tablespoons olive oil
1 tablespoon white wine vinegar
grated rind of $\frac{1}{2}$ lemon
salt and freshly ground black pepper

Garnish
green pepper rings

Cut the meat into very thin slices and then into neat julienne strips about 0.3 m ($\frac{1}{8}$ in) wide. Cover the tomatoes with boiling water and leave for 2 minutes, peel off skins, discard cores and seeds and finely chop the flesh. Peel and very finely chop the garlic. Combine the tomatoes, garlic, parsley, chervil, olive oil, vinegar and lemon rind and mix well. Season with salt and pepper. Add the meat and toss with a fork until all the ingredients are combined. Chill for at least 2 hours. Pile the meat salad into a serving dish and garnish with thin rings of green pepper.

Three-Star Chef's Salad

SERVES 4–6

175 g (6 oz) cooked tongue
175 g (6 oz) thin green beans
2 small courgettes
2 small carrots
75 g (3 oz) farmhouse Cheddar
75 g (3 oz) red Cheshire cheese
75 g (3 oz) white Cheshire cheese

12 black olives
2 small dill-pickled cucumbers
2 small firm tomatoes
4 spring onions
1 small iceberg lettuce
150 ml ($\frac{1}{4}$ pt) vinaigrette

Cut the tongue into very thin matchstick strips. Top and tail the beans and cook in a little boiling water for 6 minutes. Refresh them at once under cold running water and pat dry on kitchen paper. Trim the courgettes and grate into long shreds. Peel the carrots and grate into long shreds. Coarsely grate the Cheddar and cut the red and white Cheshire cheeses into small cubes (don't worry if they are a bit crumbly). Halve the olives and remove the stones. Cut the cucumbers into thin diagonal slices. Thinly slice the tomatoes, slice the spring onions lengthwise and shred the lettuce. Arrange the lettuce on a shallow serving platter. Arrange the ingredients in diagonal strips starting with the courgettes, then strips of beans, tongue, Cheddar, red Cheshire, cucumber, white Cheshire, and so on. Chill well and pour over the dressing just before serving.

Salade Ecossaise

SERVES 4
Plate 28, illustrated
facing page 193.

450 g (1 lb) fresh salmon
6 tablespoons olive oil
salt and freshly ground black pepper
1 clove garlic
1 head crisp lettuce (preferably cos)
$\frac{1}{2}$ teaspoon Dijon mustard
juice of $\frac{1}{2}$ lemon
pinch sugar

450 g (1 lb) young French beans
3 firm tomatoes
8 black olives
2 sliced hard-boiled eggs
50 g (2 oz) tin anchovy fillets

Garnish
2 tablespoons finely chopped chives

Brush the salmon with 2 tablespoons olive oil, season with salt and pepper, wrap in foil and bake in a hot oven (200°C / 400°F / Reg 6) for about 20 minutes until just cooked. Leave to cool, remove skin and bones and break into eight pieces. Rub a salad bowl with the garlic clove. Remove outer leaves from the lettuce, cut the heart into eight pieces and arrange in the bottom of the bowl. Combine the mustard, the remaining olive oil, lemon juice, sugar and seasoning and mix well. Top and tail the beans, cook until just tender in boiling, salted water, drain well and toss in the dressing while still warm. Arrange the beans in the centre of the lettuce, top with salmon, tomatoes, hard-boiled eggs and drained anchovies. Sprinkle with the chives and serve well chilled.

Plate 27. Grated Carrots with Spinach, Bacon and Mushrooms

Plate 28. Salade Ecossaise

Clarabelle

SERVES 6

A summer dish that is so cool to look at that it really sharpens any appetite. The jellied mould can be filled in the centre with any number of delicious variations. A mixture of watercress and prawns, for instance, with a sharp French dressing; or try pasta shells mixed with mayonnaise and chopped tongue, or ham and tomatoes and black olives. A fish salad in a cocktail sauce would be good or cold chicken, diced, with a curried mayonnaise.

1 tablespoon gelatine powder
300 ml ($\frac{1}{2}$ pt) water
150 ml ($\frac{1}{4}$ pt) white wine
juice of 1 lemon
1 large cucumber
salt

150 ml ($\frac{1}{4}$ pt) double cream
1 tablespoon finely chopped dill
1 tablespoon finely chopped chives
4 spring onions (white parts only) finely chopped
pinch caster sugar

Mix the gelatine with a little of the water and heat gently, stirring, until it dissolves. Combine the gelatine, water, wine and lemon juice and refrigerate until just beginning to set. Peel and coarsely grate the cucumber, put into a sieve and sprinkle generously with salt. Leave to stand for 30 minutes, then rinse and drain well. Whip the cream until thick. Add the cucumber, dill, chives and spring onions to the jellied mixture with the sugar and mix lightly. Season with pepper. Mix in the cream and pour into a ring mould. Refrigerate until set and turn onto a serving dish.

Tasmanian Chicken Salad

SERVES 4–6

1 onion
1 boiling fowl
1 chicken stock cube
1 lemon
bouquet garni
salt and freshly ground black pepper
450 g (1 lb) tin water chestnuts

2 green peppers
2 spring onions
2 crisp eating apples
300 ml ($\frac{1}{2}$ pt) mayonnaise
1 teaspoon lemon juice
lettuce leaves
25 g (1 oz) split almonds, roasted

Peel and slice the onion. Cook the chicken until tender in enough water to cover, with the stock cube, the lemon cut into quarters, onion, bouquet garni and seasoning. Leave to cool in the stock and cut the meat into neat cubes when cold. Drain and thinly slice the water chestnuts. Discard core and seeds from the green peppers; chop the flesh of one and cut the other into thin strips. Chop the spring onions. Peel, core and dice the apples. Put the mayonnaise in a large bowl, add the lemon juice and check seasoning. Add the chicken, apple, water chestnuts and chopped pepper. Arrange on crisp lettuce leaves in a serving dish, sprinkle with the roasted almonds and decorate with the strips of green pepper. Chill and serve.

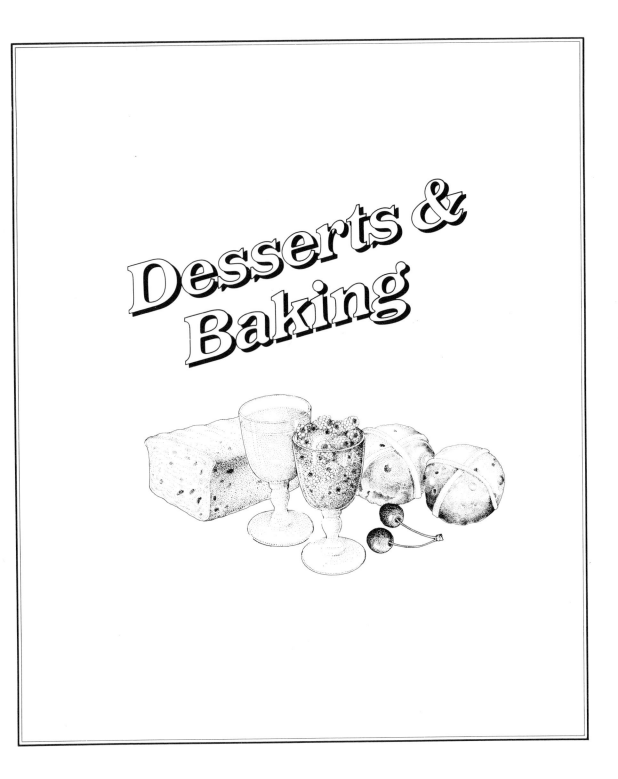

Desserts & Baking

January Fruit Salad
SERVES 6

8–10 clementines or satsumas
1 orange
175 g (6 oz) frozen raspberries

150 ml (¼ pt) water
175 g (6 oz) caster sugar
1 tablespoon kirsch (optional)

Peel the clementines and cut them into thin slices, removing any pips. Place the fruit in a glass bowl. Very thinly pare off the skin from the orange, remove any white membrane and cut the peel into very, very thin strips. Blanch the peel in boiling water for 10 minutes and drain. Combine the raspberries, water and sugar in a saucepan, bring to the boil and simmer for 10 minutes. Rub through a fine sieve to remove the raspberry pips. Add the orange peel and the juice of the orange to the raspberry juice, poor it over the clementines, add the kirsch and leave to cool. Serve well chilled.

Melon and Grape Slices
SERVES 6

1 melon
100 g (4 oz) black or green grapes
450 ml (¾ pt) orange juice

1 tablespoon gelatine powder
1 tablespoon sugar

Halve the melon and remove the seeds. Scoop out the flesh with a small ball scoop and reserve the melon shells. Halve the grapes (peel them if the skins are tough) and remove the pips. Fill the melon shells with the combined melon balls and grapes. Heat 2–3 tablespoons orange juice and dissolve the gelatine in it. Add the sugar, then stir into the remaining juice. Pour the jelly over the fruit in the melon shells and chill in the fridge until set firm. Some of the liquid will be absorbed into the melon skin and any extra jelly should be poured over the fruit after it has been left to set for about 30 minutes. Serve the melon cut into slices.

Ananas au Kirsch
SERVES 6

1 large ripe pineapple
3 crisp Cox's apples
3 pieces preserved ginger
juice of ½ lemon

50 g (2 oz) caster sugar
1 tablespoon kirsch
2 tablespoons ginger syrup

Carefully peel the pineapple and cut off six thin slices from the bottom. Neatly remove the core from the centre of the slices and arrange the slices on a serving dish. Peel, core and dice the apples and peel and dice the remaining pineapple. Chop the ginger. Combine the diced apples, pineapple, chopped ginger, lemon juice, sugar, kirsch and ginger syrup, in a bowl, toss lightly and leave to marinate for at least 2 hours. Pile the diced fruit in the centre of the pineapple slices, chill well and pour over any juices just before serving.

Tropical Frenzy
SERVES 8

10 passion fruit
3 tablespoons hot water
1½ tablespoons gelatine powder
5 eggs, separated
175 g (6 oz) caster sugar

450 ml (¾ pt) double cream

Decoration
1 ripe mango
3 kiwi fruit

Halve the passion fruit and scrape out the flesh into a sieve over a bowl. Rub the pips until you have extracted all possible juices. Put the water into a small pan, sprinkle over the gelatine and stir over a low heat to dissolve. Put the egg yolks and sugar into a bowl over a pan of hot water and whisk until the mixture is almost white and the sugar is completely dissolved. Remove from the heat, add the passion-fruit juice and whisk until cool. Whip the egg whites until stiff and beat the cream until thick. Add the gelatine to the egg yolk mixture and mix well. Lightly fold in the cream and egg whites and turn into a dampened circular mould or cake tin. Chill until set firm. Turn out the mousse by dipping it into very hot water and inverting the mould onto a circular serving dish. Peel the mango and cut the flesh off the stone into thin slices. Peel and thinly slice the kiwi fruit. Decorate the mousse with the mango and kiwi fruit and serve chilled.

Figs with Ginger Cream
SERVES 6

6 large ripe figs
150 ml (¼ pt) double cream
1 tablespoon caster sugar
grated rind of 1 orange

pinch ground ginger
pinch ground cinnamon
1 piece preserved ginger, finely chopped

Wash the figs and cut them into thin slices from the stalk end through to within a matchstick's width of the base. Gently fan them out and arrange on a flat serving dish. Whip the cream until stiff and mix in the caster sugar, half the orange rind, ginger, cinnamon and preserved ginger. Spread the cream over the figs, sprinkle with the remaining orange rind and chill well.

Gingered Strawberries
SERVES 4

This recipe has only 40 calories per serving.

450 g (1 lb) strawberries
pinch ground ginger

225 ml (8 fl oz) dry ginger ale
few mint leaves

Slice the strawberries and divide them between four glass goblets. Add a pinch of ginger to the ginger ale and pour the liquid over the strawberries. Chill in the fridge for an hour and serve topped with mint leaves.

Watermelon Fresco
SERVES 6–8

The green skins of these large melons make attractive, natural bowls for serving a dessert; fill the centre with a mixture of rose-coloured flesh, sliced fresh peaches and black grapes.

1 small watermelon
2 peaches
juice of ½ lemon

225 g (8 oz) black grapes
2 tablespoons sugar
2 tablespoons sherry

Using a sharp knife, cut a serrated pattern around the melon about a third of the way from the top. Remove the lid and scoop out the inside. Remove the seeds and dice the flesh. Peel and slice the peaches and sprinkle them with lemon juice to prevent them discolouring. Halve the grapes and remove the pips. Combine the fruits and sprinkle over the sugar and sherry. Fill the melon shell, cover with foil and chill for at least 2 hours before serving.

Raspberry Simbelle
SERVES 6

450 g (1 lb) raspberries
juice of 2 oranges
2 tablespoons brandy
4 tablespoons caster sugar

150 ml (¼ pt) double cream
1 tablespoon icing sugar
2 drops vanilla essence

Divide the raspberries among six large wine glasses. Pour over the orange juice and brandy and sprinkle with caster sugar. Chill in the fridge for at least an hour. Whip the cream until thick, stir in the icing sugar and vanilla essence. Spoon the cream over the raspberries and serve.

Caramel Oranges
SERVES 6–8

8 oranges
225 g (8 oz) sugar

150 ml ($\frac{1}{4}$ pt) cold water
150 ml ($\frac{1}{4}$ pt) warm water

Thinly cut the rind from 1 orange without removing any white pith or membrane. Cut it into thin strips, blanch in boiling water for a minute and drain well. Using a sharp knife, cut the skin and membrane from all the oranges until they are pared down to the flesh only. Cut into slices, removing any pips. Place in a glass bowl and sprinkle with strips of blanched peel. Combine the sugar with the cold water in a heavy saucepan and heat over a low flame, without stirring, until the sugar turns to a rich, golden-brown caramel. Remove from the heat and, protecting your hand from splatters with a cloth, pour in the warm water, stirring to dissolve the caramel. Leave to cool. Pour the cooled caramel mixture over the oranges and chill well before serving.

Orange Strawberry Pudding
SERVES 4

4 thin-skinned oranges
3 tablespoons strawberry jam

juice of 1 lemon
50 g (2 oz) slivered blanched almonds

Peel the oranges, removing all the pith and membrane, and cut into very thin slices. Remove any pips and arrange the fruit in four glass bowls or goblets. Heat the strawberry jam until melted, mix with the lemon juice and pour this over the orange slices. Brown the almonds for a few minutes in a hot oven until golden crisp and when cool, sprinkle over the fruit. Chill the pudding before serving.

Baked Orange
SERVES 1

1 large orange
1 teaspoon lemon juice

1 tablespoon brown sugar
dot of butter

Put the orange in a saucepan of boiling water and cook until its skin is tender, about 20 minutes. Drain, cool and cut in half. Place the halves, cut side up in a baking dish, remove the pips and pour the lemon juice into the centres. Cover the tops with brown sugar, dot with a little butter and bake in a hot oven or under the grill for 10–15 minutes, until the sugar has melted and is bubbling. The skin as well as the flesh can be eaten.

Wine-Simmered Plums
SERVES 4

Serve hot or cold with whipped cream flavoured lightly with vanilla. Or you can remove the stones, purée the plums and use them as a base for a delicious autumn ice-cream, or serve the purée as a rich, pungent sauce with roast pork, gammon, duck or game, cooking the purée by boiling it over a high heat for a few minutes, stirring to prevent burning.

700 g (1½ lb) cooking plums
175 g (6 oz) granulated sugar
300 ml (½ pt) dry white wine
strip of lemon rind

¼ teaspoon ground cumin
pinch ground cloves
pinch grated nutmeg

Remove the stalks from the plums and place the fruit in a saucepan with the other ingredients. Bring gently to the boil and then simmer over a low heat for about 20 minutes, or until the plums are soft.

Plum and Blackberry Compote
SERVES 4–6

Serve hot or cold with cream.

450 g (1 lb) cooking plums
1 tablespoon water
150 ml (¼ pt) port

225 g (8 oz) sugar
450 g (1 lb) blackberries

Place the plums in a baking dish with a tablespoon of water. Pour over the port and cover with the sugar. Bake in a moderate oven (180°C / 350°F / Reg 4) for 20 minutes, then add the blackberries and mix them gently into the plums and continue to bake for a further 10 minutes. Add more sugar if necessary.

Highland Fling
SERVES 4

4 fresh peaches
juice of 2 lemons
2 tablespoons honey

2 tablespoons whisky
150 ml (¼ pt) double cream

Peel the peaches by nicking them, covering with boiling water for 30 seconds, draining and sliding the skins off. Remove the stones and cut the flesh into thin slices. Arrange in four glasses or goblets. Combine the lemon juice and honey in a saucepan and heat gently, stirring well until the honey is melted. Add the whisky and pour this over the peaches. Leave until cold and top with the cream, whipped if liked.

Italian Stuffed Peaches
SERVES 4

4 large peaches
2 tablespoons caster sugar
15 g ($\frac{1}{2}$ oz) unsalted butter
1 egg yolk

75 g (3 oz) macaroons
1 teaspoon lemon juice
1 teapoon brandy

Peel the peaches by nicking them, covering with boiling water for 30 seconds, draining and sliding the skins off. Cut them in half, remove the stones and scoop out a little of the peach flesh to make room for the filling. Cream the sugar with the butter until the mixture is smooth. Add the egg yolk and beat well. Crush the macaroons with a rolling pin. Combine the butter mixture with the macaroons, lemon juice and brandy and press into the peach cavities. Place the peaches in a lightly buttered baking dish and bake in a moderate oven (180°C / 350°F / Reg 4) for 20 minutes. Serve warm with cream.

Banana, Apricot and Lemon Pancakes
SERVES 6

90 g (3$\frac{1}{2}$ oz) plain flour
1 egg
1 egg yolk
300 ml ($\frac{1}{2}$ pt) milk
40 g (1$\frac{1}{2}$ oz) butter

6 bananas
2–3 tablespoons apricot jam
juice of 1 lemon
caster sugar
double cream, for serving

Combine the flour, egg, egg yolk and milk and blend or process until smooth. Melt half the butter and mix it into the batter. Leave the batter to stand for 30 minutes, then blend again. Smear a thin film of oil over a non-stick pan and heat until smoking. Pour about 2 tablespoons of the batter into the pan, swirling it around until the bottom of the pan is evenly covered. The covering should be almost transparent. Cook over a medium heat until the pancake is set, toss and cook until golden brown on the other side. Slide onto a heated plate and keep warm while cooking the remaining pancakes. Peel the bananas. Spread apricot jam on each pancake, then place a banana in the centre, sprinkle with lemon juice and then caster sugar. Roll up the pancakes neatly. Place them in an ovenproof serving dish, dot them with the remaining butter, sprinkle them with caster sugar and heat through in a hot oven (200°C / 400°F / Reg 6) for 10 minutes. Serve at once with cream.

Desserts & Baking

My New Instant Pud
SERVES 6

50 g (2 oz) butter
100 g (4 oz) sugar
juice of 1 lemon or lime
grated rind and juice of 1 orange

3 tablespoons whisky
6 bananas (preferably a bit on
   the green side)

Melt the butter in a saucepan, add all the ingredients excluding the bananas and stir for 10 minutes over a high heat until the sauce is thick and fudgy. Place the unpeeled bananas in a baking dish and bake in their skins in a hot oven (200°C / 400°F / Reg 6) for about 20 minutes, until their skins are black and beginning to split. Place each banana on a plate, pull off a strip of skin and pour over some of the sauce. Serve at once.

Banana Happiness
SERVES 4

4 large bananas
juice of 1 lemon
2 tablespoons honey

1 tablespoon brandy
150 ml ($\frac{1}{4}$ pt) double cream

Peel and thinly slice the bananas and toss in the lemon juice to avoid discoloration. Arrange the slices in four glass dishes. Heat the honey gently until just runny, stir in the brandy and leave to cool. Whip the cream until stiff, spread it over the bananas then spoon over the honey mixture. Chill before serving.

Banana Flambé
SERVES 8

8 bananas
juice of 1 lemon
25 g (1 oz) slightly salted butter
225 g (8 oz) soft brown sugar
1 glass red wine or port
1 teaspoon each cinnamon and nutmeg

pinch allspice
grated rind of 1 large orange
25 g (1 oz) chopped almonds
2 crushed macaroons
2 tablespoons rum

Peel the bananas and cut each into quarters lengthwise. Brush with lemon juice and fry gently in the butter for 2 minutes. Arrange the bananas in a lightly greased baking dish. Combine the sugar, red wine, spices and orange rind in a saucepan and simmer gently until the mixture is thick and syrupy. Pour this over the bananas and top with almonds and the macaroons crushed into small pieces. Bake for 20 minutes in a moderate oven (180°C / 350°F / Reg 4). Before serving, heat the rum to boiling point, pour it over the bananas, set light to it at once and bring it flaming to the table.

Rhineland Baked Apples

SERVES 4

4 large cooking apples
25 g (1 oz) sultanas
25 g (1 oz) mixed candied peel
50 g (2 oz) brown sugar
25 g (1 oz) butter

150 ml ($\frac{1}{4}$ pt) brown ale
150 ml ($\frac{1}{4}$ pt) double cream
1 tablespoon caster sugar
1 drop vanilla essence

Neatly remove the apple cores and place the apples in a well-buttered shallow baking dish. Finely chop the sultanas and mix with the peel, 40 g (1$\frac{1}{2}$ oz) brown sugar and the butter. Pack the mixture into the centres of the apples and pour over the beer. Sprinkle the remaining sugar around the apples and bake in a moderately hot oven (190°C / 375°F / Reg 5) for 45 minutes to an hour until the apples are soft but not bursting out of their skins. Transfer to a serving dish, spoon over the juice from the dish and serve with a last-minute topping of cream whipped until thick and flavoured with caster sugar and vanilla essence.

Apple and Blackberry Crisp

SERVES 4

In this recipe, the top layer of apples prevents the juice of the blackberries seeping through the crisp, crunchy topping.

3 cooking apples
450 g (1 lb) blackberries
2 tablespoons sugar
finely grated rind and
    juice of 1 orange
150 g (5 oz) flour

40 g (1$\frac{1}{2}$ oz) sugar
75 g (3 oz) butter
$\frac{1}{2}$ teaspoon ground cinnamon
15 g (1 oz) finely chopped
    blanched almonds

Peel, core and slice the apples. Wash and dry the blackberries if necessary. Arrange half the apples in the bottom of a lightly buttered ovenproof dish, add the blackberries, mixed with 2 tablespoons sugar, and cover with the remaining apples. Pour over the orange juice. Mix the flour and 40 g (1$\frac{1}{2}$ oz) sugar together and rub in the butter with the fingertips until the mixture resembles breadcrumbs. Add the orange rind, cinnamon and almonds and sprinkle the mixture over the fruit. Bake in a hot oven (220°C / 425°F / Reg 7) for about 20 minutes, until crisp and golden brown.

Rhubarb Crunch

SERVES 4

A most unusual fruit crunch, a 'crumble' where the cake topping is replaced by a mixture resembling a soft flapjack. (A pinch of cinnamon and some seedless raisins can be added to the topping if you want to spice it up!)

450 g (1 lb) rhubarb
225 g (8 oz) sugar
150 ml ($\frac{1}{4}$ pt) water

50 g (2 oz) butter
1 dessertspoon golden syrup
100 g (4 oz) rolled oats

Cut the rhubarb stalks into 1 cm ($\frac{1}{2}$ in) pieces and combine with water and 150 g (5 oz) sugar in a saucepan. Bring to the boil, cover and simmer gently for 5–10 minutes. Place in an ovenproof dish and leave to cool. Melt the butter and golden syrup together until runny. Add the rolled oats and remaining sugar and cook over a low heat, stirring continuously until the sugar has dissolved. Distribute the flapjack mixture evenly over the rhubarb and cook in a moderate oven (180°C / 350°F / Reg 4) for 20 minutes, or until the topping is golden brown. Serve hot or cold with custard or cream.

Old English Syllabub

SERVES 6

A pure syllabub should be made with milk fresh from the cow and mixed with the eggs and sugar while still foaming. If you don't have a cow at your doorstep, excellent results can be obtained by using bottled milk and single cream, providing the egg whites are only added at the very end.

2 eggs, separated
100 g (4 oz) caster sugar
150 ml ($\frac{1}{4}$ pt) milk
300 ml ($\frac{1}{2}$ pt) single cream

150 ml ($\frac{1}{4}$ pt) sherry
finely grated rind of $\frac{1}{2}$ lemon
grated nutmeg

Beat the egg yolks with the sugar until light and pale. Gradually add the milk and cream, beating all the time until the mixture is smooth. Blend in the sherry, add the lemon rind and leave to stand for an hour. Just before serving, whip the egg whites until stiff, fold them into the syllabub and sprinkle with a little grated nutmeg.

Mango Fool
SERVES 4

2 large, or 4 small mangoes
100 g (4 oz) sugar
150 ml ($\frac{1}{4}$ pt) water
juice of $\frac{1}{2}$ lemon or lime

150 ml ($\frac{1}{4}$ pt) milk
1 egg
150 ml ($\frac{1}{4}$ pt) double cream

Peel the mangos, slice the flesh off the stones and chop the flesh. Combine the mangoes with sugar, water and lemon juice in a saucepan and simmer for 20 minutes. Purée the fruit and leave to cool. Heat the milk and beat it into the egg. Put into a small heavy pan and stir constantly over a low heat until the mixture thickens into a smooth thick custard. Cool. Whip the cream until stiff. Stir the custard into the mango purée, fold in the cream and spoon into four goblets. Chill the fool well before serving.

Avocado and Macaroon Cream
SERVES 4

100 g (4 oz) macaroons
150 ml ($\frac{1}{4}$ pt) double cream
50 g (2 oz) pistachio nuts

2 ripe avocados
juice of $\frac{1}{2}$ lemon
50 g (2 oz) sugar

Crush the macaroons. Whip the cream until thick. Chop the pistachio nuts and roast them in a hot oven for about 3 minutes until crisp. Peel and stone the avocados and mash to a smooth purée with the lemon juice. Add the macaroons and sugar and mix well. Lightly fold in the cream and pile the mixture into four glass goblets. Sprinkle over the roasted pistachio nuts and chill in the fridge for at least 30 minutes before serving.

Stone Cream
SERVES 6

150 ml ($\frac{1}{4}$ pt) milk
1 tablespoon gelatine powder
4 egg yolks
600 ml (1 pt) double cream

3 tablespoons raspberry or
    strawberry jam
50 g (2 oz) toasted flaked almonds

Combine the milk and gelatine in a small saucepan and stir over a low heat until the gelatine has dissolved (on no account boil the milk, or the mixture will curdle). Beat the egg yolks until smooth. Heat the cream to just below boiling point and gradually beat it into the egg yolks. Blend in the milk and gelatine mixture. Spread the jam over the bottom of an ovenproof serving dish and pour over the custard mixture. Bake in a moderately slow oven (170°C / 325°F / Reg 3) for 2–3 minutes, until golden brown. Cool and scatter the almonds over the top of the cooled cream. Serve chilled.

Mocha Cream Pudding
SERVES 4

This is very rich and requires no cooking at all. It must be put in the fridge or a very cold larder for a couple of hours before it is required.

sponge fingers
sherry
100 g (4 oz) caster sugar
100 g (4 oz) butter
2 eggs

2 tablespoons strong coffee
150 ml (¼ pt) single cream

Decoration
grated chocolate

Line a pudding basin with sponge fingers and sprinkle with sherry. Cream the sugar and butter well and add the eggs one at a time, always beating well all the time. Add the coffee slowly, beating until the mixture is soft. Pour into the lined basin and top with more sponge fingers. Press down with a plate. Chill until required, when it should be turned out and covered with the cream. Grate chocolate over the top.

Blackcurrant Jelly
SERVES 4

This can be made in a round mould, masked with sweetened whipped cream, and with just a suspicion of vanilla essence added, then sprinkled with toasted split almonds. You cut the jelly like a cake and the contrast of white cream and dark jelly is stunning.

450 g (1 lb) blackcurrants
4 tablespoons water
225 g (8 oz) granulated sugar
1 tablespoon gelatine powder
2 tablespoons port

200 ml (7 fl oz) double cream
1 tablespoon caster sugar
2 drops vanilla essence
40 g (1½ oz) slivered blanched almonds

Combine the blackcurrants, water and sugar in a saucepan. Bring to the boil, cover and simmer until the fruit is soft. Rub through a fine sieve and make up the resulting purée to 600 ml (1 pt) with water. Stir the gelatine in a little water over a low heat until dissolved. Mix the gelatine and port with the purée and pour into a mould. Chill until set. Whip the cream until stiff, sweeten with caster sugar and flavour with vanilla essence. Mix well. Dip the mould into very hot water, turn out the jelly onto a serving dish and mask with whipped cream. Toast the almonds under a hot grill until golden brown, cool and scatter over the pudding.

Lemon Wine Jelly
SERVES 4

Surround the jelly and fill the centre with sliced or chopped fresh fruit. My favourite combination is a mixture of sliced bananas sprinkled with lemon juice to prevent discoloration and halved, pipped black grapes. Whipped cream can also be used to decorate the jelly.

300 ml ($\frac{1}{2}$ pt) water
juice of 2 lemons
1$\frac{1}{2}$ tablespoons gelatine powder

2 tablespoons sugar
300 ml ($\frac{1}{2}$ pt) white wine
1 tablespoon sherry

Combine water, lemon juice, gelatine and sugar in a saucepan and heat over a low flame until the gelatine and sugar are dissolved. Add the wine and sherry and pour into a ring mould. Chill until set and turn out onto a serving dish.

Egg and Sherry Jelly
SERVES 2

Light, smooth puddings such as junket or jellies all slip down well when you are feeling off colour.

300 ml ($\frac{1}{2}$ pt) water
juice and rind of 1 lemon
1 tablespoon gelatine powder

40 g (1$\frac{1}{2}$ oz) sugar
2 egg yolks, very well beaten
2 tablespoons sherry

Combine the water, lemon rind, gelatine and sugar in a saucepan and heat over simmering water until the gelatine is dissolved. Strain to remove the lemon rind, add the lemon juice and pour this over the well-beaten yolks. Cook in a pan set over simmering water, stirring continually without boiling until the mixture is thick and creamy. Add sherry, pour into a mould and leave to set.

Fruit and Honey Jelly
SERVES 4

1 tablespoon gelatine powder
300 ml ($\frac{1}{2}$ pt) hot water
juice of 1 lemon

175 g (6 oz) clover honey
150ml ($\frac{1}{4}$ pt) cold water
chopped apple or orange segments

Dissolve the gelatine in a little of the hot water, then mix with remaining hot water. Add the lemon juice and honey and stir until dissolved. Add cold water and fruit and pour into a mould. Chill until set firm.

Banana Mousse

SERVES 6

1 tablespoon gelatine powder
juice of 1½ lemons
4 eggs, separated
175 g (6 oz) caster sugar

4 bananas
grated rind of ½ lemon
300 ml (½ pt) double cream
50 g (2 oz) mixed shelled nuts

Stir the gelatine in the lemon juice over a low heat until dissolved. Beat the egg yolks with the sugar until light and creamy. Mash 3 bananas in a bowl with a fork. Add the bananas, lemon rind and gelatine mixture to the creamed egg yolk. Whip the cream until thick and fold it into the mixture with the fourth banana cut into small pieces. Chill until beginning to set. Beat the egg whites until stiff. Fold them lightly into the banana mousse and transfer to a soufflé dish. Finely chop the nuts, roast in a moderately hot oven and scatter over the mousse.

Crème de Menthe Mousse

SERVES 6

This recipe is equally good made with rum, brandy, chartreuse, Grand Marnier or other orange flavoured liqueur.

2 tablespoons chopped almonds,
    hazelnuts or walnuts
300 ml (½ pt) double cream

100 g (4 oz) icing sugar
2 egg whites
4 tablespoons crème de menthe

Roast the nuts in a hot oven for 2–3 minutes until crisp. Beat the cream until it begins to thicken, mix in the icing sugar and continue to beat until the cream is light but not quite stiff. Beat the egg whites until stiff and lightly fold them into the cream with the crème de menthe. Spoon into glasses, top with nuts and chill until firm.

Soufflé Milanaise

SERVES 6

1 tablespoon gelatine powder
juice of 2 lemons
3 eggs, separated
225 g (8 oz) sugar
450 ml (¾ pt) whipping cream

Decoration
toasted chopped almonds
whipped cream (optional)

Tie a band of greaseproof paper around a soufflé mould. Add the gelatine to the lemon juice and heat to dissolve. Whisk the egg yolks and sugar to a thick cream and add the gelatine solution. Whip the cream and fold it into the mixture. Whisk the whites to a stiff foam and blend in. Put the soufflé into the mould and allow to set. Remove the greaseproof paper and decorate with toasted almonds around the side. It may be further decorated with whipped cream if desired.

Plate 29. Liqueur Water Ice

Plate 30. Cherry-Picker Flan

Raspberry Bavarois

SERVES 6

450 g (1 lb) frozen raspberries
100 g (4 oz) caster sugar
3 egg yolks
300 ml ($\frac{1}{2}$ pt) milk

1 tablespoon gelatine powder
juice of $\frac{1}{2}$ lemon
1 tablespoon hot water
300 ml ($\frac{1}{2}$ pt) double cream

Defrost the raspberries in their container as slowly as possible. Reserve a few for decoration. Beat the sugar with the eggs yolks until light and creamy. Bring the milk to the boil and whisk it into the egg yolk mixture. Transfer the custard to the top of a double saucepan and stir with a wooden spoon over hot (not boiling) water until the custard is thick enough to coat the back of the spoon. Remove from the heat and leave to cool. Sprinkle the gelatine over the surface of the combined lemon juice and hot water, leave to stand for a few minutes and then stir until the gelatine has dissolved. Add the gelatine mixture to the custard and mix well. Leave in the fridge until beginning to set. Purée the raspberries through a sieve and blend them into the custard. Whip the cream until stiff and fold two-thirds of the cream lightly into the raspberry mixture. Turn into a dampened mould and chill until set firm. Dip the mould into very hot water for a few seconds only, turn out onto a serving dish and surround with the remaining cream dotted with reserved raspberries.

Cold Pineapple and Ginger Soufflé

SERVES 4

This can be done at least 24 hours in advance. To add an extra golden touch, decorate the pudding with mandarin orange segments.

225 g (8 oz) tin pineapple in syrup
4 pieces crystallised ginger
1 tablespoon gelatine powder
juice of $\frac{1}{2}$ lemon

2 eggs
50 g (2 oz) caster sugar
300 ml ($\frac{1}{2}$ pt) double cream
  whipped until thick

Drain the pineapple, reserve 150 ml ($\frac{1}{4}$ pt) syrup and chop the fruit into small pieces. Finely chop the ginger. Dissolve the gelatine in a little hot water and add to the fruit syrup mixed with the lemon juice. Separate the eggs and beat the yolks with sugar until light and creamy. Add the gelatine mixture, chopped fruit and ginger and fold in the whipped cream. Whip the egg whites until stiff, fold them into the pudding and pour the mixture into a mould. Chill until set and turn out before serving.

Omelette Glacé Surprise
SERVES 6–8

900 ml–1.2 litres (1½–2 pts)
   orange water ice, preferable made
   with the juice of blood oranges
2 egg yolks

3 tablespoons caster sugar
1 tablespoon double cream
3 egg whites

When the water ice is frozen, pack it into a soufflé dish, half-filling the dish, and return it to the freezer. Beat the egg yolks with a tablespoon of sugar and the cream. Whisk the egg whites until really stiff and fold lightly into the yolks. Tie a band of greaseproof paper around the top of the soufflé dish, pour in the soufflé mixture and sprinkle with the remaining sugar. Stand the dish in a larger dish and pack it around the sides with ice cubes. Bake the soufflé in a hot oven (220°C / 425°F / Reg 7) for 5 minutes, until well risen and golden brown on top. Remove the paper and serve at once.

Paprika's Surprise
SERVES 4

4 large oranges
350 g (12 oz) fresh
   strawberries or raspberries
4 teaspoons sugar

2 tablespoons brandy
2 egg whites
100 g (4 oz) caster sugar
whipped cream, for serving

Cut a slice off the top of each orange and scoop out the inside, leaving a clean shell. Press the pulp through a sieve and reserve the juice. Hull and slice the strawberries thinly. Fill the oranges with the strawberry slices, sprinkle with the sugar and pour over the brandy and a dessertspoonful of orange juice for each orange. Chill in the fridge. Whip the egg whites until frothy, add half the caster sugar and continue to beat until really stiff. Lightly fold in the remaining sugar and pile the meringue on top of the filled oranges. Bake in a hot oven (220°C / 425°F / Reg 7) for about 4–6 minutes, until the meringue is just set and lightly browned. Serve at once with cream.

Lemon Soufflé
SERVES 4

50 g (2 oz) butter
1 tablespoon flour
200 ml (7 fl oz) milk
grated rind and juice of 1 lemon

2 teaspoons brandy
75 g (3 oz) caster sugar
2 large eggs, separated
whipped cream

Melt the butter, add the flour and mix well. Gradually add the milk, stirring continuously, until the mixture is thick and smooth. Beat in the lemon rind and juice, brandy and sugar. Add the egg yolks one at a time, beating until they are well-blended into the basic soufflé mixture. In a clean bowl, beat the egg whites until stiff but not dry and fold them into the soufflé base with a fork. Pour the mixture into a lightly greased soufflé dish about 18 cm (7 in) across. Place the dish in a roasting tin half filled with hot water and bake in a moderate oven (180°C / 350°F / Reg 4) for 40 minutes. Serve at once with a dollop of whipped cream.

Liqueur Water Ice
SERVES 6

Plate 29, illustrated facing page 208.

These are fairly expensive to make, but next time you really want to splash out and make an impression and don't want to break your back doing so, here is a sweet which is made in minutes and is blatantly luxurious. Use crème de menthe, crème de cassis or Grand Marnier. Serve the ice in fine glass goblets, topped with a littled sweetened whipped cream. Pour over a little more liqueur just before serving and hand round a plate of almond biscuits to go with it.

350 g (12 oz) sugar
600 ml (1 pt) water

juice of 1 lemon
150 ml (¼ pt) liqueur

Combine the sugar and water, bring slowly to the boil and then boil as fast as possible for 5 minutes. Leave to cool and mix in the lemon juice. Pour into a freezing tray and freeze, stirring every now and then as the sides become solidified. When the mixture is all granulated, mix in the liqueur and continue to freeze until almost solid.

Plum Sorbet with Melon

SERVES 4

700 g (1½ lb) wine-simmered plums (see page 200)
2 tablespoons frozen orange juice concentrate

2 egg whites
75 g (3 oz) caster sugar
2 small melons, with the seeds removed

Remove the stones from the plums and purée the fruit, and then stir the purée over a high heat until it thickens. Leave to cool. Beat in the orange juice. Beat the egg whites until thick, then gradually beat in the caster sugar until the whites are smooth and shiny. Fold in the fruit purée, cover tightly with foil and freeze for about an hour. Remove from the freezer, beat until smooth and light and then freeze for at least another 2 hours. Five minutes before serving, pile the sorbet in the middle of the melon halves and serve.

Sorbet Vallée d'Auge

SERVES 4–6

This is one of the lovely tricks of cookery that looks highly complicated but is in fact surprisingly easy to produce.

juice of 1½ lemons
6 large Golden Delicious or Granny Smith apples
350 g (12 oz) sugar

1 tablespoon Calvados (optional)

Decoration
mint leaves

Put the juice of ½ lemon in a bowl. Cut a cap off the top of the apples. Brush the exposed apple flesh with lemon juice to prevent it from browning (brush the flesh all the time you are working). Using a small pointed knife, cut around the edge of the apple flesh, and with a teaspoon, scoop out the flesh from the apple, going to within 0.5 cm (¼ in) of the skin. Brush the inside of the apple cases with lemon juice and freeze the cases and apple tops until the filling is ready. Combine the apple flesh, the juice of 1 lemon and 2 tablespoons water in a saucepan, bring to the boil and simmer until the apple is tender. Rub the apple pulp through a sieve to get rid of the cores and pips. Pour the apple purée into a measuring jug, add sugar and then enough water to measure 1.2 litres (2 pts) of purée and liquid. Return to a clean pan and stir over a medium heat until the sugar has dissolved. Mix well, cool and pour into a freezer proof container. Freeze until semi-solid and then turn into a bowl and beat with a rotary beater or blender until the sorbet is light, white and fluffy. Freeze until solid. Beat once more to stabilise the mixture and freeze again. Brush the frozen apple cases with Calvados and spoon in the sorbet. Replace the tops and decorate with mint leaves.

Orange and Lemon Sorbet

SERVES 6

Serve with chocolate mints.

90 g (3½ oz) sugar
150 ml (¼ pt) water
2 teaspoons gelatine powder

juice of 2 lemons
600 ml (1 pt) orange juice
1 egg white

Combine the sugar and water and slowly bring to the boil, stirring to dissolve the sugar; leave to cool. Dissolve the gelatine in the lemon juice over a low heat. Combine the syrup, orange and lemon juices, mix well and pour into a freezer proof container. Freeze until crystals have formed but the mixture is still not quite solid. Beat to a mush. Whip the egg white until stiff, fold it into the fruit juice and return to the freezer. Freeze until firm and serve in glasses or goblets which have been previously chilled.

Peach Ice-Cream

SERVES 4

350 g (12 oz) peeled, stoned and
  sliced ripe peaches or nectarines
100 g (4 oz) icing sugar
juice of ½ lemon

juice of ½ orange
300 ml (½ pt) double cream
150 ml (¼ pt) single cream

Combine the fruit, sugar and fruit juice in a blender or food processor until smooth. Whip the double and single creams together until stiff and light, fold in the fruit and turn into a freezer proof container. Freeze until half solid, break into a bowl and beat until smooth and creamy. Return to the freezer and freeze until firm. Remove the ice-cream from the freezer 10 minutes before serving.

Desserts & Baking

Bombe Princesse
SERVES 6

An attractive-looking ice-cream cake with an evocative flavour and texture – something really different. If you don't like making meringues, don't be put off by this recipe. Bought meringues can be substituted; or if you make them yourself and they discolour or break, it doesn't matter in the least.

3 egg whites
175 g (6 oz) caster sugar
450 ml (¾ pt) double cream
4 pieces of preserved ginger

2 tablespoons caster sugar
grated rind of 1 lemon
3 tablespoons kirsch

Whisk the egg whites until stiff. Add half the sugar and continue beating for 1 minute. Fold in the remaining sugar with a fork. Well oil a baking sheet with olive oil. Drop dollops of the meringue mixture onto the sheet from a tablespoon. Bake the meringues in a cool oven (110°C / 225°F / Reg ¼) for 2 hours, until firm. Turn off the heat, leave to dry out for 15 minutes. Remove from the baking sheet and break into small pieces when cool. Whisk the cream until it forms light peaks. Finely chop the ginger. Fold the ginger, caster sugar, lemon rind, kirsch and meringue into the cream. Lightly oil a cake tin with a removable base. Spoon in the cream mixture and smooth it down with the back of a wooden spoon. Cover tightly with foil and freeze for at least 4 hours. Turn out the ice-cream cake 10 minutes before serving.

Kiwi Ice-Cream with Strawberries
SERVES 6

150 ml (¼ pt) water
100g (4 oz) light brown sugar
6 ripe kiwi fruit
juice of 1 lemon
4 eggs
300 ml (½ pt) single cream
150 ml (¼ pt) double cream

350 g (12 oz) strawberries
1 orange
1 tablespoon brandy

Decoration
sprigs of mint

Combine the water and sugar in a saucepan and stir over a medium heat until the sugar has dissolved; leave to cool. Peel and roughly chop the kiwi fruit and combine it with the syrup, lemon juice, eggs and both creams in a blender, and work until smooth. Turn into a plastic container and freeze for an hour. Beat the ice-cream until smooth and return to the freezer until frozen through. Soften for 30 minutes in the fridge before serving. Thickly slice the strawberries and divide them between six glass goblets. Squeeze the orange and pour the juice together with the brandy over the strawberries, sweetening if necessary with a little sugar. Top the strawberries with scoops of ice-cream and decorate with sprigs of mint.

Desserts & Baking

Rhubarb and Ginger Ice-Cream
SERVES 4

450 g (1 lb) rhubarb
150 ml (¼ pt) water
150 g (5 oz) sugar
2 teaspoons lemon juice

4 pieces preserved ginger
1 egg white
1 tablespoon icing sugar
300 ml (½ pt) double cream

Cut the rhubarb stalks into 1 cm (½ in) pieces and combine with water and sugar in a saucepan. Bring to the boil, cover and simmer until rhubarb is tender. Cool and chill in fridge. Add the lemon juice to the chilled rhubarb, pour into a freezer proof container and freeze until ice crystals have formed and the mixture is solidifying around the edges. Beat the partially frozen rhubarb with a rotary whisk until smooth and mushy. Finely chop the ginger and mix it into the rhubarb. Whisk the egg white until stiff, blend in the icing sugar and fold it into rhubarb mixture. Whip the cream until stiff and fold into mixture. Return to the container and freeze until firm.

Apple Charlotte
SERVES 4–5

The success of a charlotte depends on using clarified butter – you obtain it by melting the butter until foaming, then straining through a muslin to remove impurities.

700 g (1½ lb) cooking apples
15 g (½ oz) butter
grated rind of ½ orange
grated rind of ½ lemon
2 teaspoons lemon juice
175 g (6 oz) granulated sugar

pinch ground cinnamon, cloves and nutmeg
8–10 slices crust-free white bread
100 g (4 oz) clarified butter
1¼ tablespoons demerara sugar

Peel and core the apples and roughly chop them. Combine them with 15 g (½ oz) butter, orange and lemon rind, lemon juice, granulated sugar and spices, and cook over a moderate heat, stirring until the apples are reduced to a thick pulp. Brush some of the slices of bread in the clarified butter and use them to line a soufflé dish. Fill the centre of the dish with apple mixture and top with the remaining bread slices (you may have to cut them to shape) brushed with clarified butter on both sides. Bake the charlotte in a hot oven (200°C / 400°F / Reg 6) for 20 minutes, by which time the bread topping should be crisp and golden brown. Sprinkle with the demerara sugar and return to the oven for a further 5 minutes. Serve hot or warm.

Apple Pudding
SERVES 4–6

Serve the pudding hot from the basin with cream.

175 g (6 oz) self-raising flour
75 g (3 oz) shredded suet
pinch salt
450 g (1 lb) cooking apples

juice of 1 lemon
150 g (5 oz) soft brown sugar
75 g (3 oz) melted butter

Combine the flour, suet and salt and rub the suet into the flour with your fingers until the mixture resembles coarse breadcrumbs. Add enough water to make a firm dough and knead until smooth. Roll out the pastry and use two-thirds of it to line a well-buttered 900 ml (1½ pt) basin. Peel, core and roughly chop the apples and place them in the lined pudding basin. Add the lemon juice, sugar and melted butter. Roll out the remaining pastry to make a top, dampen the edges and pinch them firmly together. Cover with a piece of buttered greaseproof paper, tie down the paper firmly and over-wrap with foil. Steam the pudding in a saucepan for 2½ hours, or in a pressure cooker at low pressure for about 1 hour.

Steamed Suet and Apple Pudding
SERVES 4

This has a spicy and pungent aroma. It is particularly good after a rather light main course.

200 g (7 oz) self-raising flour
pinch salt
90 g (3½ oz) shredded suet
cold water
450 g (1 lb) cooking apples

1 tablespoon sultanas
100 g (4 oz) caster sugar
grated rind of ½ lemon
pinch cinnamon and nutmeg

Combine the flour with the salt and suet and mix well. Gradually mix in enough cold water to make a stiff dough. Turn onto a floured board and knead until smooth. Reserve one-third of the pastry for the lid. Roll out the remaining pastry and line a well-greased 900 ml (1½ pt) pudding basin. Peel, core and slice the apples. Combine the sultanas and sugar with the lemon rind and spices. Arrange layers of apples in the basin, sprinkling each layer with the sugar mixture. Roll out the remaining pastry; top the pudding, dampen the edges and press firmly together. Cover tightly with a buttered paper, over-wrap with foil and stand the basin in a saucepan filled two-thirds of the way up with boiling water. Steam for 2½ hours or cook at low pressure for 1 hour in a pressure cooker. Add boiling water as required during the steaming.

Apricot Devonshire Pudding
SERVES 4

A sponge-pudding mixture and tinned apricots are combined to make a light, moist fruit cake which melts in the mouth. Serve with cream or a sauce of melted raspberry jam thinned with a little lemon juice and water.

3 eggs
75 g (3 oz) soft brown sugar
75 g (3 oz) flour

425 g (15 oz) tin apricot halves
grated rind of ½ lemon

Separate the eggs and beat the yolks with sugar until pale and creamy. Mix in the flour and blend well. Beat the egg whites until stiff and fold into the mixture (don't worry if it looks a bit lumpy). Drain off the juice from the apricot halves, mix them with the lemon rind into the sponge base and turn into a lightly buttered baking dish. Bake in a moderate oven (180°C / 350°F / Reg 4) for about 30 minutes until firm to the touch and golden brown on top.

Lemon Pudding
SERVES 4

This is so good, I get asked for it again and again.

200 g (7 oz) self-raising flour
pinch salt
90 g (3½ oz) shredded suet
cold water

2 small lemons
150 g (5 oz) brown sugar
75 g (3 oz) butter

Combine the flour with the salt and suet and mix well. Gradually mix in enough cold water to make a stiff dough. Knead on a floured board until smooth and set aside one-third of the dough for the pudding lid. Roll out the remaining pastry and use it to line a well-buttered pudding basin, allowing room for it to rise. Cut each lemon into quarters. Put about one-third of the sugar and butter into the bottom of the pudding, cover with the lemons and top with the remaining sugar and butter. Roll out the remaining pastry, cover pudding, dampen edges and press firmly to seal. Cover tightly with foil and place the basin in a saucepan, adding enough water to come two-thirds up the basin sides. Steam for 2 hours, or cook at low pressure for about 1 hour in a pressure cooker.

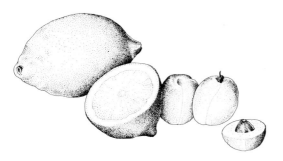

Pear Meringue Flan
SERVES 4

shortcrust pastry made with
100 g (4 oz) flour
700 g (1½ lb) cooking pears
2 tablespoons water
juice and rind of ½ lemon

75 g (3 oz) granulated sugar
50 g (2 oz) butter
2 eggs, separated
50 g (2 oz) caster sugar

Line an 18 cm (7 in) flan case with thinly-rolled pastry; peel, quarter and roughly chop the pears. Combine the pears in a saucepan with the water, lemon juice and rind. Bring to the boil and simmer until soft. Purée the pulp through a sieve and return to a clean pan with the granulated sugar and butter. Beat the egg yolks and add to the pan. Stir over a low heat until well-mixed; pour the purée into the flan case and bake in a moderate oven (180°C / 350°F / Reg 4) for about 30 minutes, until the pear mixture is set. Beat the egg whites until stiff, lightly fold in the caster sugar and pile the meringue on top of the pear filling. Dredge with extra caster sugar. Cook in a slow oven (140°C / 275°F / Reg 1) for about 30 minutes, until the meringue is set and golden brown.

No-Crust Lemon Cheese Pie
SERVES 4

225 g (8 oz) cottage cheese
2 eggs, separated
40 g (1½ oz) sugar
25 g (1 oz) flour

300 ml (½ pt) milk
grated rind and juice of 1 lemon
¼ teaspoon vanilla essence
50 g (2 oz) caster sugar

Press the cottage cheese through a fine sieve. Beat the egg yolks with the sugar, flour and about 2–3 tablespoons milk until the mixture is smooth. Heat the remaining milk to boiling point and pour it slowly into the egg mixture, beating all the time. Pour this custard into a clean pan and bring slowly to the boil, stirring continuously. Remove from the heat. Leave to cool for about 5 minutes and add the lemon juice and rind, cottage cheese and vanilla essence. Pour into a pie dish and top with a meringue made by whisking the egg whites until stiff and then folding in the caster sugar. Bake in a moderate oven (180°C / 350°F / Reg 4) for 20 minutes until lightly browned. The pie can be served hot or cold.

Lime Chiffon Pie

SERVES 6

4 tablespoons raspberry jam or
  redcurrant jelly
20 cm (8 in) baked flan case
3 eggs, separated
150 g (5 oz) caster sugar

finely grated rind and juice of
  2 large or 3 small limes
2 tablespoons gelatine powder
3 tablespoons hot water
300 ml ($\frac{1}{2}$ pt) double cream

Spread the jam over the flan case. Combine the egg yolks and sugar over a saucepan of hot (not boiling) water and whisk over a medium heat until the mixture is light, pale coloured and fluffy. Remove from the heat and whisk until cool. Mix in the lime rind and juice. Soften the gelatine in the hot water and stir until dissolved. Add the gelatine mixture to the yolks. Whisk the egg whites until stiff. Beat the cream until thick. Fold the cream into the yolk mixture and then lightly fold in the egg whites. Spoon the mixture into the flan case and chill in the fridge until firm (about an hour).

American Apple Pie

SERVES 6

The pie can be served hot or cold and is traditionally served with a sharp-tasting Cheddar cheese on the side – lashings of cream are also in order.

shortcrust pastry to line a 23 cm (9 in)
  flan case and top it
900 g (2 lb) cooking apples
1$\frac{1}{2}$ tablespoons cornflour
100 g (4 oz) dark brown sugar

$\frac{1}{2}$ teaspoon ground cinnamon
$\frac{1}{2}$ teaspoon grated nutmeg
1 tablespoon lemon juice
40 g (1$\frac{1}{2}$ oz) butter
$\frac{1}{2}$ teaspoon vanilla essence

Line a flan case with thinly rolled out pastry. Peel, core and thickly slice the apples. Sieve the cornflour and add it to the apples with the brown sugar, cinnamon, nutmeg and lemon juice, tossing the ingredients to mix. Melt the butter and add the vanilla, add to the apple mixture and mix well. Pile the ingredients into the flan case. Roll out some more pastry to cover the pie, dampen the edges and press them firmly together. Prick in two or three places with a fork and bake in a hot oven (200°C / 400°F / Reg 6) for about 40 minutes, until the crust is golden brown and the apples are soft (test by sliding a sharp knife through the crust).

Apple and Mincemeat Turnovers

SERVES 6

2 large cooking apples
75 g (3 oz) granulated sugar
150 ml (¼ pt) dry white wine
3 generous tablespoons mincemeat
400 g (14 oz) packet frozen
  puff pastry, thawed

1 egg, beaten
caster sugar
cream, for serving

Peel, core and roughly chop the apples and combine them in a saucepan with the sugar and wine. Cook over a low heat until the apples are soft and the liquid has been absorbed (the apples will turn a marvellous golden colour). Combine the apples with the mincemeat, mix and leave to cool. Roll out the pastry very thinly and cut into six circles 15 cm (6 in) in diameter. Dampen the edges. Divide the apple mixture into mounds to one side of the centre of each circle and fold over the pastry. Press the edges firmly together and crimp with the back of a fork. Brush with the beaten egg and bake in a hot oven (200°C / 400°F / Reg 6) for about 20–30 minutes until well puffed and golden brown. Sprinkle with caster sugar and serve with cream.

Cherry-Picker Flan

SERVES 6

Plate 30, illustrated
facing page 209.

225 g (8 oz) shortcrust pastry
450 g (1 lb) cherries
grated rind of 1 lemon
2 tablespoons granulated sugar
3 tablespoons water

2 small eggs
100 g (4 oz) ground almonds
100 g (4 oz) caster sugar
icing sugar, for dusting

Roll out the pastry thinly and line a 25 cm (8 in) flan case with greaseproof paper. Fill with dried peas or beans and bake blind in a hot oven for 15 minutes until firm. Remove the peas and paper and leave to cool. Stone the cherries and combine them in a saucepan with the lemon rind, granulated sugar and the water. Cook the fruit over a medium heat for 5 minutes and leave to cool. Beat the eggs and mix with the ground almonds and caster sugar to make a thick paste. Arrange the cherries in the flan case, cover with the almond paste and bake in a moderately hot oven (190°C / 375°F / Reg 5) for 30 minutes until the pastry and topping are golden brown. Dust with icing sugar and serve warm.

Desserts & Baking

Pecan Pie
SERVES 6

Serve warm or cold with plenty of cream.

*shortcrust pastry to line a 23 cm (9 in)
  flan case*
175 g (6 oz) shelled pecan nuts
90 g (3½ oz) soft brown sugar
150 g (5 oz) golden syrup

175 ml (6 fl oz) maple syrup
3 eggs, beaten
½ teaspoon vanilla essence
50 g (2 oz) butter, melted

Line the flan case with thinly rolled-out pastry. Roughly chop 100 g (4 oz) of the nuts and spread them over the bottom of the case. Combine the sugar and syrups in a saucepan and heat over a low flame, stirring until the sugar has dissolved. Leave to cool and then combine with the beaten eggs, vanilla essence and melted butter and mix well. Pour the mixture over the nuts in the case and arrange the remaining halved pecan nuts in a pattern over the top. Bake in a moderately hot oven (190°C / 375°F / Reg 5) for about 40 minutes until the filling is set.

Profiteroles
SERVES 4–6

Choux pastry, which makes the gloriously sophisticated éclairs and profiteroles, is a dough the inexperienced cook believes to be difficult and arduous to make. Without an electric mixer or food processor, it is hard work to give the lightness and puffiness that is the essence of this pastry.

300 ml (½ pt) water
65 g (2½ oz) butter
200 g (7 oz) plain flour

4 large eggs
whipped cream or ice-cream
chocolate sauce

Combine the water and butter in a saucepan and heat until the butter has melted. Bring to a fast boil, remove from the stove and add the flour all at once. Beat vigorously with a wooden spoon until the mixture becomes smooth and forms a ball which comes cleanly away from the side of the pan. Beat the eggs until smooth with a rotary whisk. Add to the paste a little at a time, beating continuously until each addition has been absorbed and the mixture is no longer slippery – the final result should be elastic and light, and a small quantity pulled on a spoon should stand erect.

Push neat rounds of the paste from a dessertspoon onto a lightly oiled baking sheet. Bake in a hot oven (200°C / 400°F / Reg 6) for 10 minutes. Reduce the heat to 180°C / 350°F / Reg 4 for about 15 minutes or until the cooked shells are well risen, a uniform golden yellow, and feel light and hollow when tapped on the bottom. Turn off the oven and leave the shells, with the door open, to dry off for 10 minutes, then cool on a wire rack. Split half-way through the centres, fill the shells with whipped cream or ice-cream. Pile into a pyramid on a serving dish and pour over chocolate sauce just before serving.

Rupert's Florentine Cake

SERVES 8

175 g (6 oz) butter
175 g (6 oz) granulated sugar
2 tablespoons thick honey
50 ml (2 fl oz) double cream
25 g (1 oz) plain flour
100 g (4 oz) chopped almonds

50 g (2 oz) chopped hazelnuts
65 g (2½ oz) cut mixed peel
100g (4 oz) plain chocolate
glacé cherries
300 ml (½ pt) whipping cream

Cover three large baking sheets with non-stick baking paper. Draw an 18 cm (7 in) circle on each with a waterproof pen. Combine the butter, sugar, honey and double cream in a saucepan. Slowly bring to the boil, stirring to dissolve the sugar and melt the butter. Using a kitchen thermometer, heat to a temperature of 150°C / 300°F. Add the flour, nuts and candied peel and stir over a high heat until the mixture leaves the sides of the pan. Spread the mixture to within 2 cm (¾ in) of the drawn circles and bake in a moderately hot oven (190°C / 375°F / Reg 5) for 7 minutes. Remove from the oven, draw the mixture back into the circles with a knife where it has spread over the edge, and return to the oven for a further 7 minutes until the layers are a rich golden brown. Leave to cool, shaping the layers again if necessary with a knife, and then strip off the non-stick paper. Break up the chocolate into small pieces and melt it in a saucer placed on top of a saucepan of hot, not boiling, water. Spread the chocolate over one of the Florentine layers and decorate with glacé cherries. Whip the cream until thick and spread half on one of the plain Florentines, top with a second layer of biscuit, cover with the remaining cream and finish with the chocolate-covered layer. Serve chilled and cut into wedges.

Raspberry and Walnut Meringue Gateau

SERVES 6–8

Plate 31, illustrated facing page 224.

75 g (3 oz) shelled walnuts
   plus extra for decoration
5 egg whites
pinch salt
250 g (9 oz) granulated sugar
100 g (4 oz) plain flour

finely grated rind of 1 large lemon
2 tablespoons medium-dry sherry
300 ml (½ pt) double cream
1 tablespoon caster sugar
350 g (12 oz) raspberries

Line the base and sides of a 23 cm (9 in) loose-bottomed cake tin with non-stick baking paper. Very finely chop, mince or grind the walnuts. Whisk the egg whites and salt until the mixture forms stiff peaks. Sprinkle the sugar over the surface and whisk lightly until the sugar is incorporated into the meringue. Sprinkle the flour, walnuts and lemon rind over the top of the mixture and fold it into the egg whites with a fork until the mixture is light and mixed (you don't want to have lumps of flour but on the other hand, you want to incorporate the ingredients as gently as possible). Turn the mixture into the cake tin, banging it to settle the ingredients. Bake in a moderate oven 180°C / 350°F / Reg 4 for 40 minutes until a skewer plunged into the cake will come out clean. Leave the cake to settle in the tin for 15 minutes then turn onto a wire rack and leave to cool. Chill the cake in the refrigerator for 20 minutes and cut it in half horizontally using a sharp long-bladed knife dipped in hot water to make cutting easier.

Sprinkle the sherry over the cut sides of the gateau. Whip the cream until stiff and lightly mix in two-thirds of the sugar and the raspberries, reserving a few for decoration. Sandwich the gateau with two-thirds of the cream and top with the remaining cream. Decorate with the reserved raspberries and the walnuts. Chill before serving.

Strawberry Cream Gateau
SERVES 6–8

Puff pastry is such a time-consuming thing to make that I have no compunction in buying a frozen one and I defy anyone to tell the difference. This gateau impressed me because of its exotic appearance, which completely belies the simplicity with which it is made.

450 g (1 lb) puff pastry
300 ml (½ pt) double cream
50 g (2 oz) caster sugar
2 drops vanilla essence

450 g (1 lb) strawberries, hulled
  and sliced
icing sugar

Roll out pastry very thinly and cut into three circles about 20 cm (8 in) in diameter. Brush the surface of each with a little water and sprinkle over a very thin dusting of caster sugar. Place them on dampened baking sheets and bake in a very hot oven (230°C / 450°F / Reg 8) for 5–10 minutes until well risen and golden brown. Leave to cool on the baking sheet and then split each circle carefully in two with a long sharp knife. Whip the cream until stiff and mix in the sugar and vanilla essence. Spread pastry circles with whipped cream, cover with strawberries and sandwich the layers neatly together. Sift a little icing sugar over the top and chill in the refrigerator until ready to serve.

Desserts & Baking

Rich Fruit and Carrot Cake

150 g (5 oz) sultanas
150 g (5 oz) currants
150 g (5 oz) stoned raisins, chopped
50 g (2 oz) cut mixed peel
100 g (4 oz) glacé cherries, halved
350 g (12 oz) carrots, peeled and
 coarsely grated
50 g (2 oz) chopped almonds

$\frac{1}{2}$ teaspoon ground mace
$\frac{1}{2}$ teaspoon ground cinnamon
225 g (8 oz) plain flour
225 g (8 oz) butter
225 g (8 oz) soft brown sugar
grated rind of 1 lemon
4 large eggs
4 tablespoons brandy

Combine the fruit, carrots and nuts and mix well. Mix the spices with the flour. Cream the butter, sugar and lemon rind until light and fluffy. Beat the eggs and add them, a little at a time, to the butter and sugar mixture, beating well after each addition of egg. Mix in 2 tablespoons of the brandy and lightly fold in half the flour. Fold in the remaining flour and finally mix in the fruit mixture. Turn into a 20 cm (8 in) cake tin lined with two thicknesses of non-stick paper. Bang the tin hard to make sure all the ingredients settle without air pockets and make a small hollow in the centre. Tie two thicknesses of brown paper around the outside of the tin and put it on another two thicknesses of brown paper on a baking sheet. Bake in a slow oven (150°C / 300°F / Reg 2) for 1$\frac{1}{2}$ hours. Then cover the top with greaseproof paper to prevent any burning and continue to bake for a further 2$\frac{1}{4}$ hours until a skewer plunged into the centre comes out clean. Turn onto a rack and leave to cool. Prick the top lightly with a skewer and sprinkle with the remaining brandy.

Devonshire Apple Cake

Dorset Apple Cake is similar, but also includes 50 g (2 oz) currants and 25 g (1 oz) mixed peel; the top is sprinkled with brown sugar rather than granulated.

225 g (8 oz) self-raising flour
1 teaspoon salt
100 g (4 oz) butter
100 g (4 oz) caster sugar

450 g (1 lb) peeled, cored and
 sliced cooking apples
2 eggs, lightly beaten
25 g (1 oz) granulated sugar
jam, to fill

Mix the flour and salt, rub in the butter and add the caster sugar and apples. Add the lightly beaten eggs and spoon into two 20 cm (8 in) sandwich tins; sprinkle with granulated sugar and bake in a hot oven (200°C / 400°F / Reg 6) for 30–40 minutes. Sandwich together with jam.

Plate 31. Raspberry and Walnut Meringue Gateau

Plate 32. Cucumber Jelly, Raspberry Vinaigrette for Summer Salads

Ginger Cake

225 g (8 oz) plain flour
2 teaspoons ground ginger
1 teaspoon bicarbonate of soda
100 g (4 oz) butter
50 g (2 oz) soft brown sugar
50 g (2 oz) black treacle

175 g (6 oz) golden syrup
150 ml ($\frac{1}{4}$ pt) milk
2 eggs
75 g (3 oz) blanched almonds,
  finely chopped
50 g (2 oz) preserved ginger, chopped

Sift flour, ginger and bicarbonate of soda into a bowl. In a saucepan, gently warm butter, sugar, treacle and syrup until butter is melted. Stir in milk then cool. Beat eggs and mix into cooled mixture. Add this to the flour, blending in with a wooden spoon. Stir in chopped almonds and ginger. Pour into a greased, lined 20 cm (8 in) square cake tin. Bake in the centre of a slow oven 150°C / 300°F / Reg 2 for 1$\frac{1}{4}$ hours. Remove from tin when cool and leave at least one day before cutting.

Easter Fruit Cake

These quantities are for two cakes.

150 g (5 oz) softened butter
150 g (5 oz) lard
100 g (4 oz) caster sugar
75 g (3 oz) soft dark brown sugar
5 eggs, beaten
350 g (12 oz) self-raising flour

350 g (12 oz) raisins
50 g (2 oz) glacé cherries
75 g (3 oz) walnuts
grated rind of 1 orange
75 g (3 oz) ground almonds

Cream the butter and lard with the sugars until smooth and fluffy. Beat the eggs into the butter and sugar. Gradually mix in the flour. Add the raisins, cherries, walnuts, orange rind and ground almonds and mix well. Turn into two well-oiled and floured 26 × 9 cm (10$\frac{1}{2}$ × 3$\frac{1}{2}$ in) loaf tins and bake in a moderately slow oven (170°C / 325°F / Reg 3) for about an hour, until a skewer plunged into the centre of the cakes comes out clean. Turn out onto wire racks and store, when cool, in airtight tins.

Desserts & Baking

Lucy's Rich Currant Bread

Serve this warm, cut into slices spread with butter, or treat it just like a rich fruit cake. It's deliciously rich and everyone loves it.

50 g (2 oz) butter	1 teaspoon mixed spice
450 g (1 lb) sultanas	1 teaspoon ground cinnamon
450 ml ($\frac{3}{4}$ pt) water	350 g (12 oz) whole wheat flour
350 g (12 oz) soft brown sugar	2 teaspoons baking powder

Combine the butter, sultanas, water and sugar with the spice and cinnamon in a saucepan, bring to the boil and boil over a high heat for 5 minutes. Remove from the heat and leave to cool. Mix in the flour and baking powder. Divide the mixture between two well-greased and floured loaf tins and bake in a moderate oven (180°C / 350°F / Reg 4) for about $1\frac{1}{4}$ hours or until a skewer plunged into the loaves comes out clean.

Banana Bread

This is best eaten warm, cut into thick slices with plenty of soft butter.

3 ripe bananas	225 g (8 oz) plain flour
100 g (4 oz) butter	1 teaspoon bicarbonate of soda
225 g (8 oz) caster sugar	pinch salt
2 eggs, lightly beaten	

Mash the bananas until smooth. Cream together the butter and sugar until light, smooth and fluffy. Add the eggs and bananas and mix well. Sift the flour, bicarbonate of soda and salt. Add to the banana mixture a little at a time, folding lightly until the ingredients are well mixed. Turn into a well-oiled loaf tin and bake in a moderate oven (180°C / 350°F / Reg 4) for about an hour until a skewer plunged into the middle will come out clean.

Potato Cakes

450 g (1 lb) mashed potatoes	2 tablespoons plain flour
15 g ($\frac{1}{2}$ oz) melted butter	salt and freshly ground black pepper
1 tablespoon grated raw onion	lard or dripping for frying

Mix the mashed potatoes with the melted butter, grated onion and flour. Season with salt and pepper. Shape the potato mixture into a roll on a well-floured board and cut into 2.5 cm (1 in) thick slices. Press the slices into flat cakes about 1 cm ($\frac{1}{2}$ in) thick. Fry in hot fat until brown on both sides. The potato cakes will retain their shape a lot better if they are chilled for an hour or more before frying.

Desserts & Baking

Almond Shortbread

150 g (5 oz) plain flour
25 g (1 oz) ground rice
50 g (2 oz) caster sugar

pinch salt
100 g (4 oz) butter
40 g (1½ oz) flaked almonds

Combine flour, ground rice, sugar and salt in a bowl and mix well. Add the butter, taken straight from the fridge and grated into flakes through the coarse blades of a grater. Rub the butter into the flour mixture using the fingertips until the mixture resembles fine breadcrumbs. Press the mixture firmly into an 18 cm (7 in) sandwich tin patting down until flat. Prick the top with a fork and with a knife mark into 8 even slices. Sprinkle over flaked almonds, cover with a circle of greaseproof paper and chill in the refrigerator for 1 hour before baking. Bake in a slow oven 150°C / 300°F / Reg 2) for an hour; remove the greaseproof paper for the last 15 minutes of baking time. Cool in the tin, turn onto a wire rack and break into pieces when cold. The shortbread can be dusted with sugar before serving.

Orange Almond Flapjacks

Flapjacks have always been amongst my favourite teatime treats and they couldn't be easier to make. In this recipe I have added variety by including some chopped almonds and orange peel to the ingredients; they are so popular they disappear like magic into hungry mouths.

100 g (4 oz) golden syrup
75 g (3 oz) butter
50 g (2 oz) soft brown sugar

175 g (6 oz) rolled oats
50 g (2 oz) chopped almonds
grated rind of 2 oranges

Combine the syrup and butter in a saucepan and cook gently until the butter is melted. Mix in the sugar, cook for a further 2 minutes and stir in the oats, nuts and orange rind. Pour the mixture into a well-greased tin measuring about 28 × 18 cm (11 × 7 in) and press down firmly with the back of a wooden spoon. Bake in a moderate oven (180°C / 350°F / Reg 4) for 30 minutes until golden brown. Remove from the oven and cut, while still hot, into neat finger slices about 2.5 cm (1 in) wide. Cool in the tin and turn out when hard.

Desserts & Baking

Alpenjacks

100 g (4 oz) soft brown sugar
100 g (4 oz) butter
1 tablespoon golden syrup

175 g (6 oz) muesli
¼ teaspoon ground ginger
pinch ground cinnamon

Combine the sugar, butter and syrup in a saucepan and heat over a low flame, stirring occasionally, until the butter has melted. Mix well and stir in the muesli, ginger and cinnamon, mixing well to combine all the ingredients. Spoon the mixture into a well-greased shallow baking tin and spread it out thinly to the depth of about 1 cm (½ in). Press the mixture down firmly and evenly. Bake the Alpenjacks in a slow oven (150°C / 300°F / Reg 2) for 45 minutes. Leave the mixture in the tin for about 10 minutes to settle, cut into squares and leave to set firm.

Sweet Sultana Scones

225 g (8 oz) plain flour
2½ teaspoons baking powder
40 g (1½ oz) sugar
40 g (1½ oz) butter)

50 g (2 oz) sultanas
150 ml (¼ pt) milk
plus extra for brushing
1 small egg

Sieve the flour, baking powder and sugar into a bowl. Add the butter cut into small pieces and rub it into the dry ingredients until the mixture resembles coarse breadcrumbs. Stir in the sultanas and mix to a dough with the milk beaten with the egg. Press out the dough on a floured board to a thickness of 1 cm (½ in) and cut into circles with a pastry cutter. Brush the tops with a little extra milk and bake in a very hot oven (230°C / 450°F / Reg 8) for 8 minutes until well-risen and golden brown. Leave the scones to cool for a few minutes. Split them and spread each half generously with butter and serve.

Drop Scones

2 tablespoons golden syrup
2 eggs
450 g (1 lb) plain flour
1 teaspoon baking powder

pinch salt
75 g (3 oz) caster sugar
300 ml (½ pt) milk
oil for frying

Warm the syrup intil runny. Beat the eggs until smooth. Combine the syrup and eggs with the remaining ingredients (except the oil) and beat with a rotary whisk until smooth. Put a heavy pan (preferably a cast-iron frying-pan) over a high heat and rub it with kitchen paper dipped in oil. When the oil is smoking, drop tablespoons of the batter onto the pan in circles, cook until bubbles appear, turn over and press down lightly with a fish slice and cook until the underside is golden, and the scones are firm all the way through. As soon as each batch is cooked wrap in a napkin and keep warm while you make the rest.

Desserts & Baking

Bread Rolls

150 ml ($\frac{1}{4}$ pt) milk
25 g (1 oz) butter
150 ml ($\frac{1}{4}$ pt) water
20 g ($\frac{3}{4}$ oz) fresh yeast

1 teaspoon sugar
450 g (1 lb) plain flour
1 teaspoon salt
1 egg, beaten

Heat the milk, butter and water together in a saucepan until the butter is melted. Cream the yeast and sugar together. Add the warm liquid and leave for 5 minutes. Sift the flour and salt together. Add half the flour to the yeast and liquid and beat until a smooth batter is formed. Add the rest of the flour and beat in. Turn the dough onto a floured board and knead for 10 minutes until smooth and elastic. Put the dough in an oiled bowl. Turn, to make sure the surface of the dough is well-oiled. Cover with a cloth and leave in a warm place for 40 minutes or until doubled in bulk. Punch down the dough. Knead lightly and form into 20 small rolls. Place on a greased baking sheet. Cover and leave in a warm place for a further 20 minutes or until again doubled in size. Brush with beaten egg and bake in a hot oven (220°C / 425°F / Reg 7) for 15 minutes. For immediate use cook for a further 5 minutes or so until golden brown. To freeze: cool after 15 minutes. Pack in polythene bags, seal and label. To use: place frozen rolls on a baking sheet. Bake in a hot oven (220°C / 425°F / Reg 7) for 10 minutes or until golden brown.

French Bread

450 g (1 lb) plain flour
1 teaspoon salt
25 g (1 oz) butter
25 g (1 oz) fresh yeast

1 teaspoon sugar
300 ml ($\frac{1}{2}$ pt) warm milk
2 eggs
a little melted butter

Sift the flour and salt into a large bowl. Rub in the butter with the fingertips and place in a slow oven for 3 minutes to warm. Cream the yeast and sugar. Stir in the warm milk and 1 beaten egg. Add the liquid to the flour and beat well. Turn onto a board and knead until smooth. Grease a bowl with melted butter. Put in the dough . Brush the top with melted butter. Cover and leave to rise in a warm place for about an hour until doubled in bulk. Shape into plaits or long rolls. Leave to prove on a greased baking sheet for 10 minutes. Brush with beaten egg and bake in a hot oven (200°C / 400°F / Reg 6) for 20 minutes until golden brown.

Scottish Baps

300 ml (½ pt) milk and water
  combined
25 g (1 oz) fresh yeast
1 teaspoon caster sugar
450 g (1 lb) plain flour

large pinch salt
25 g (1 oz) butter
25 g (1 oz) lard
milk for glazing or flour
  for dusting

Heat the milk and water to blood temperature. Cream the yeast with the sugar and gradually add the liquid, stirring well until the mixture is smooth. Leave the yeast mixture in a warm place until foaming. Sieve the flour and salt into a warmed mixing bowl and rub the butter and lard (cut into small pieces) with the fingertips until the mixture resembles coarse breadcrumbs. Make a well in the centre of the flour mixture, add the yeast and work it into the flour with a spoon. Knead the dough and then turn it onto a floured board and knead again for a few minutes until smooth. Place the dough in an oiled basin, cover with a cloth and leave to rise in a warm, draught-free place for about an hour until doubled in size. Turn out the dough onto a floured surface, knead lightly this time and shape into rounds about 7.5 cm (3 in) in diameter. Place on an oiled baking sheet, and brush with milk or dust with flour, leave to rise for 20 minutes, press a finger into the centre of each bap and then bake in a hot oven (200°C / 400°F / Reg 6) for 15 minutes until golden.

Your Own Hot Cross Buns

1 teaspoon and 3 tablespoons
  clear honey
100 ml (4 fl oz) milk
1 tablespoon dried yeast
350 g (12 oz) strong white flour
½ teaspoon salt
1 teaspoon mixed spice

½ teaspoon ground cinnamon
65 g (2½ oz) butter
1 egg, beaten
75 g (3 oz) mixed dried fruit
shortcrust pastry for making crosses
1 tablespoon milk
1 tablespoon caster sugar

Combine 1 teaspoon honey with 3 tablespoons warm milk and mix in the yeast. Leave in a warm place until foaming. Combine flour, salt and spices in a large bowl and leave in a warm place until yeast mixture is ready. Combine remaining milk and honey with butter and heat to blood temperature. Add yeast, beaten egg and warm milk mixture to flour. Mix well and work into soft dough. Knead for 5 minutes, place in buttered bowl, cover and leave to rise in warm draught-proof place for about 40 minutes until dough has doubled its size. Add the dried fruit and knead well. Divide into 12 balls and press into bun shapes. Place on baking sheets, well spaced out, cover with a floured cloth and leave to rise again for 20 minutes. Cut pastry into thin strips, dampen and place a cross on top of the risen buns. Bake in a hot oven (220°C / 425°F / Reg 7) for 15 minutes until golden. Brush with milk and sugar and cool.

Sauces & Preserves

White Sauce

A white sauce forms the basis of a good many other classic sauces and, providing the right procedure is followed, is quick and easy to make. Many cookery books recommend taking the saucepan from the stove once you have formed a roux from butter and flour but I find this tends to make the sauce lumpy. I make my white sauces over a hot flame stirring vigorously to prevent the sauce colouring.

25 g (1 oz) butter
2 tablespoons flour

300 ml (½ pt) milk
salt and white pepper

Melt the butter in a small saucepan. Add the flour and stir with a wooden spoon until the mixture forms a ball and comes cleanly away from the sides of the pan. Gradually beat in the milk, stirring continuously over a high heat until the sauce is thick and smooth. Lower the heat and simmer gently, stirring for 3 minutes. Season with salt and pepper.

Variations
Use half stock and half milk.
Enrich the sauce by beating 1 egg yolk and 2 tablespoons of double cream into the finished sauce and stirring over a low heat until thick and shining.
Give extra flavour by simmering the milk with an onion and bouquet garni before straining it and adding it to the sauce.
Some white wine can be used to replace some of the milk.

Lemon Sauce with Fresh Tarragon

This sauce goes well with egg, fish and chicken dishes and can be used to pep up cold tongue or ham.

40 g (1½ oz) butter
1 tablespoon flour
300 ml (½ pt) milk or half milk
  half chicken stock
2 teaspoons lemon juice

2 tablespoons finely chopped tarragon
salt and freshly ground black pepper
1 egg yolk
1–2 tablespoons double cream

Melt the butter in a saucepan, add the flour and mix well. Gradually beat in the milk (or milk and stock) stirring continuously over a medium heat until the sauce comes to the boil and is thick and smooth. Add the lemon juice and tarragon, salt and pepper, and simmer gently for 4 minutes. Beat the egg yolk with the cream, add the mixture to the sauce and mix well, stirring continuously over a low heat – do not allow to boil.

Mustard Sauce

To serve with pork, bacon or ham dishes.

300 ml (½ pt) milk
1 slice onion
1 slice carrot
1 bay leaf
sprig of parsley
small pinch grated nutmeg

salt and freshly ground black pepper
25 g (1 oz) butter
1½ tablespoons flour
2 teaspoons Dijon mustard
5 tablespoons double cream

Combine the milk in a pan with the onion, carrot, bay leaf, parsley, nutmeg and seasoning. Bring to just under boiling point, as slowly as possible to allow the flavouring ingredients to infuse into the milk. Remove from the heat and strain through a fine sieve. In a clean pan, melt the butter, add the flour, mix well and gradually add the warm milk, stirring continuously over a medium heat until the sauce comes to the boil and is thick and smooth. Blend in the mustard and simmer very gently for 3 minutes. Whip the cream until thick and whisk it into the sauce.

Olive and Almond Sauce

This sauce adds piquancy to any plain grilled or poached fish.

40 g (1½ oz) butter
3 tablespoons flour
300 ml (½ pt) chicken stock
8 olives

150 ml (¼ pt) single cream
½ tablespoon lemon juice
50 g (2 oz) shredded almonds
salt and white pepper

Melt the butter in a saucepan. Add the flour, mix well and gradually blend in the stock. Stir continually over a medium heat until the sauce is thick and smooth. Simmer for 3 minutes. Stone the olives and cut the flesh into thin strips. Add the cream to the sauce (do not boil) and mix with the lemon juice, almonds and olives. Season with salt and pepper.

Egg Sauce

An old-fashioned English sauce which is delicious with fish.

2 hard-boiled eggs
1 small onion
40 g (1½ oz) butter
1 tablespoon flour

300 ml (½ pt) milk
1 teaspoon made English mustard
salt and freshly ground black pepper
2 tablespoons finely chopped parsley

Chop the hard-boiled eggs. Peel and very finely chop the onion. Melt the butter in a saucepan. Add the onion and cook over a low heat until soft and transparent. Add the flour and mix well. Gradually blend in the milk, stirring continually until the sauce is thick and smooth. Add the mustard, season with salt and pepper, bring to the boil and simmer for 3 minutes. Fold in the hard-boiled eggs and parsley and serve at once.

Special Apple Sauce

A special sauce to serve with pork or duck that has far more flavour than the rather insipid concoction that is usually unstrained apple purée. I use Cox's apples in this recipe, finding the slightly sharp and well-knit texture of the fruit ideal for cooking.

4 Cox's apples
2 tablespoons water
1 teaspoon lemon juice
40 g (1½ oz) butter

2 tablespoons redcurrant jelly
¼ teaspoon sage
salt and white pepper

Peel, core and roughly chop the apples. Combine with the water and lemon juice in a small, heavy saucepan. Bring to the boil, cover tightly and simmer gently until the apples are soft. Beat the apples to a purée with a wooden spoon, blend in the butter, redcurrant jelly and sage and stir over a low heat until the jelly has melted. Simmer for a further 10 minutes to allow the flavour of the sage to infuse into the sauce. Season lightly with salt and pepper.

Sauce Infernale

A delicious accompaniment which adds excitement to roast game, roast chicken, steak or even hamburgers.

1 chicken liver
2 teaspoons finely chopped parsley
2 teaspoons finely grated lemon rind
1 very finely chopped shallot
6 tablespoons red wine

1 teaspoon Dijon mustard
2 teaspoons lemon juice
salt and freshly ground black pepper
pan juices from roast or fried meat

Finely chop the liver and mash it with a fork. Add all the ingredients to the juices left in the pan from the roast game, poultry, steak or hamburgers. Mix really well and simmer for 3 minutes.

Sauce Finiste

Serve this quickly made sauce with grilled meat or fish.

225 g (8 oz) tin tomatoes
40 g (1½ oz) butter
¼ teaspoon made English mustard

pinch cayenne pepper
1 teaspoon lemon juice
1½ teaspoons Worcestershire sauce

Drain and reserve the juice of the tomatoes and finely chop the flesh. Heat the butter in a saucepan until brown and add the remaining ingredients and the tomato juice. Mix well and simmer for 5 minutes.

Bread Sauce

To serve with poultry.

1 onion	75 g (3 oz) white breadcrumbs
2 cloves	15 g ($\frac{1}{2}$ oz) butter
450 ml ($\frac{3}{4}$ pt) milk	$\frac{1}{2}$ teaspoon finely grated lemon rind
5 peppercorns	pinch grated nutmeg
salt	pinch dried mixed herbs
1 bay leaf	

Remove onion skin and stick the cloves into the onion. Combine the onion, milk, peppercorns and a little salt in a saucepan with the bay leaf. Bring slowly to boiling point and then leave to stand in a warm place for 20 minutes to allow the flavours of the onion, cloves and bay leaf to infuse into the milk. Strain into a clean pan. Return the onion to the milk and add the breadcrumbs, butter, lemon rind and a tiny pinch of grated nutmeg and mixed herbs. Cook slowly over a low heat for 15 minutes. Remove the onion, mix the sauce well with a wooden spoon and check to see if it needs more salt.

Shrimp and Butter Sauce

To serve with plainly cooked fish.

1 small carton potted shrimps	1 tablespoon very finely chopped
50 g (2 oz) butter	parsley
juice of $\frac{1}{2}$ lemon	salt and freshly ground black pepper

Thaw the potted shrimps completely if they are frozen. Heat the butter until melted but do not allow to brown. Add the potted shrimps and stir continuously over a low heat until the butter from the shrimps has also melted. Add the lemon juice and parsley, check the seasoning and serve at once.

Caucasian Sauce

A colourful alternative to the more mundane horseradish sauce, to serve with roast beef, smoked mackerel or smoked trout.

2 tablespoons redcurrant jelly	salt and freshly ground black pepper
1 teaspoon made English mustard	150 ml ($\frac{1}{4}$ pt) sour cream
1 tablespoon horseradish sauce	

Melt the redcurrant jelly over a low heat until liquid. Cool and mix in the mustard and horseradish sauce. Season with salt and pepper and fold in the sour cream.

Sauces & Preserves

Cumberland Sauce

Traditionally, this accompanies lamb.

1 lemon
1 orange
100 g (4 oz) redcurrant jelly

1 tablespoon Dijon mustard
150 ml ($\frac{1}{4}$ pt) port
salt and freshly ground black pepper

Thinly remove the rind from the lemon and orange with a potato peeler and cut the rind into very thin julienne strips. Squeeze the juice of the orange and of half the lemon. Blanch the peel in boiling water for 5 minutes and drain well. Combine the redcurrant jelly, mustard, port, rinds and fruit juice in a saucepan, season with salt and pepper and heat through, stirring until the jelly has all melted. Bring to the boil and then remove from the heat and leave to cool.

Maltese Tomato Sauce

Serve with pasta or try serving it with haddock or cod.

400 g (14 oz) tin tomatoes
3 cloves garlic
2 small red chilli peppers
  (fresh or dried)
1 tablespoon olive oil
pinch thyme

pinch sage
2 bay leaves
1 tablespoon finely chopped mint
1 tablespoon tomato purée
1 tablespoon capers
salt

Finely chop the tomatoes, reserving all the juice. Peel and very finely chop the garlic cloves. Finely chop the red chilli (wash your hands immediately as the chilli sticks to your fingers, and if it gets into your eyes, it can be extremely uncomfortable). Heat the oil, add the garlic and cook over a very low heat for 2 minutes. Add the remaining ingredients, season with a little salt, mix well and simmer slowly for 20 minutes. Remove the bay leaves before serving.

Sharp Tomato Barbecue Sauce

This quick, extremely delicious and sharp sauce is easiest made in a blender. It is ideal to serve with any barbecued or grilled meat or fish.

1 onion
2 cloves garlic
225 g (8 oz) tin tomatoes

salt and freshly ground black pepper
$\frac{1}{4}$ teaspoon oregano
2 teaspoons vinegar

Combine the onion and garlic cloves and tomatoes in a blender until the onion is very finely chopped. Transfer to a saucepan, season with salt and pepper, add oregano and vinegar and simmer over a low heat for 30 minutes.

Speedy Spaghetti Sauce

Serve this sauce with spaghetti and sprinkle with Parmesan cheese.

1 large onion
1–2 cloves garlic
2 tablespoons olive oil
4 anchovy fillets
400 g (14 oz) tin tomatoes
1 tablespoon tomato purée

450 g (1 lb) minced beef
4 tablespoons red wine
¼ tablespoon dried mixed herbs
½ beef stock cube
freshly ground black pepper

Peel and finely chop the onion. Crush the garlic. Heat the oil in a saucepan. Add the onion and garlic and cook over a low heat until soft and transparent. Drain the oil from the anchovies and very finely chop the fillets. Add the tomatoes, tomato purée, minced meat and wine to the onions and mix well. Stir in the anchovy fillets, herbs and stock cube, bring to the boil and simmer for 20 minutes, stirring occasionally. Season with pepper.

Chive Sauce

100 g (4 oz) unsalted butter
1 tablespoon finely chopped shallot
4 tablespoons dry white wine

2 tablespoons double cream
salt and freshly ground black pepper
1 bunch chives, chopped

Put 15 g (½ oz) butter in a small saucepan over a moderate heat, add the shallot, then cook slowly for a minute without colouring. Add the white wine and then the cream, bring to the boil and reduce by half. When reduced, turn the heat down and slowly whisk in the remaining butter in pieces until it is incorporated in the sauce. Season with salt and pepper, add the chives and serve.

Hollandaise Sauce

To serve with any vegetable.

4 egg yolks
3 tablespoons boiling water
175 g (6 oz) softened unsalted butter

1 tablespoon lemon juice
salt and white pepper

Whisk the egg yolks with 1 tablespoon of boiling water in the top of a double saucepan over hot, not boiling, water for 3 minutes. Gradually whisk in the softened butter, a teaspoon at a time, allowing the egg yolk and butter to emulsify before the addition of more butter. When all the butter has been used, add the remaining boiling water and beat in the lemon juice. Season with salt and pepper and pour it over cooked, well-drained vegetables. Ideally the sauce should be served at once, but if you do have to keep it, cover with a lid and leave it over warm water. If your sauce should curdle because you hurried too much or used too high a heat, it can quickly be re-emulsified by adding a few teaspoons of boiling water and beating vigorously.

Beurre Blanc

This classic French sauce is a winner for almost all poached fish.

1 shallot or small onion
2 tablespoons white wine vinegar

salt and white pepper
150 g (5 oz) butter

Peel and finely chop the shallot. Combine the shallot and vinegar in a saucepan, season with salt and pepper and cook over a high heat until the liquid is reduced to about a quarter. Add a quarter of the butter and mix well, keeping the pan over the heat. Bring to the boil, remove immediately and add the remaining butter, a little at a time, cut into small pieces, whisking with a wire whisk. The sauce should thicken and become the consistency of thin mayonnaise.

Sancréed Sauce

Serve this delicious sauce with cold smoked mackerel.

½ cucumber
salt
150 ml (¼ pt) double cream
2 tablespoons Dijon mustard

2 tablespoons horseradish sauce
1 tablespoon finely chopped chives
*   or spring onion tops*
freshly ground black pepper

Peel the cucumber and grate the flesh through a coarse grater, sprinkle with a little salt and leave to sweat in a colander or sieve for 30 minutes. Squeeze off any excess liquid and pat dry on kitchen paper. Lightly whip the cream until thick but not stiff. Mix in the mustard and horseradish sauce and fold in the cucumber and chives. Season and chill.

Sauces & Preserves

Seafood Sauce

Serve this instead of tartare sauce with hot or cold fish. It will make even mundane fried frozen fish fingers seem like something worthy of a four-star restaurant.

2 egg yolks
1 teaspoon mustard
salt and freshly ground black pepper
½ tablespoon lemon juice
1 tablespoon finely chopped dill weed

300–450 ml (½–¾ pt) olive oil
2 tablespoons finely chopped sweet
 pickles
1 teaspoon finely chopped parsley
1 teaspoon finely chopped capers

Beat the egg yolks with the mustard, a little salt and pepper and a drop of the lemon juice, until smooth and shiny. Soak the dill weed in the remaining juice. Gradually blend the olive oil, drop by drop, into the egg yolk mixture, beating like mad until a stiff mayonnaise is formed. When all the oil has been used up, mix in the dill weed with lemon juice, sweet pickles, parsley and capers. Check for seasoning, add a little more lemon juice if necessary and keep cool until the sauce is to be used.

Tartare Sauce

A delicious sauce for fish.

2 tablespoons capers
2 gherkins
300 ml (½ pt) lemon-flavoured
 mayonnaise

2 tablespoons finely chopped chives
1 teaspoon Dijon mustard
salt and freshly ground black pepper

Very finely chop the capers and gherkins and add them to the mayonnaise with the chives and mustard. Mix well and season if necessary with salt and pepper.

Vera's Mayonnaise Sauce

Lobster, crab and all shellfish are so rich in flavour that sometimes a plain home-made mayonnaise can be a little too bland. This is a sharper sauce with a bit of a bite to it to give the extra contrast needed.

300 ml (½ pt) home-made mayonnaise
2 tablespoons Dijon mustard
1 tablespoon tomato ketchup
½ teaspoon dried dill weed

2 drops Tabasco or chilli sauce
salt and freshly ground black pepper
juice of ½ lemon

Add the ingredients to the mayonnaise and mix well. Leave to stand in a cool place for about an hour before serving.

Sauces & Preserves

Pinkerton Sauce

Serve with a seafood cocktail.

1 clove garlic
2 tablespoons mango chutney or
  sweet pickle
1 teaspoon grated raw onion
1 tablespoon tomato ketchup

1 tablespoon finely chopped green
  or red pepper
200 ml (7 fl oz) mayonnaise
few drops Worcestershire sauce
  (optional)

Peel the garlic clove and squeeze through a garlic press or crush with a fork. Chop the chutney until fine. Add the onion, garlic, tomato ketchup, pepper and chutney to the mayonnaise and mix well. If a really piquant flavour is required mix in a few drops of Worcestershire sauce.

Spiky Sauce

This goes equally well with charcoal-grilled steak or hamburgers.

4 sprigs parsley
8 pimiento-stuffed olives
1 teaspoon capers
1 small garlic clove

1 teaspoon finely grated raw onion
1 teaspoon made English mustard
300 ml ($\frac{1}{2}$ pt) home-made mayonnaise
salt and freshly ground black pepper

Remove stalks from the parsley and finely chop the leaves. Very finely chop the olives and capers. Squeeze the garlic through a garlic press or crush with a fork. Combine all ingredients, mix well and season.

Sauce Selina

A sauce more subtle than tartare sauce to serve with fried fish.

2 egg yolks
freshly ground black pepper
$\frac{1}{2}$ teaspoon dry English mustard
300 ml ($\frac{1}{2}$ pt) olive oil
2 sprigs parsley
$\frac{1}{4}$ teaspoon tarragon
1 teaspoon lemon juice

1 tablespoon finely chopped capers
1 tablespoon finely chopped green
  pepper
1 tablespoon finely chopped chives
1 finely chopped anchovy fillet
pinch cayenne pepper

Beat the egg yolks until smooth. Season with pepper and add the mustard. Gradually beat in the olive oil, drop by drop at first, then a teaspoon at a time, until the sauce thickens and emulsifies after each addition of oil. Blanch the parsley sprigs in boiling water for 2 minutes, then drain and chop very finely. Soak the tarragon in lemon juice for 5 minutes. Beat the tarragon and lemon juice a little at a time into the egg-oil mixture. Mix in the capers, green pepper, chives and chopped anchovy fillet. Add a pinch of cayenne, check the seasoning and leave to stand for at least 15 minutes to mature before serving.

Smetana Dressing

This can be used on mixed salads but goes especially well with cold chicken or meat salads – try a combination of cold chicken, diced apple and cooked, diced new potatoes.

½ *bunch watercress*
½ *teaspoon lemon juice*
about 5 tablespoons milk

150 ml (¼ pt) sour cream
salt and freshly ground black pepper
50 g (2 oz) chopped walnuts

Remove the stalks from the watercress (add these to stock for flavouring) and finely chop the leaves. Blend the lemon juice and milk with the sour cream and season with salt and pepper. Fold in the watercress and walnuts and refrigerate for about 30 minutes before serving. If the dressing is too thick add a little extra milk.

Slimline Salad Dressing

150 ml (¼ pt) yoghourt
1 teaspoon grated raw onion
1 teaspoon lemon juice
1 teaspoon made English mustard

2 teaspoons finely chopped mint
1 teaspoon finely chopped fresh tarragon
salt, pepper and a pinch cayenne

Combine all the ingredients, season, mix well and chill before serving.

Raspberry Vinaigrette for Summer Salads

Plate 32, illustrated facing page 225.

Use the dressing for a crisp mixed green salad of shredded cos and round lettuce. Extra dressing can be stored in a screw-top jar in the refrigerator.

175 g (6 oz) fresh or frozen raspberries
3 tablespoons water
1 teaspoon white wine vinegar
½ *teaspoon dry English mustard*

3 tablespoons olive or sunflower oil
½ *teaspoon sugar*
salt and freshly ground black pepper
pinch dried mixed herbs

Combine the raspberries and water in a saucepan, bring to the boil and simmer until the fruit is tender. Rub through a fine sieve to extract the juice. Combine all the ingredients in a screw-top jar and shake well until mixed.

Devonshire Clotted Cream

2.4 litres (4 pints) gold top milk or rich, creamy fresh milk

Put the milk into a large enamel bowl that can be put over a flame (or use a flameproof dish) and leave to settle in a cool place for 24 hours until all the cream has risen and settled on the surface. Put the milk over a *very* low heat until bubbles rise to the surface forming a ring around the top of the pan (this is one of those pieces of cooking magic that it is impossible to describe but you will see the ring, the same size as the bottom of the pan, clearly as it forms). The length of time this takes depends on the depth of the pan, but on no account must the milk be allowed to boil. Carefully remove the pan from the heat and leave it in a cool place to settle for a further 24 hours. Use a slotted spoon, carefully skim off the crusty cream from the top of the pan and put it in a bowl, keeping it in the refrigerator until it is required. Use the buttermilk or skimmed milk from below the cream for baking or for soups or sauces.

Butterscotch and Almond Sauce

A rich, glistening sauce which needs long cooking. Serve it hot or cold over vanilla, chocolate or coffee ice-cream.

100 g (4 oz) unsalted butter
150 g (5 oz) soft brown sugar
1 tablespoon lemon juice

150 ml ($\frac{1}{4}$ pt) double cream
50 g (2 oz) slivered blanched almonds
2 drops vanilla essence (optional)

Cut the butter into small pieces and combine it in the top of a double saucepan with the sugar, lemon juice and cream. Stir over hot, not boiling, water until the butter has melted. Cook over a low heat for 30–45 minutes, stirring occasionally, until the sauce is thick and shining. Toast the almonds under a hot grill until golden brown. Add the vanilla essence, if used.

Brandy Butter

Serve hot with mince pies.

75 g (3 oz) unsalted butter, softened
75 g (3 oz) icing sugar

3 tablespoons brandy

Beat the butter well, gradually adding the sugar and continuing to beat until the butter is almost white and very fluffy. Gradually add the brandy, still beating all the time.

Egg Custard Sauce

Quite a different thing altogether from powdered or tinned custard and delicious to serve with old-fashioned steamed puddings.

2 eggs
1 tablespoon caster sugar

300 ml (½ pt) milk
2 drops vanilla essence

Whisk the eggs and sugar together until smooth and creamy but do not allow to become frothy. Heat the milk to just below boiling point and add to the mixture, stirring. Stir in the vanilla. Pour into a heavy saucepan and cook over gentle heat, stirring constantly, until the custard is thick enough to coat the back of a spoon.

Pear and Ginger Sauce

A delicious concoction to pour over ice-cream or pancakes.

2 ripe pears
75 g (3 oz) preserved ginger in syrup

165 g (6 oz) golden syrup
½ teaspoon ground ginger

Peel and halve the pears, remove the cores and cut the flesh into small dice. Finely chop the preserved ginger. Pour the golden syrup into a saucepan, heat until melted and mix in the ground ginger. Add the pear and ginger pieces and cook over a low heat for about 15 minutes until the pear is soft but still firm. Serve hot.

Caramel Sauce

This is the simplest of sauces good for serving over ice-cream, a baked custard or even to disguise broken meringues.

225 g (8 oz) granulated sugar
4 tablespoons water

juice of ½ lemon

Put the sugar in a heavy-based saucepan and cook without stirring over a medium heat until it melts and turns a dark brown, about 5 minutes. Add the water taking care that you do not burn your hand as the mixture will bubble up. Stir over the heat until smooth and then add the lemon juice, mixing it well in.

Creamy Marmalade Sauce

This is delicious served with steamed puddings.

2 tablespoons marmalade   *1 tablespoon brandy*
5 tablespoons double cream

Combine the marmalade and cream in a saucepan and heat over a low flame, stirring continuously, until the marmalade has melted. Do not allow the sauce to boil. Stir in the brandy and serve.

Basic Orange Marmalade

MAKES ABOUT
4 kg (9 lbs)

1.5 kg (3 lb) Seville oranges   *3.6 litres (6 pts) water*
(6–10 oranges)   *2.7 kg (6 lb) granulated sugar*

Cut the oranges in half and remove the pithy core and pips. Slice the halved oranges thinly. Tie the pips and pith in a piece of muslin and add it to the oranges in a large heavy pan about double the size of its ingredients. Cover with the water and leave to stand overnight. Bring to the boil and simmer for 1 hour until the fruit is tender. Remove muslin bag, pressing it against the pan with a wooden spoon to extract the juices. Add the sugar to the oranges, stir over a medium heat until all the sugar has dissolved. Bring to the boil and cook over the highest possible heat for about 20 mintues or until a little of the marmalade put onto a cold saucer will set firmly. Leave to cool, stir well and then put in scrupulously clean jars, cover with waxed discs and exclude all air by a layer of self sealing covers. You can always store oranges during a glut in the freezer until you are ready to tackle the time-consuming process of marmalade making. They can be frozen whole (wipe with a damp cloth and pack in polythene bags). For easier handling slice oranges that have been frozen before they are completely thawed.

Budget Breakfast Preserve

MAKES
2.3 kg (5 lb)

1 lemon
2 grapefruit skins
2 orange skins

900 g (2 lb) windfall apples
1½ teaspoons ground ginger
1.5 kg (3 lb) sugar

Squeeze the lemon and reserve the juice. Chop all the citrus peel and simmer in 600 ml (1 pt) of the water in a covered pan. When tender add chopped apples and cook until apples are tender. Mix ginger with sugar and stir into boiling fruit. Add lemon juice and boil gently for 30 minutes. Bottle in the usual way.

Rhubarb and Mint Jam

MAKES
1 kg (2 lb)

For an extra minty flavour a little finely chopped fresh mint can be added to the jelly.

900 g (2 lb) young rhubarb
700 (1½ lb) sugar

3 sprigs mint

Wash and chop the rhubarb. Put it in a saucepan with a little water to prevent it sticking to the pan and cook for about 15 minutes until the fruit is pulpy (the time for this varies according to the tenderness of the fruit used). Stir the fruit well, and add the sugar and mint. Bring to the boil and cook until the jelly thickens, remove mint and leave to cool before pouring into small pots.

Cucumber Jelly

MAKES
1.5 kg (3 lb)

Plate 32, illustrated
facing page 225.

If you cannot obtain borage leaves use a few drops of green colouring to give the jelly its translucent jade colour.

900 g (2 lb) cucumbers　　　*handful borage leaves*
900 g (2 lb) sugar　　　*6 tablespoons white wine vinegar*
2 pieces fresh ginger root　　*2 tablespoons gelatine powder*
grated peel and juice of 2 lemons　*4 tablespoons water*
4 large sprigs mint　　　*2 tablespoons brandy*

Do not peel the cucumbers. Cut them into thin slices and arrange them on a flat tray. Spread over the sugar and leave to stand for 24 hours. Combine cucumbers and sugar in a large heavy pan with the ginger root roughly broken into pieces, the lemon peel and juice, mint, borage and vinegar. Bring to the boil and continue boiling very gently for 2 hours or until a little of the preserve dropped onto a saucer will form a skin on the surface within 5 minutes if left in a coolish place. Sprinkle the gelatine over the water and leave to stand, then stir into the hot cucumber liquid to dissolve. Strain through a fine muslin or sieve and pour into scrupulously clean, warmed jars. Pour a thin layer of brandy over the top of each jar and seal at once. Store in the refrigerator. (The brandy will help to preserve the jelly and give it an extra flavour.) Ring the changes by adding 2 tablespoons finely chopped mint to the jelly after straining and when the jelly has begun to thicken, or the cucumber can be left in the jelly. Do not strain the jelly but remove the borage, mint sprigs and ginger.

Damson Cheese

This preserve used to be very popular in the Victorian era and with good reason. Fruit pulp is cooked with enough sugar to make a thick, rather coarse jelly which keeps well. The cheese can be cut into wedges and served with cream, or a sweet cream cheese, as a pudding; it can be cut into small squares and rolled in caster sugar, and it also goes well with cold cuts of meat such as ham, tongue or cold lamb. The Victorians also used damson cheese as one of the accompaniments to a curry.

Damsons, sugar, water

Wash the fruit, remove the stalks and place it in a pan with enough water to come half-way to the top of the fruit. Bring to the boil and simmer gently for about an hour until the damsons are thoroughly tender. Rub the fruit through a fine sieve or a food mill and weigh the pulp. Add 450 g (1 lb) sugar to each 600 ml (1 pt) of pulp and return to a clean pan. Bring to the boil and simmer very gently for $1\frac{1}{4}$ hours, stirring every now and then to prevent sticking or burning. Leave to cool, spoon into small bowls, cover with cellophane and tie down with rubber bands. Store the cheese in a cool place.

Apple Chutney

MAKES
1.8 kg (4 lb)

1.8 kg (4 lb) cooking apples
225 g (8 oz) onions
1 clove garlic ·
450 g (1 lb) sultanas
1 tablespoon mustard seed

grated rind and juice of 1 lemon
2 teaspoons ground ginger
900 ml (1½ pt) malt vinegar
900 g (2 lb) brown sugar

Peel and core the apples and cut the flesh into small dice. Peel and finely chop the onions and garlic. Combine the apples, onions, garlic, sultanas, mustard seed, lemon juice and rind and ginger in a saucepan with half the vinegar. Bring to the boil, cover and simmer for 30 minutes until all the ingredients are soft. Combine remaining vinegar with the sugar and stir over a medium heat until sugar has dissolved. Add this mixture to the chutney and continue to simmer for about a further 15 minutes until the chutney is thick and glossy. Cool, pack into sterilised jars and seal tightly. Store in a cool dark place and leave for at least three weeks before using.

Pickled Plums

MAKES
1 kg (2 lb)

If you have never enjoyed the contrast of pickled fruit with cold meat then you have missed an experience well worth having. Pickled plums go well with almost any meat. Kilner or bottling jars make the best containers for the fruit, which should be left to mature for at least 2 months before using.

1.5 kg (3 lb) firm ripe plums
1½ tablespoons ground ginger
1 teaspoon ground cinnamon
1 tablespoon salt

350 g (12 oz) soft brown sugar
600 ml (1 pt) vinegar
3 tablespoons allspice
1 tablespoon cloves

Wash the plums, remove the stalks and dry well. Prick each plum in about half a dozen places with a large darning needle or cocktail stick. Combine the ginger, cinnamon, salt, sugar and vinegar in a saucepan, bring slowly to the boil, stirring every now and then until the sugar has dissolved. Add the fruit and simmer gently for about 10 minutes until the plums are tender but not soft. Strain off the liquid and gently pack the plums into hot bottling jars. Return the liquid to a clean pan; add the allspice and cloves, bring to the boil and boil for about 20–30 minutes until thick and syrupy. Strain and pour over the plums while still hot. Cover and seal.

First Catch Your Crocodile
31 JULY 1977

BEING MARRIED TO an explorer is a very lonely life, and after eighteen years the awful thing is that I haven't learned to cope with it at all. Robin was just 20 when we got engaged, and the following day he went away for nine months. I used to send him telegrams saying 'Can't possibly marry you. Can't remember what you look like'.

This time he has now been away for two and a half months of a fifteen-month expedition, and it's rather the same; and, shaming though it is, I have to admit that I have succumbed to loneliness and rather cut myself off from the world. Now, I am going out to visit him but I'm determined, once I return from Borneo, to start going out again.

We had been married for twelve years before we reached the joint conclusion that it was ridiculous that I had never travelled with him. So we went to South America together, and spent three months almost entirely in the jungle, only weeks after our son was born. I had been very ill and everyone said I was mad, but as it turned out it was the right decision. It got me on my feet and toughened me incredibly. If I hadn't gone I'm convinced I'd be a chronic invalid.

We had to visit thirty-three isolated jungle tribes in Brazil on a fact-finding mission for Survival International, of which Robin is chairman. And it was tough initiation. It meant sleeping in hammocks in the jungle, being covered in mosquito bites, going for hours on foot in the most horrible conditions.

I've always been terrified of snakes. I was scared stiff of flying across the jungle in tiny planes, in electric storms (something like thirty-two of these little planes go down a year over the Amazon jungle and they don't even bother to go out to look for them).

One tribe was very difficult indeed . . . They stoned us. I was armed with a Beretta, but Robin will never carry a gun. It was my first experience of handling a weapon; I practised with a cigarette packet at ten yards. My great moment of glory was shooting a crocodile. We were camping by an infested river and we couldn't get near the water for crocodiles; no, I didn't bring it back as a handbag – we ate its tail, though, which was really filthy. We were ten days from anywhere and it would have rotted, so I bought a handbag to compensate.

First Catch Your Crocodile & other articles

Our next trip together was to Indonesia, and much more exciting because the tribes were 50,000 strong. Lovely stark-naked spear-carrying head-hunters. Three months was too long and after two, I became exhausted. We had to go five days without any food whatsoever and I developed anorexia because by then I found I just couldn't eat ... I weighed eight stone before I left England and eventually went down to six stone.

How it came about was that we had sailed by Chinese tramp steamer to a remote island of head-hunters called Seram and had a tremendously difficult trip into the interior. It was grotesque: the rivers were swollen and we had to swim through them, in the sort of pouring rain you can't see through. I wasn't afraid. I was just so fed up I wanted to die. I did say to Robin, 'Leave me, leave me, all I want to do is die ... let me float down stream.' I lost all will to go on.

It was first mountainous and then a malarial swamp full of mosquitos and leeches. Being leeched is horrible. You are supposed to scrape them off with a knife or flick them – but if you pull them, as I have done, in disgust, you'll end up with a lot of scars, like me. We came down very quickly to catch the boat, and when I passed out from exhaustion I was dragged along by a lovely head-hunter. No, he didn't want mine, but my word they had a lot of other people's.

When we got on the boat the voyage took five days; the boat owners were terribly poor and had only a handful of rice a day each, which they would have shared – but we couldn't take theirs. After that the anorexia took hold.

It is a great excitement to be taking the children for the first time. Lucy is 17 and Rupert will be seven during the trip. Robin has been given a fibreglass jet-boat by New Zealand, which he is taking up rapids that nobody has ever navigated before. He says it leaps like a salmon over a waterfall. Rupert and I are going to do this, too. And Rupert, who has always been afraid of the water, has had to learn to swim in a six-week crash course. I'm excited for him because *he* is so excited.

He asked an anthropologist if he could ask him a 'private question'. 'If it's called the rain forest, does that mean it rains every day? And if so, should I take *two* mackintoshes?'

I've eaten some extraordinary things in the jungle. I've eaten very large red ants, fried to a crisp and served with manioc, a poisonous starch ... you pulp, wring out and boil ... jungle roulette. I've discovered the two basic requirements of travelling with Robin ... take a tin of sardines, it can last three days and so prevent anorexia, and a large supply of celery salt, because jungle food is very tasteless ...

Apart from the tail of the crocodile I shot, I've eaten snake, I've eaten monkey, a lot – it's quite good, like rabbit. I'm real dustbin material, fortunately. I will eat literally anything useful in the jungle, where you have to. I've eaten iguana – quite delicious, like very tender chicken – and I have eaten dog, I'm ashamed to say, in Indonesia. It was very sad for an English person.

But far worse than the food is the drink. In Indonesia after the rice harvest they have these terrible drinking sessions where they drink rice wine and force you to drink enormous quantities of this very unpleasant stuff. Girls with ears weighted down to their knees force you to drink.

What does one take on the jungle, people ask? You literally need only two pairs of jeans and two tee-shirts with long sleeves because of the mosquitos; tennis shoes are the only possible footwear – you've got to have something you can get off quickly because of the leeches; it's no good having boots because it's a helluva job getting them off when inside there are fifty leeches packed round your legs. I also take very full Victorian nightdresses because one is often sleeping with assorted sexes, and you can use them as a sort of tent to change under. Other than that nothing, except a blanket both for comfort and warmth. Everything rots. Within two days everything is covered with mould. The other thing is, I never take a looking-glass because you can't bother with your appearance.

It will be the first time that Robin and I have not been alone together and it will be interesting to see how I fit into the tight community of scientists in the long house Robin is building.

Snake And Chips
4 SEPTEMBER 1977

Dear Everyone

I have exchanged one kitchen for another, so that the cook here can take things easily for a bit, and become an avid gardener as well. Both jobs are very satisfactory as the plants literally spring up overnight (courgettes planted today will be eight inches high in three days' time) and Rosemary (the New Zealand girl cooking here) and I are coping with about twenty people for meals on restricted rations.

Tins are very expensive and getting stores up river is a problem, so we are discovering fresh vegetables which will last, jungle greens, fish, wild boar and even python meat. (From a snake over twenty feet long, we had to pressure cook it for three hours and served up snake and sweet potato chips.)

The long house which Robin has built is in the traditional style, with ten small rooms, a long verandah with a central balcony sticking out. A T-shaped area with a walkway leads to the kitchen which has open sides and, until I arrived, two small kerosene stoves. I brought a couple of Calor gas burners up with me which have made life easier.

The settlement here, which includes Punans and Berawans, some of their wives and children, must number about fifty people and more are pouring in all the time because we are having a housewarming party and the news has spread.

Our lot are mostly scientists who come and go from here at base camp to the sub-camps, some of which are three or four days' walk away. Most of them are 'bug' men and the unscientific of us get kind of nervous when cockroaches the size of hen's eggs walk across our toes, two-inch long ants invade the kitchen and the inside of the lavatory pan – a loo on stilts over a deep pit – and get a bit on edge over the number of 'nasties' that crowd around the lights at night, but the experts shout with excitement at every unpleasant new arrival.

The natives who work for us are cheerful and incredibly strong, carrying loads that none of our men could even lift. They are enchanting with Rupert, my seven-year-old son, whom they take fishing, bathing and swimming – he prefers being with them.

Needless to say, it rains in the rain forest which is only yards from our door. We have a system in Heath Robinson style, to catch water from the roof and yesterday filled up three large petrol drums in under five minutes. It also came into all the rooms but by now one has stopped trying to keep clothes dry or mould-free.

We wash from a raft moored in the river. The water is clear and surprisingly cool and the only hazards are a crocodile upstream, pit vipers that swim through the water, and little fish which find soap a great delicacy and nibble the most surprisingly private parts of one's body. Keeping scrupulously clean is vital as every bite (and one's arms, legs, neck and feet are covered with bites) turns septic very quickly.

Washing up is the usual bore but keeping the long house clean is almost a pleasure, as all you do is sweep the dirt through the bamboo slats. The house is on stilts because not only is that cooler but also, although we are about thirty feet above the river, when the rains really come the ground around will flood. The stilts are also supposed to discourage rats but last night we saw three in the house for the first time. Lord Medway, who arrived today, is however, a rat fanatic and he, at least, is thrilled. A buffalo has been killed for our party and the very high but magnificent head will be mounted in the long house.

The Berawans have been busy fermenting some rice wine, 'borak', for us and it looks as though it is going to be quite a thrash with two large helicopter loads of officials and other important Malaysians coming up in the morning to join us.

Love to you all and I hope everything is well with everyone,

Marika

Ten Day's Hard Labour
25 JUNE 1978

AN ADVERTISEMENT IN the *Denver Post* read, 'FOR THE TRAVELLER WHO HAS DONE ALMOST EVERYTHING – If you would like to spend ten days and nights on an English country estate as the guest of Marika Hanbury Tenison ... Have breakfast served to you in bed ... Take walks in glorious Cornish gardens ... be lavishly entertained by local British Society ... and learn gourmet cooking all the while ... *WE'RE GOING YOUR WAY.*'

Seven Denver ladies were hooked and my latest survival scheme

First Catch Your Crocodile & other articles

was launched. In desperation I had joined the great British tourist bonanza because although my home is no 'stately' affair (it's a kind of glorified farmhouse in the middle of Bodmin Moor), it shares with Woburn and other great homes the problems of rising damp, rotting windows and antiquated plumbing.

You have to have a gimmick for this kind of thing, and since lions, veteran cars and portraits of my ancestors were out I settled for a lavish version of 'The Good Life' with home-grown produce, cookery lessons, local gardens and as many friends as I could persuade to masquerade as 'British Society'.

An elaborate itinerary filling every minute of the ten days merely evoked curt cables requesting 'swimming and tennis facilities', and I discovered my home needed a facelift if guests were to pay £45 a day for the privilege of staying there.

Eighteen years of accumulated junk was turfed out of my study and made an extra bedroom; lights usually switched on by crawling under beds had to be re-wired; the house was scrubbed and painted – and I even had a new bathroom installed for the water-loving Americans.

The garden was trimmed with nail scissors and the gardener mumbled darkly about the dangers of 'Colorado beetles'.

Arrival day – and seven ladies with twenty-four large pieces of luggage had to be met at the station in a red minibus with steering problems. I gave a final briefing to my assembled 'staff': 'You must wear shoes', to daughter Lucy and her friend Melanie disguised as chambermaids; 'Smile all the time', to housekeepers Valerie and Julie who already looked exhausted; 'If you don't know the answer to a question, make one up', to secretary Clare; 'Measure out the gin', to my Saturday gardener, Michael, transformed in a snazzy striped waistcoat; and 'Don't panic' to Anna, a borrowed cook who remained enviably cool as one of the labradors ate the raised pies she had made that morning.

I hadn't expected the ladies or their wardrobes to be so big; my bedrooms shrank and the £15 I had spent on new hangers became a drop in the ocean. American voices filled the house and I could sense them wondering whether they were going to get their money's worth as some of them banged their heads on ancient worm-filled beams.

The day began at 5.30 am, with lunch to get out of the way before the morning 'cookery demonstration and chat-in', arrangements for the day's visit to famous gardens or real stately home. I had to move out of my bedroom to a camp bed in the passage to make room for visiting 'British Society' who would be staying the night.

Breakfasts were the worst thing. Seven trays with seven butter dishes, salts and peppers, coffee pots and milk jugs. Who had muesli and who wanted cooked breakfast? Who had asked for hot water and who for hot milk? Mrs Long liked bourbon but did she like muffins? Eight o'clock came; Lucy and Melanie had no shoes on and everyone was sleepy and bad-tempered.

On the second day I woke up with a violent tummy bug and staggered about being sick and washing my hands in Dettol, terrified that Mrs Foster, aged 80, might catch it, trying to be enthusiastic about making an old-fashioned treacle tart and organising an Edwardian picnic, complete with damask tablecloths, in the bluebell woods.

The picnic was a triumph, so I left them and crawled into bed for the afternoon to be able to face a cocktail party for eighty and dinner for eighteen. The Cornish loved the Americans and the Americans loved the Cornish; two bottles of gin disappeared in about ten minutes.

The enthusiams and energy of those ladies amazed me but my itinerary beat them. By day six they frankly admitted they never wanted to see another rhododendron and Mrs Foster nearly didn't make it to the castle on St Michael's Mount.

The ladies wanted to shop so I revised the itinerary to lunch in a 'quaint' old English pub and a spending spree in Fowey, followed by yet another dinner party, and a film about the Seychelles.

That evening was a near disaster. The screen fell on top of Mrs Ampter, the main water pipe burst in the boiler house, I fell into five feet of water trying to turn off the boiler which was threatening to explode, and the labrador developed a liking for the salmon which was cooling for lunch the next day. My guests were unruffled and, thanks to Mogadon, slept through the bangs of the pipes when the plumber eventually turned up at 4.30 am.

Breakfasts became easier when I discovered no one liked kedgeree; still suffering from my 'bug' and having lost nine pounds I demonstrated how to make roulades, brandy snaps shaped like water lilies and Victorian bombes. My guests began to help themselves to drinks and they assured me they actually *liked* Lucy's bare feet. Suddenly it was day ten and we were gloating over the generous tips of £153.

We had champagne on Bodmin Road station with hugs and

kisses all round, and even a tear or two. I had succeeded in giving my guests what they described as 'the time of their life' – my final triumph being able to scrape up six single men for my last dinner party and a knees-up around my ancient piano.

The house was silent, the labrador scorned such mundane fare as Cornish pasties for lunch and I slept for forty-eight hours. Financially I was well in the red but next year I'm hoping to increase the trade and – who knows – my venture into the tourist bonanza may even lead to my being able to renew the plumbing.

Back to School
13 AUGUST 1978

M Y SCHOLASTIC CAREER is not something I am proud of. My parents were politely asked to remove me from my third and final school ('We feel that Marika has outgrown the Francis Holland and the Francis Holland has outgrown Marika') when I was 14-years-old.

That was the end of my education, which I regret. I wasn't stupid; I just couldn't conform like the other girls.

Imagine, then, getting a letter from the High Mistress of a well-known London girls' school inviting me to give a talk on cooking and exploring. The High Mistress told me she had been following my career with interest and asked if I remembered her.

I was flattered but could not, although the name rang a faint bell. I found the invitation irresistible, especially as I was informed I would be following such figures as Margaret Thatcher and the American Ambassador.

As the time drew nearer, however, I wished to God I had never accepted the invitation. Ostrich-fashion, I pretended it wasn't going to happen and so did nothing about planning my talk.

I have done a fair amount of public speaking but always to older audiences of Women's Institutes and ladies luncheon clubs where I could get away with quite a lot because I was usually younger than most of my audiences. But this was quite different: how on earth was I to keep the attention of a hundred odd brilliant girls, all winging their way towards Oxbridge, when I couldn't spell 'sausage' without looking it up and had never learnt even the date of the Magna Carta?

First Catch Your Crocodile & other articles

Dressed in what I hoped was a good combination of the trendy and the Establishment I sat in the train desperately writing headings on stiff cards ('my career, attitudes towards food, cooking for an explorer', and so on). I tried to steady my hand with a couple of gin and tonics but threw them down the lavatory because I felt that to arrive reeking of gin would be inexcusable.

Mistiming brought me outside enormous wrought-iron gates and a glowering red-brick building twenty minutes early. My skirt was creased, my nose shining and I had no make-up with me.

By the time the High Mistress was ready to receive me I felt I was going to be sick. I slid around in a leather chair, juggled with an elegant tea cup and a cigarette (for which there was no ashtray) and felt inordinately scruffy in the presence of the tall, elegantly dressed woman whose face I was still desperately trying to place. I searched for clues as we chatted politely but failed to come up with any answer.

A bell rang outside: it was zero hour. I trailed after the High Mistress through imposing passages lined with golden lists of girls who had 'made it', passing elegant creatures who looked as though they belonged on the pages of *Vogue* rather than in a classroom; girls who were obviously far too liberated to be interested in the mechanics of making a soufflé or whipping a lemon syllabub.

The auditorium was enormous; a hundred girls stared at me; I couldn't decide whether to sit or stand. The High Mistress began her introduction – and I realised with horror that I had left my notes on the train.

'I last met Marika when I was teaching her English and I know you will all be most interested to hear what she has to say . . . ' The penny dropped. How could I have forgotten that gorgeous creature I had had a crush on and who had been by far my favourite teacher at my last school?

Suddenly I was 14 again; I pulled myself together, faced my audience and even began to relax a little when the girls giggled at a resumé of my scholastic career, laughed at an account of trying to cook a piranha fish in Brazil and gasped when I told them of starving in Indonesia.

To my delight they really were interested in cooking and food. I managed thirty-five minutes – my allotted time – without too much pain; and even the embarrassing nervous tic in my left eye had subsided when the time came for questions. Did I think we would all be living on food pills by the twenty-first century? What did I consider was a healthy eating pattern? How balanced was the diet of an isolated tribal people? How did I view the subject of vegetarianism? The questions, I felt, reflected the school's academic reputation – and I was relieved I had only a short time to discuss them.

'Thank you for your stunning talk here', wrote the High Mistress a week later. 'You were much appreciated and it was heart -warming to see you again – only different.'

I haven't felt so proud of myself since the same lady gave me an A-plus for an essay on people from another planet!

The Lesser Evel
15 OCTOBER 1978

WOULD YOU SPEND over £100 on a present for a small boy? I have always been terrified of spoiling my children, so you might think it strange that for my son Rupert's eighth birthday I indulged in one which cost the princely sum of £160.

Rupert is small for his age (as a premature baby he weighed about two pounds at birth and has not yet caught up) but he is full of bounce and the holidays stretched wearily ahead. We live in an isolated area; there are few other children of the same age around and with a father exploring Borneo and a mother who is useless at cricket, football or rough-housing, the summer looked like being pretty dull for poor Rupert.

Until, that is, I was persuaded to buy him a motorbike, a real one with automatic gears, a two-stroke engine and a speed of up to thirty miles per hour.

Motorbiking for kids round here is becoming quite the rage and, while the thought of an eight-year-old bombing about on an Evel Knievel-type machine at first filled me with terror, friends who have already succumbed convinced me that a 'bike' really was the answer. 'Much cheaper to run than a pony,' they pointed out. 'No shoeing, grooming coats in the winter and precious grass in the summer, no vet's bills or guess who ends up looking after the bloody thing.'

I negotiated for a second-hand Italian machine, a grown-up's motorbike in miniature, of shining blue and silver. Rupert, equipped with yellow crash helmet, visor, knee and arm pads (like those used for skateboarding) was unable to say a word he was so excited. After a wobbling and slightly nervous start he began to get the hang of it, skidding on the lawn and crashing down unhurt. Gradually he gained confidence and by the end of the first day was able to rise in the saddle over the bumps and put a foot to the ground to help guide him around sharp bends.

The effect of the machine has been almost miraculous. Suddenly Rupert, always too small to fight other boys of his own age and permanently lagging behind on the games field, has gained enormous confidence; the mechanics of the bike fascinate him and he is quite happy to clean and oil it and talk knowledgeably about the petrol mix.

Obviously he is not allowed on the road but, living on a farm, he has a large area of fields and tracks to ride over and he has become invaluable for taking messages to the farm workers. He can even get to the village, two miles away across country, and buy an ice cream with his pocket money.

As with all grown-up toys, there have to be rules. He has to tell me exactly where he is going, for how long (I get sick with terror at the thought of him coming off in some remote place and being stuck underneath the bike unable to move). He has to keep the machine cleaned and oiled; he is not allowed on the lawn when the grass is wet; and he has to dismount and wheel the bike across the road which splits the farm in half. My greatest surprise is how grown up he is about these rules; they are accepted without question and the threat of 'do this or you won't be able to ride your bike tomorrow' is a one-hundred per cent winner.

The bike has also opened up a new social horizon. Rupert and his bike now go to stay with friends, who also have bikes, for weekends of scrambling around improvised courses.

The only problem (and it's the same one that crops up with ponies) is that already, after only a month, Rupert has outgrown his bike and needs another one with more power and more gears. Meanwhile, he's setting up a wooden ramp and a line of Dinky cars to jump over as a surprise for when his father comes home.

A Case of Telephonitis
24 DECEMBER 1978

BRRR BRRR . . . GRRR GRR!

I DON'T GET ON with the telephone. I have a hate relationship with the instrument because it doesn't play any games by my rules.

My way of living may be a little eccentric but it is not *that* way out; yet the rules of the Post Office and Telecommunications Services make it virtually impossible for me ever to make a business call.

I wake up early, and rise at 5 am and work through the morning until midday when I sprint into the kitchen to make the lunch. The mornings, of course, are the time when telephone calls are prohibitively expensive; so much so that in our household we have had to put an embargo on making anything but a local call before 1 pm. But at that time everyone in their right mind has gone out to lunch, and in the publishing world (my world) they seem to remain at lunch until 3 or 4 pm.

My afternoons are spent in a dormouse-like way. At 2 pm, exhausted by my early start to the day, I retire to bed and sleep like a baby until five. My secretary says I am out 'at a meeting' or 'having by hair done' but in reality I am happily dossed down with hot water bottles and dreams of a telephoneless world. By the time I come to, anyone who is anyone seems to have left his office for home while I am back at my desk raring to go again.

I'm not much good at telephone gossip either. It never seems to be the right moment and inevitably friends catch me in the middle of making pastry, watching a soufflé rise of mixing a game pâté with my hands. Finding me rather short and distant (someone else has to hold the telephone for me while I go on mixing or rolling my dough) they tend, quite quickly, to give up ringing me just to have 'a cosy chat'.

Telephone bills get me down, too. Robin, my husband, loves the machine. He actually rushes to answer the rings while I cringe away, always fearful of bad news. Despite our morning embargo he is usually found glued to the machine for most of the day until I can almost hear the machinery totting up the bills. Yet, when he was away for fifteen months and I was avoiding both ringing out and accepting calls the bill was almost exactly the same as it had been when he was at home.

First Catch Your Crocodile & other articles

Then there is the actual line to our rather remote farm house on Bodmin Moor in Cornwall. Crackles, waterfalls and eerie howls are commonplace and recently (having been caught by a morning call) £1500 which I thought I had been offered for an article (we had even celebrated with an expensive night out) turned out to be only £15 when the letter arrived.

Another dirty trick we have to suffer is the similarity of our number to that of a local weather station. Six thirty on a Sunday morning is the popular time for callers to get it wrong. Wearily and slightly hung over from a Saturday night party, one of us reaches for the receiver, panicking at the thought of children or parents ill, of accidents and death, only to hear a hearty voice inquire if the weather is suitable for a sail/surf/picnic on the North/South coast of Cornwall. 'It's raining', we say flatly, 'and it probably won't stop raining until May'.

Not long ago some fault or other kept me awake all night. Robin was in Borneo and when the telephone rang at 1 am I knew it must be him. I groped for the receiver and got only the sound of the Atlantic breakers rolling towards the shore, a sound I might just as well have got from holding my ear against a conch shell. The ringing was repeated at half-hourly intervals throughout the night and, in the morning when the men came to investigate they found – would you believe? – that we had been 'interfered with by mice'.

I thought I had problems but a recent holiday in Ireland gave me some small measure of cheer. Ours, it seems, is by no means the worst telephone service in Europe; that honour is reserved for the Irish one. I was there not long ago and a man I met at a party told me a story which made me, on the Cardinham exchange, feel I was making mountains out of molehills.

This chap's telephone wires had been completely severed by a fallen tree. After waiting in vain for two months for the wires to be mended, he decided to take the matter into his own hands. He got hold of a ladder and a pair of rubber gloves and spent a satisfactory afternoon joining all those little coloured wires together. Having got the lot married up he bound them tightly with electrical tape and went triumphantly back to his house. Lifting the receiver he was enchanted to find a dialling tone but when he rang a number in Dublin and the telephone was answered at the other end, all he got was gobbledegook. Furious, he flung the telephone to the other end of the room, shattering it into six pieces and silencing the 'bloody thing'.

When he reported a smashed telephone the engineers came at once. 'How did it happen?' they asked. 'Well, you see,' my friend replied, 'It was like this; a cow came through the window and kicked the telephone and the thing was smashed to pieces.'

'Ah, yes, is that so,' asked the Irish telephone engineers, 'that's very understandable,' and they installed a new telephone at once. It was still, however, another month before they mended the broken line.

Meanwhile, back on the farm, my telephonitis continues, a particularly difficult phobia as we have no fewer than ten telephone extensions, a burglar alarm attached by telephone to the police and an outsize outdoor telephone bell that echoes through the garden where I, ostrich fashion, hide my head in the rhododendrons and hope that someone else will answer the call.

Lady of Diplomatic Sauces
4 FEBRUARY 1979

VERONICA MACLEAN IS IN her late fifties but she looks a lot younger. Trim and elegant, she is a delight to meet – witty, amusing and yet comfortably cosy; she bubbles with enthusiasm and possesses plenty of what is called 'charisma'. It is easy to see how she gathered the multitude of very good friends that contributed to her first two cookery books, *Lady Maclean's Cook Book* and *Diplomatic Dishes*.

We met at her publishers where I found her flipping through a pile of reviews, the result of her latest cookery book *Sauces and Surprises,* with the eagerness of a teenager. 'I've been away for six weeks so I'm a bit out of touch and these are terribly exciting.'

She and her husband Sir Fitzroy Maclean (travel writer, expert on Russia and Yugoslavia, biographer, historian and former Conservative MP) had been on a whistle-stop tour of America. 'Fritz was lecturing on Russia and East/West relations and we ended up in Hawaii, at the World Business Council in America, where he was presented with a medal for his contribution to World Understanding.' I gave one lecture, not on cooking but on the Caucasus; and while Fitz was busy I filled in my time by going to college classes.'

Coming back as she was from the warmth of Hawaii to the snow and strikes of Britain I was not surprised to find her enthusiastic about American life. 'Everything works there; life is so easy and no one is frightened of machines. Most of the people we stayed with had no servants but they were so efficient; everyone lent a hand and they were all so well organised.

'We had some marvellous meals but the best of all was a lunch party given by a Japanese gentleman. We started with fresh caviar from the Sacramento River. It was the most delicious I have ever tasted and I am quite a caviar queen; it was better than good Russian caviar. To finish we had a whole Brie cheese studded with pine nuts, hundreds of them; it was a wonderful combination of Japanese and Western food.'

Lady Maclean was brought up at the castle of her father (Lord Lovat) in Scotland where she had what sounded like the most romantic and enchanted childhood. She watched her father's private army, the Lovat Scouts, parading and playing the bagpipes, loved fishing and instead of going to school was taught at home by a French governess who took her to France when she was twelve. There she learned to cook simple dishes. 'I loved snails the first time I tried them and the first dish I ever made was mayonnaise. I have been very lucky; at home we had a French chef who used to catch salmon on a bent pin; we always had good food and so did my first husband's family. When Alan Phipps and I married (he was killed in the war leaving me with two young children), he was earning only £350 a year so I did the cooking and loved it.'

Writing cookery books happened rather by chance. She had done some travel writing and had also been a monthly contributor on cookery to *Vogue*.

Her first book was written to help raise money for her husband's constituency and was so successful that Collins suggested publishing it for general distribution. Her latest book *Sauces and Surprises* was written because 'I felt there was a gap to be filled in this field. Sauces are so important and since they are such a personal thing I have often included two or three different recipes for the same sauce.'

Having travelled widely with her husband, she is now an expert on the East. And as if their life wasn't full enough already she and her husband own a hotel, the Creggans Inn, at Strachur in Scotland. 'We inherited it as part of the estate and increased its size and improved its comfort. We now have twenty-six bedrooms. I do the hiring and firing, take care of the decorating, the menus and in emergencies, do the cooking; basically it is country house cooking and we try to concentrate on serving good, plain food and giving a warm welcome.'

Her energy filled me with admiration and envy; she has four children, a husband who is shortly to be involved in the filming of his Russian trilogy for American television, who flies across the world at the drop of a hat; they have a house on the Dalmation coast and a flat in London, as well as the estate in Scotland – yet at 58 she still has time to consider starting a new career in non-cookery journalism. She deserved, I felt at the end of our lunch, every success.

Manners Still Rule
6 MAY 1979

LETTERS ARE STILL arriving in every post as a result of my recent article 'No smiles, please, we're British'. It seems I was not alone in decrying the lack of manners, friendliness and caring in much of Britain today; it is obviously a subject close to many people's hearts. Many of the letters did, however, offer some hope and cheer; and if you are thinking of moving away from the churlishness of the Big Smoke, country villages or the smaller town seem to offer a far better way of life.

In the North of England and in Scotland smiles, my correspondents tell me, are still plentiful and there were some lovely stories of people, especially the elderly, being treated with respect and given a helping hand when necessary. Down in the South-East of England, too, politeness is still considered important. The ticket collectors at the station at Robertsbridge in Sussex, Mrs Bleche, a grandmother of five, tells me, are always 'happy to pass the time of day' and she suggested that perhaps I 'can't be meeting the right people'.

Dr Peter Jack left England in 1954 because he saw many of the things I described 'beginning to happen then'. He suggested I visit Rhodesia where, despite their problems, 'manners, courtesy and a friendly smile are still the order of the day'.

Strangely enough it was from Northern Ireland that I had most letters reassuring me that in one part of Britian at least, smiles, friendliness and thoughtfulness towards one's fellow man are still very much in evidence. Do you remember that war time song 'Pack Up Your Troubles In Your Old Kit Bag and Smile, Smile, Smile'? That appears to be one of the many slogans of a country torn by strife, death and terror. Lady Fisher, one of the co-chairmen of the Women Caring Trust says: 'You may be surprised to know that in Belfast you will find many people with mouths that turn up and not down!'

Many people blamed violence and bad language on television for much of the deterioration of manners among children these days. Some blamed me – and there were suggestions from an elderly gentleman who gets smiles from all sides that perhaps I should have a sex change.

At least it does seem that all in Britain is not lost and there must be hope for the future, if my overflowing postbag is anything to go by. In London last week I even had a couple of kisses blown at me from obvious *Sunday Telegraph* readers as I battled with the bad-temperedness of the rush-hour traffic – and found my mouth definitely turning up.

Fairyland For The Over-40s
3 JUNE 1979

WHATEVER OTHER PEOPLE may say about 'life begining at 40', I woke up on my 40th birthday with an overwhelming sensation of deep depression.

I was halfway through my life, still countless things left undone that I had planned to do, beginning to get stiff when I walked up hills, no longer having the satisfaction of an occasional wolf whistle when I passed a team of road workers, thickening a bit around the middle and getting slightly leathery around the eyes and neck because I never bothered to feed my skin with the dedication I lavished on my stomach. Not a particularly pretty picture and not one which, like a good claret or even a parquet floor, had any hope of improving with time.

Spring automatically makes a woman think of swimsuits, toning up the body a bit, having a face pack or two and buying summer clothes. This year I felt something far more drastic than a do-it-yourself, in-between chores, personal spring-clean was required. I needed professional help, and after twenty-one years of marriage, a teenage daughter and a small son, felt entitled to have it. I needed to get away all by myself, somewhere I could sleep until midday if I wanted to, have a respite from housework and cooking, be thoroughly pampered and cosseted and perhaps realise a miracle that would indeed make me believe life at 40 had begun rather than ended.

The choice lay between a health hydro or a beauty farm hotel which would provide beauty treatment with a low calorie but delicious diet. I chose the latter. I had been before to health farms and, marvellous as they undoubtedly are for losing excess weight, a strict regime of hot water and little else combined with the spectacle of other overweight middle-aged manic depressives wandering around all day in their dressing gowns was not what I needed. I needed comfort, pampering and more than a little luxury. So with Robin, my husband, conveniently away on business, Lucy in London and Rupert at school, I packed my most glamorous clothes and, feeling like a guilty school girl playing truant, set off.

The place I had chosen for my escape from middle age was an hotel of the old school with large elegant rooms, a delightfully Edwardian air of grace and discreet luxury, enough stars to make one feel extravagant and a sophisticated health, beauty and slimming course thrown in.

For someone continually surrounded by people and who leads what others see as a remarkably full and busy life, finding oneself completely alone was a strange experience. I 'took' tea, complete with cucumber sandwiches, in the lounge, feeling invisible, almost overcome by the sensation of sitting down and being waited on in the middle of the afternoon with nothing else to do. Later I had a solitary drink (I dared not have more than one in case the barman thought me a middle-aged alcoholic) and then a solitary dinner in the chandeliered dining room, carefully dressed in discreet black jersey and stretching a glass of house wine through the delicious meal which a friendly waiter assured me had a calorie count of less than 500.

After self-consciously reading a book in a corner of the softly lit lounge, now transformed into a ballroom complete with band, singer and a repertoire of old favourites, I fled to the reassurance of a large double bedroom complete with armchairs, a colour television and a balcony and went to sleep before midnight for the first time in years.

Three glorious days of pampering followed. Early morning tea and breakfast in bed (together with the newspapers I never normally see before lunchtime), a routine of a sauna, cold needle-sharp shower, face massage, face packs, the glory of first underwater massage and then a body massage were all utterly just what I had longed for. It was like being a child and having a nanny all over again. 'Get undressed' 'get dressed', 'relax' in a giant bath while a high power hose was directed on to my fleshier parts, nudging away years of abuse, and having the tensions in the back of my neck eased away as an attractive 25-year-old rubbed me with scented oil and eased out the creases from my aging elbows. It was a glorious orgy of self-indulgence with the first pedicure of my life, three manicures, the frivolity of a lightening rinse on hair that had dulled and an inch cut off the straggles at the back.

My masseuse told me her clients poured out their problems to her as they lay on the massage table, so I joined their ranks – chuckled over, comforted and gossiped with – as my skin grew softer and, despite the good living, I shed those flabby pounds.

'At Home' For Charity
9 AUGUST 1979

COUNTRY OPEN DAYS and fêtes are still one of the best ways of raising money for charity. A fortnight ago we made our first attempt to 'do our bit', to throw open our surroundings to the public, to pray for sunshine and to fret about where to put the 'Ladies', about whether the borrowed tea urns would turn up in time and, even more important, to worry whether indeed any of the public would bother to come to such a do-it-yourself occasion.

We had spent a good month planning for our 'Open Day' in aid of the Boys' Clubs. My explorer husband, Robin, got together his 'exploriana', gathered over years of travelling – spears, clubs, feather headdresses, hammocks and evil-looking parangs – and arranged them tastefully on the whitewashed walls of a barn, and I, meanwhile, made ginger cake after ginger cake and the hundreds of mini-meringues that were to make up our 50p teas.

Lunch times became council meetings, afternoons were spent dead-heading the roses, and there were at least a couple of panics an hour as the day drew near. Having reached 250 meringues, I gave up and negotiated with a local bakery for the remaining 250.

'Could they please try to see they were not too perfect?', I begged, but they arrived looking pristine and immaculately twirled beside my homespun creations. We tried out the barbecue and found the wind blowing smoke straight into our eyes; and we managed to lose the raffle tickets, drawing-pins and sticky tape.

'Open Day' was Sunday. Three o'clock that morning I woke, after a two-week heatwave, to the sound of torrential rain. By the backdoor light I could see phlox being flattened and sweet peas drooping. I could smell the pungent odour of a cess pit that always overflows when the skies open. Sleep was out of the question, so I busied myself making great piles of pancakes for my cookery demonstrations.

The rain stopped, the helpers arrived in droves until we were not sure what to do with them all. Robin became maniacal about putting up notices saying 'no entry' all over the place.

For a moment we were all able to relax with a hasty buffet lunch and a magnum of champagne being produced to encourage the workers, but not for long. Down the drive one hour early came the first of our guests, and the hostess lost her cool. 'Go away', I shouted rudely. 'We don't start until two o'clock'. They went and didn't come back.

We had thought there would not be many visitors, but in fact our wildest hopes were exceeded. By two o'clock sharp they were pouring in. The tea ladies feverishly buttered more bread, the raffle tickets were selling like hot cakes, the tombola was making a bomb, Robin had to turn away parties from his exhibition of exploriana, and my pancakes had an audience of more than a hundred.

We had aimed for the princely sum of £200; instead we grossed over £900 – a miracle as it was collected from over 500 people. And no litter had been left, no cigarettes stubbed out on my carpet, no *object* or flower cutting had been pinched. They had all behaved as delightfully as only an English crowd at an English fête can.

Value for money seems to be the over-riding factor of our successful day.

My advice to other fête-holders is to ask a high entrance fee, but provide free entertainments for the price. Make the prizes of good quality and odds on the side-shows reasonable. The public, I discover, come to an event of this sort with a specified amount of money in their pockets to spend – the trick is to make them spend it *all*. Our tombola offered a 9–1 chance of winning a prize of up to the value of around £25 for 15p; the orange stall provided a 5–1 chance for 5p of winning three oranges (surely good value).

Leftover Lolly
9 SEPTEMBER 1979

I AM NOT ASHAMED to reveal that no one is more eager to make what the Americans call a 'quick buck' than I am.

Well, these days you have your eye open for the main chance, don't you? Unfortunately my schemes for making a little cash on the side seldom bear fruit and usually end up by actually costing me money.

My latest venture, however, really does seem to have the germs of financial success. It began because as a cookery writer, I have a basic problem. Most of my days are spent inventing recipes or trying them out, with the result that the refrigerator is nearly always filled with platefuls of goodies and, despite my household indulging in what appears to outsiders to be an almost continuous moveable feast, we just cannot consume the amount of dishes I have to make each day.

So what do I do with the leftovers? Well, occasionally I behave like Lady Bountiful and give them to my friends; some can be frozen to serve when I am in bed with 'flu or away; but some of the food, to my shame since I abhor waste, was ending up tossed into the dustbin.

Then the unthought of happened. Our local town has never been what one might call a gastronomic oasis, so the opening of a wine bar which offered not only a good selection of wines and spirits but also a very respectable cold collation lunch of pies, quiches, cold cuts and salads was something of an event. Since it is run by my hairdresser's brother-in-law, I had advance warning of the opening and was there to give advice, rather bossily, on both the decor and the food. Sipping a glass of very passable *vin ordinaire*, I had my brainwave and approached my hairdresser's brother-in-law, Brian King. Would he, I asked, be interested in some of my better leftovers?

'Would I!' he replied with warming flattery. 'Nothing I would like better; give the place some class, raise the whole tone, which is exactly what I want to do.'

Glowing, I rushed home to knock up the remains of a dressed salmon with an elegant garnish (which had been used to experiment on for some upper class recipes), a couple of rather exotic salads and a sea bass *Delange* which has just been featured in a television interview and was still quite fresh but redundant.

Working out the price per portion was more a question of hit-and-miss than a computerised evaluation, but Brian was happy to fork out £9 in cash for the salmon, £5 for the sea bass and £1 each for the salads.

The following week I produced Golden Tomato Soup and a deliciously viridescent watercress-and-leek soup. This resulted in Brian, who hadn't really considered serving hot food, getting a carpenter back in to make counter space for hot plates, the soups and a whole new set of soup bowls.

But it was over the Bank Holiday weekend that I really got into my stride. I was naturally out to impress my visitors and since we live in Cornwall, I pointed out to my husband we *had* to give them lobster for at least one meal. 'We can't afford it,' he said firmly in his 'No-arguments-are-going-to-make-me-change-my-mind' tone of voice, and my streak of stubbornness inherited from my mother sent me straight back to the kitchen where I had been preparing a remould of Tamar Salmon with Celeriac and Mayonnaise, a galatine of chicken and ham with parsley, and other mouth-watering cold dishes for my weekend guests.

Unfortunately I was carefully arranging the dishes in the car when the first visitors swept up to find me all set to sell at least two of their meals. 'You can't take it away', they wailed in unison, 'it looks delicious'.

But I could and an hour later (having heard the galantine described as a 'guillotine') triumphantly in possession of £38 in 'oners' I was on my way to pick up the £30 of lobster already ordered and waiting for me. What is more, I made an excellent lobster bisque from the tails, roes and claws of the shellfish and flogged that next day.

Now a whole new source of income beckons me and I am seriously contemplating saving up for a refrigerated van in which to distribute my no longer redundant leftovers.

She Can't Hear, with that Broken Leg!

26 APRIL 1981

H AVE YOU CONSIDERED, in this Year of the Disabled, what it would be like to be disabled yourself? I hadn't. I was sorry for the disabled and happy to help raise money for them but I hadn't actually spared a moment's thought of what it would be like to suffer the indignities, pain and frustrations of being disabled oneself. Then . . . a small piece of onion skin on the stone floor, a slip and I was down with a broken hip. In seconds I had joined their ranks, confined to a wheelchair and crutches for three months of purgatory.

In the hospital, with a steel plate in my leg and a foot-long scar, it was all right. I was a baby like everyone else, given pills, bathed and served breakfast in bed. After two weeks I was allowed home, and it was only then I realised how much freedom I was used to, how active I used to be and how nightmarish was the situation I now found myself in.

I couldn't get up or down stairs without being carried; I had to have someone to help me in and out of the bath and to dry my legs. I was in bed at first and if a book was out of reach I had to ask for it; someone had to bring me food, drinks and handkerchiefs and take me to the lavatory. Everyone was unfailingly patient. They never complained about all the times when I wanted a drink, or a newspaper or the television switched on or off, but I knew I was being a bore. I saved up things to ask for when the next person came near me, was reduced to tears when I spent more than an hour or two alone, and could hear myself becoming increasingly impossible, demanding and dictatorial.

Matters improved a little when I was able to go downstairs and either be pushed in a wheelchair or take a few hobbles on crutches. I hated those crutches – dreary wooden affairs with a hospital smell and the leather pads worn shiny by other people's armpits. I felt better after an artist friend tarted them up with royal blue velvet on the pads, shocking pink silk tassels around the tops and bottoms and the stocks themselves had been painted blue with bright primitive flowers.

The disabled, I discovered, learn tricks to improve their lot. I cooked from my typewriting chair, whizzing around the kitchen on castors, used my butcher's apron to carry out paper and books, and made the journey to the loo only four times a day.

One day I stupidly decided to make a visit to Harvey Nichols at sale time. A friend drove me there but had to leave me; suddenly I found it was impossible to walk on sticks to the lift and carry a handbag at the same time (the extra weight threw my balance out completely). 'Excuse me,' I asked a passer-by – I had already discovered that the healthy public avoids the eyes of the infirm – could you carry my bag to the fourth floor?'. One after another they turned their heads away and scurried shamefacedly past. It was a good six minutes before a young girl, looking surprised, took my bag and accompanied me in the lift.

The trip to London to see specialists revealed that life for the disabled is not cheap. No one I knew there had a lift or a bedroom on the ground floor and so I had to stay in a hotel. There, the porters and hotel staff were kindness itself, lifting the wheelchair, picking me up when I fell over, and fetching and carrying for me. But in the street people stared at me wheeling my ramshackle chair towards Knightsbridge as though I were the Hunchback of Notre Dame, and it took me twenty minutes' waiting at a set of traffic lights before I could persuade some able-bodied man to negotiate my chair over the pavement and across the road.

I found the attitude of the public more and more confusing. Going into the busy Plymouth market on a Friday lunchtime I discovered that most people don't begin to look where they are going. I was pushed and jostled until I nearly screamed in fear, because one more fall and my leg would have snapped like a dry twig. A small child hurtled into my legs sending me swaying, and was pulled back hastily by her mother who hissed savagely, 'Get away from the lady; she's different, she can't hear' extraordinary when it was my leg, not my ears, that were broken!

I went to a few cocktail parties in the wheelchair and later on sticks, and found them a nightmare. When I was in the wheelchair people talked way above my head or were forced to kneel embarrassingly at my feet to make themselves heard. I was an island of silence below a sea of noise. When I was on my sticks, leaning against a wall in a corner, I was often ignored; sickness at parties isn't very nice and I felt a bit like an animal who had been kicked out by its pack.

Next week, God and the specialists willing, I shall be able to throw away my painted sticks and stagger around on a walking stick. I am one of the lucky ones, but at least I now understand the problems of a disabled person and am able to refrain from asking someone else when I am in their company, 'Does *she* take sugar?'.

Seaside Change
10 MAY 1981

IT IS EXTRAORDINARY how people can change when they are on holiday. We once went to Portugal with a nice couple with whom we had been friends for years. Our children played happily together, she was a sweet, marvellously reliable person and he was a jolly chap who liked a couple of beers in the local pub but didn't go overboard.

Yet within two days of our arriving at our self-catering flat, they had both undergone a personality change. He was consuming unbelievable quantities of *grappa* and had taken up with a local fisherman and was out until all hours. Guess who had to look after their children? 'Marvellous holiday,' they both said at the end, 'wonderfully relaxing; we must do this again'.

So this is a word of warning. Making your only holiday a DIY affair may be the cheapest way of taking the family off for a spree, and the bonus of sharing costs with friends and their family may well appeal; but will it work out? Will your friends who are such chums when you only see them a couple of times a week turn out to be companions when you are all living at close quarters for ten days or a fortnight? Will their children be as amenable on holiday as you have found them to be at home? And will Martha or Mary prove to be the amusing, helpful and competent confidante she was over coffee in the High Street when you are together on the Costa Brava or a Greek island?

It is the chores that get you down on this type of holiday. However simply you decide to live, there has to be a certain amount of bed-making, washing-up and generally keeping things in order, especially since there usually seem to be rather more people on holiday than the house can comfortably take.

Children on holiday behave differently, too. Teenagers cause endless worry by chatting up local birds or fellas you know they wouldn't be seen dead with at home. They crash the car they borrowed without asking, drink too much cheap wine and are sick in washbasins. The younger ones cover the only bath in sand, fill the fridge with seaweed and snails, leave their clothes *everywhere* and break all the glasses, which you have to replace. And even the nicest babies get sunstroke, wasp stings or upset tummies and seem to cry all night.

A couple of years ago I went on holiday in a rented villa in Brittany with another three couples and their children. We had agreed on a rota of shopping and cooking, with one husband and wife doing shopping one day while another couple did all the cooking.

I cooked the first day; the second day Lisa, who was going to do it, discovered some friends were staying down the coast and that was the only day they could see them. So I did the cooking again. On the third day Henrietta, whose turn it was, heard that there was a festival in Quiberon to which she *had* to take her family because she was researching 'gothic feasts'; so again I was the one who did the cooking.

And so it went on. Everyone was very kind about 'taking the burden' off me by doing the shopping (and sampling the local wine, which meant they didn't get back until 2.30 pm), and the nearest I got to authentic Breton food was a gateau Breton bought in the supermarket.

Perhaps you are thinking, 'She must be impossible; she obviously can't get on with anyone'. Not so; I have had many idyllic holidays shared with other families. I am simply warning you about the importance of testing out your companions and thoroughly investigating their and their children's holiday habits before you venture off with them into the unknown.

Try to make sure that your friends have the same ideas about 'things to do' on a holiday, that they are prepared to pull their weight, share the chores and don't expect you to be their baby-minder all the time. Make a plan, and stick to it, about who will do what chores, cutting them down to a minimum, and agree on basic rules about the children and what they can and cannot do.

I may sound a bit like a school mistress, but from my experience organisation does make sense if you want to enjoy a holiday shared with friends.

My Daughter, My Friend
22 AUGUST 1982

WHIZZING TO NEW YORK and back for two days is a way of life for people like diplomats and businessmen, but for ordinary mortals like me the idea is relatively lunatic. That, however, is just what I recently did.

There is a time in every parent's life when that invisible umbilical cord has to be severed and this was, I realised, subconsciously at first, just such a time. My 22-year-old daughter, browned off with her job at Virgin Records in London, had gone off to New York to find her fortune, or whatever it was she was looking for, and I was missing her.

I hadn't realised how heartaching the break would be, how I would miss her daily telephone calls from the office, our lunches in London and the weekends when she brought home what seemed like weeks of dirty washing and when she slept until lunchtime each morning. We are both bad correspondents, and although we had talked about once every three weeks over the telephone since she went to New York, the thousands of miles between us seemed much further than just an ocean.

Then Lucy telephoned twice in one week and both times sounded homesick, tearful and miserable. I suggested she came home, but she said 'No,' she must stick it out and not give up. On an impulse I said, 'Supposing I come to New York for the weekend, would you like that?' Her cries of excitement and her tears on the other end of the line were enough to make my rash offer become a reality.

Lucy lives in The Bowery, probably one of the roughest districts of New York. She has a so-called 'loft' there, a disused warehouse, which she shares with a fella (we're just good friends, Mummy) called Dave, and I felt, for both our sakes, that it would be politic if I stayed at the more staid and comfortable Algonquin Hotel.

Having booked a room, I then booked a flight. I was too late for an Apex flight, I couldn't face going standby so, since regular New York flights are always jam-packed, I beat the system by joining an Air India flight that had come from Delhi and was on its way from London to America.

I left London at 1 pm Friday and, after a comfortable journey, was at the hotel by 5.30 pm local time. Lucy was waiting in the foyer of the hotel, mini-skirted and incredibly young looking and fatter; 'Americans like my "tussy" (bottom) Mummy,' she explained, 'They say it's cute and, anyway, don't start getting at me'. I bit my tongue.

My room was a delight, with a brass bed, a television, lots of central heating, and an excellent room service. Being used to making decisions I had planned out our weekend.

I need not have bothered; Lucy had arranged it all. Drinks that evening at the Algonquin to 'look at the people'; a table was booked. Another table was booked for dinner at the place everyone is going to at the moment, the Grand Central Station Oyster Bar. A leisurely breakfast together on Saturday morning, then shopping and lunch in Greenwich Village (the table was booked), followed by a rest for me ('I don't want to tire you'), the theatre to see Lauren Bacall in 'Woman of the Year' ('I used your American Express number to book the tickets – thought that would be suitable for you to see,') and on to the 21 Club for a late dinner.

'But darling,' I said, 'Is it all right for two women alone to go to the 21 Club at that time of night?'.

'Oh, Mummy *really*, of course it is.'

She ordered the drinks, caught waiters' eyes and gave me the run down on people around. It was Lucy who got a taxi, tipped the doorman, Lucy who pointed out that they had overcharged on our bill at the Oyster Bar, Lucy who reassured me that it was perfectly all right to order my favourite dish of raw clams for the first, second and third courses. 'New York, appreciates eccentrics like you.'

I had not expected to relinquish the maternal instinct quite so easily. I found it a delight not to have to bother with any organisation, planning or the nitty-gritty of bookings and taxi hailings. Suddenly my daughter had become not just an appendage of myself but my mentor.

On Saturday morning we went shopping at Saks, Bloomingdales and Macys. I bought her skirts, sweaters and shoes, and she insisted I bought shirts and a watch for myself. We were like two giggling schoolgirls but, instead of me, it was Lucy who led the way, bullied lady sales staff, found me chairs to sit on and insisted I try the *gnocchi* for which the Greenwich Village restaurant was famous. She even efficiently tracked down a source of American caviar from Red River sturgeon which I particularly wanted to try out, and had it packed in an insulated bag so that I could get it home in good condition.

I discovered I no longer had a daughter; instead I had a friend, a fabulous friend, if rather a bossy one, on my own level; the roles had reversed.

That evening was marvellous. Lauren Bacall was superb. ('She's amazing isn't she, Mummy? She is *even* older that you are'); but at the 21 Club, where no one looked in the least strangely at two women dining alone at that time of night, she forgot my age and we gossiped, laughed and chatted like two old friends. I have to admit to a small *frisson* of annoyance when it was just Lucy that a couple of dinner-jacketed and most attractive men tried to pick up and not both of us.

The next day after breakfast in my room we had Sunday lunch in fairyland on the top of the World Trade Centre, 107 storeys high, with the whole of New York spread out below us, and for a moment there was a glimpse of my small daughter as Lucy rushed from window to window with her camera and ate enough from the lavish buffet to make that 'tussy' even more prominent. I did raise an eyebrow at three helpings of strawberry cheesecake, but accepted the explanation that she was saving to go to LA for three weeks and this meal meant she needn't eat for three days. Lucy came with me to the airport and stayed until the last minute before the plane left.

Miraculously we, Lucy and I, had successfully weathered the storm of the inevitable changes that occur in mother-daughter relationships. I went back to London delighting in having found such a rewarding friend and companion and filled with enormous pride at knowing she was of my making. Now I can't wait for her to come home; 3,000 miles away is too far for one's best friend to live.

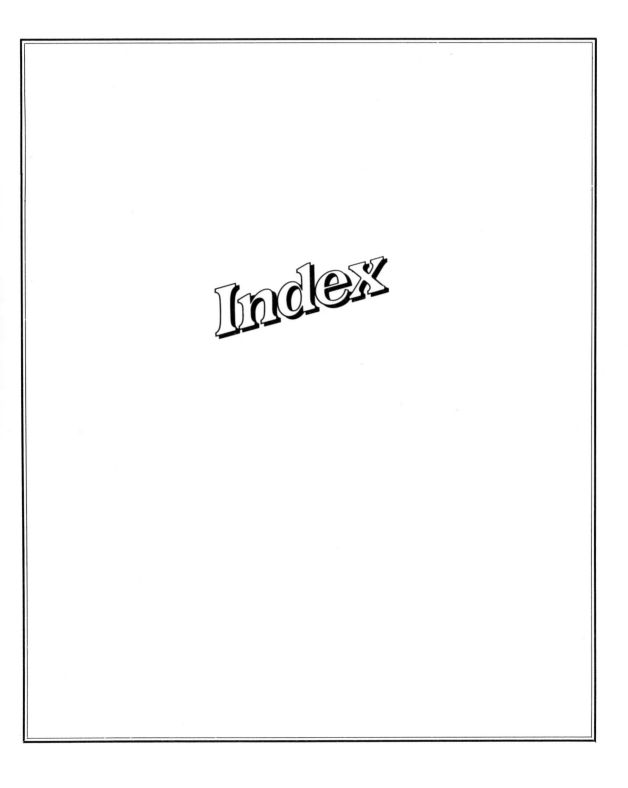

Index

Index

281

Index

Index

Index

Index

Index

Index